Cannon's Point Plantation, 1794–1860

Living Conditions and Status Patterns
in the Old South

Studies in
HISTORICAL ARCHAEOLOGY

EDITOR
Stanley South

Institute of Archeology and Anthropology
University of South Carolina
Columbia, South Carolina

ADVISORS

Charles E. Cleland
John L. Idol, Jr.
Mark P. Leone
Kenneth E. Lewis
Cynthia R. Price
Sarah Peabody Turnbaugh
John White

Cannon's Point Plantation, 1794–1860

Living Conditions and Status Patterns in the Old South

John Solomon Otto

Center for American Archeology
Kampsville, Illinois

1984

ACADEMIC PRESS, INC.
(*Harcourt Brace Jovanovich, Publishers*)
Orlando   San Diego   San Francisco   New York   London
Toronto   Montreal   Sydney   Tokyo   São Paulo

ACADEMIC PRESS, INC.
Orlando, Florida 32887

United Kingdom Edition published by
ACADEMIC PRESS, INC. (LONDON) LTD.
24/28 Oval Road, London NW1   7DX

Library of Congress Cataloging in Publication Data

Otto, John Solomon.
    Cannon's Point Plantation, 1794-1860.

    (Studies in historical archaeology)
    Includes index.
    1. Cannon's Point Plantation Site (Ga.) 2. Plantation
life--Georgia. 3. Excavations (Archaeology)--Georgia.
4. Slavery--Georgia--Condition of slaves. I. Title.
II. Series: Studies in historical archaeology (New York,
N.Y.)
F294.C36O87 1984   975.8   83-15784
ISBN 0-12-531060-9

To Charles Fairbanks, Samuel Proctor, and Jerry Milanich

John Couper (1759–1850)

Contents

Preface

This volume presents the results of historical archaeological investigations at Cannon's Point, an antebellum sea-island cotton
plantation off the Georgia coast. Because the investigations compare archaeological remains at sites once occupied by slaves, overseers, and planters—people who differed in racial, social, and economic status—this book will be of value to archaeologists for its
treatment of the problem of status patterning in the archaeological
record. And because the investigations compare the material living
conditions of the plantation's inhabitants, this book will interest
historians concerned with the treatment and daily lives of slaves in
the Old South.

Our understanding of the daily lives of slaves on Old South
plantations was, until quite recently, based upon somewhat unrelia-
ble sources. Much of what we knew came from the writings of white
visitors to antebellum plantations, but these elite observers saw only
selected aspects of the slaves' lives. Another source has been a group

of autobiographies of slaves who escaped to the antebellum North. Some were written by blacks, others were dictated by blacks to white editors, and most were published in the North as antislavery propaganda. The authors were usually young men, craftsmen, and border-state ex-slaves. Because few slaves from the Deep South, women, or field hands left autobiographies, these narratives probably were not typical of the lives of many slaves throughout the Old South. After the Civil War, further information was gathered from former slaves. During the 1930s, for example, Works Progress Administration (WPA) interviewers talked to hundreds of former slaves about their life in the South both before and after Appomattox. The narrators in the WPA project did include men and women who had worked as field slaves in the Deep South, but their reminiscences were all too often marred by lapses of memory, colored by postbellum experiences, or misconstrued by white interviewers. All these sources are more or less incomplete and biased. However, in the past decade or so scholars have begun to develop a source of new information. Led by Charles Fairbanks of the University of Florida, some historical archaeologists are now examining the unwritten legacy of the slaves—their ruined cabins, their lost or discarded tools and other artifacts, and what is left of their food remains and other garbage.

The goal of excavating slave cabins—as with most other archaeological excavations—is to recover tangible evidence concerning the housing, possessions, foods, crafts, recreation, and lifestyle of the former residents. Unlike many written sources, which are often directed toward posterity, archaeological remains are rarely falsified or intentionally biased. When they discarded their kitchen garbage 150 years ago, these slaves had no idea that it would eventually interest archaeologists. Archaeological evidence does have limitations, however. Not all materials survive over time. Clothing, wood, and plants often decay, whereas iron, ceramics, and bones usually survive. But by combining the incomplete archaeological record with the incomplete written record, we may achieve a clearer appreciation of how slaves lived. Our comparison of written and archaeological sources also permits us an evaluation of the accuracy of the narratives and reports left by plantation owners and white visitors.

We were able to pursue this approach at Cannon's Point, an abandoned cotton plantation that operated from 1794 to 1861. Cannon's Point contains the ruins of two sets of four slave cabins and their refuse middens. At one of these cabins we exposed the foundations and much of the refuse midden, which contained nonperishable possessions and food remains discarded by two generations of slaves. Surviving written sources available from Cannon's Point (and other sea-island cotton plantations) include plantation accounts, letters written by the planter family, and descriptions of the plantation left by such visitors as Aaron Burr, Basil Hall, Fanny Kemble, and Charles Lyell. The documents attest to the presence of an elite planter family, the Coupers, and their hired middle-class overseers on Cannon's Point Plantation. The ruins of houses once occupied by these two groups were revealed by survey, and refuse middens were found at the houses of each group. Because planters, overseers, and slaves differed in racial, social, and economic status, they enjoyed or suffered differential access to the material wealth of the plantation—cash crops, food crops, and livestock. Their differential access to material wealth is reflected in the archaeological record of their material living conditions—house ruins and the discarded artifacts and food remains of the middens. The written and material record of Cannon's Point Plantation thus offers a rare opportunity not only to examine the material living conditions of the Old South, but also to observe a substantial example of status patterning in the archaeological record.

Acknowledgments

Charles Fairbanks of the Department of Anthropology, University of Florida, initiated plantation archaeology with his excavations at Kingsley Plantation, Ft. George Island, Florida, and Rayfield Plantation, Cumberland Island, Georgia. His excellent articles on slave cabin archaeology were the source of many of the research hypotheses in this book. Throughout the long period of research and writing, Dr. Fairbanks generously shared his vast knowledge of historical archaeology.

During the months of analysis and writing, Samuel Proctor and Jerry Milanich of the Florida State Museum spared time from their own research. Sam Proctor was especially helpful, relying on his comprehensive knowledge of Southern history to aid me in locating historical sources.

Stephen Cumbaa, a highly talented zooarchaeologist at the National Museum of Natural Sciences in Ottawa, unselfishly offered aid and encouragement to me as I analyzed the Cannon's Point faunal remains in the zooarchaeological laboratory of the Florida State Museum. Elizabeth Wing graciously provided me with work space and access to the comparative faunal collections.

Stanley South, editor of the *Studies in Historical Archaeology* series, offered invaluable criticism and advice. Moreover, he encouraged me to make the needed revisions. In addition, South's numerous publications proved indispensable in writing the chapters.

The archaeological research that made this book a reality was funded by National Science Foundation and Sea Island Company grants awarded in 1973 to Charles Fairbanks and Jerry Milanich. The Sea Island Company, of Sea Island, Georgia, the owners of Cannon's Point, also furnished meals and quarters for the archaeological field crews.

Student crew members of the University of Florida Archeological Field Schools excavated the plantation sites during the spring and summer quarters of 1973 and 1974. In addition, Charles Fairbanks, principal investigator of the Cannon's Point project, and two members of the spring 1974 field school, Kathy Beidelman and Nina Thanz, mapped the standing ruins of the Couper house and kitchen and the overseer's house. Another member of the spring 1974 field school, Vincent Amanzio, aided me in reconstructing the ceramic and glass items from the plantation sites.

Because documentary research played a major role in this study, I thank the staffs of the following institutions for their cooperation: Margaret Davis Cate Collection, Brunswick Junior College, Brunswick, Georgia; Southern Historical Collection, University of North Carolina, Chapel Hill; Georgia Historical Library, Savannah; Wimberley George de Renne Library, University of Georgia, Athens; Duke University Library, Durham, North Carolina; Georgia State Archives, Atlanta; and the P. K. Yonge Library of Florida History, University of Florida, Gainesville.

I also thank the people who responded to my written requests for aid: James C. Bonner, Milledgeville, Georgia; E. M. Coulter, University of Georgia; Lilla Hawes, Director, Georgia Historical Society; James Heslin, Director, New York Historical Society; Bobby Frank Jones, Tennessee Technological University; William D. Postell, Tulane University School of Medicine; and William K. Scarborough, University of Southern Mississippi. Others contributing useful information were James Bagwell, Georgia Southwestern College; K. G. Berrie, Brunswick, Georgia; Francis A. Lord, Columbia, South Carolina; and W. H. Parker and Curtis Stevens, of St. Simons Island.

Finally, I am most grateful to Sophie Otto, who typed several drafts of the manuscript, and to Solomon Otto, who aided in proofreading and editing. In addition, Nain Anderson, Senior Administrative Archeologist, Center for American Archeology, Kampsville, aided me in editing the manuscript.

Cannon's Point Plantation, 1794–1860

Living Conditions and Status Patterns
in the Old South

CHAPTER 1

The Historical and Archaeological Significance of Plantation Excavation

In 1968 Charles Fairbanks, an archaeologist at the University of Florida, conducted excavations of a slave cabin on Kingsley Plantation, Ft. George Island, Florida; this was the first known excavation of an antebellum slave cabin in the United States. Fairbanks hoped to recover "specific information on how the slaves lived and the details of their housing, crafts, family life, and daily activities" (Fairbanks 1974:63). The following year Fairbanks and Robert Ascher, an anthropologist from Cornell University, excavated a second slave cabin on Rayfield Plantation, Cumberland Island, Georgia (Ascher and Fairbanks 1971). Fairbanks's excavations presaged the concern with the material living conditions of Old South slaves—an academic debate that dominated the historiography of slavery during the 1970s (see David *et al.* 1976; Fogel and Engerman 1974a, 1974b; Gutman 1975a, 1975b; Owens 1976; Rawick 1972).

Although both of Fairbanks's plantation excavations focused on the ruins of slave cabins, Fairbanks's 1972 excavations at Site SA 16-23—an eighteenth-century mestizo (Hispanicized Native American) dwelling site at St. Augustine, Florida—included the refuse and activity areas at the site as well as the ruins of two dwellings. As Fairbanks noted in a series of papers and articles, the "backyards" of these sites—including the refuse disposal areas, wells, privies, and outbuildings—contain much of the evidence that archaeologists need in order to explore such cultural phenomena as ethnicity, socioeconomic stratification, and status patterning in the archaeological record (Cumbaa 1976; Deagan 1974; Fairbanks 1972, 1976, 1977).

The archaeological and historical investigations at Cannon's Point Plantation (1794–1861), St. Simons Island, Georgia (Figure 1.1), were a logical development of Fairbanks's pioneering work in slave cabin archaeology and backyard archaeology. In 1972 the Sea Island Company of Georgia, which had purchased the Cannon's Point tract for a planned subdivision, questioned Charles Fairbanks about the archaeological potential of the prehistoric and historic sites located on Cannon's Point (Figure 1.2). These sites included an archaic shell ring, several late prehistoric Native American sites, and an abandoned cotton plantation that operated from 1794 to 1861. Receiving grants from the National Science Foundation as well as aid from the Sea Island Foundation, Fairbanks and Jerald Milanich of the Florida State Museum planned excavations at the threatened Cannon's Point sites. Though the excavators were primarily concerned with the prehistoric sites, several field crews conducted excavations at the plantation sites, which included several slave cabins with their associated refuse middens, an overseer's house with its associated refuse midden, and a planter's dwelling with its associated kitchen and refuse midden. Since these sites were occupied by inhabitants who differed in race, economic standing, and social status, the archaeological excavations at Cannon's Point Plantation generated information about the material living conditions of black slave and free white inhabitants as well as observations of how racial, social, and economic status differences are reflected in material living conditions.

In addition to the archaeological sites at Cannon's Point, investigators located a variety of written sources concerning the history of the plantation, its operation, and the lives of its antebellum inhabitants, which included a planter family, the Coupers, who operated the estate from 1794 to 1861; a series of hired white overseers; and dozens of black slaves.

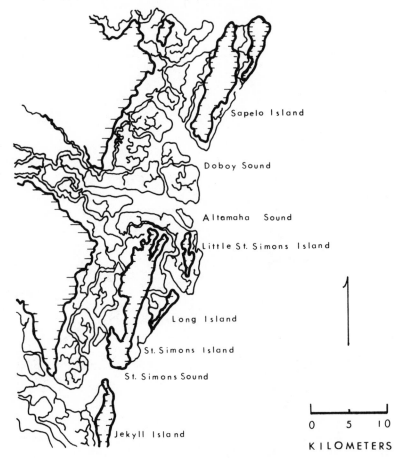

Figure 1.1. The Central Georgia sea islands. (Adapted from Reimold 1974: Figure 1.)

Therefore, the archaeological and historical resources at Cannon's Point allowed us to address two questions that loom large in both Southern history and historical archaeology: (1) What were the material living conditions of Old South slaves, and how did they differ from those of free whites? (2) How were the racial, social, and economic status differences existing among plantation inhabitants reflected in the archaeological record of their material living conditions?

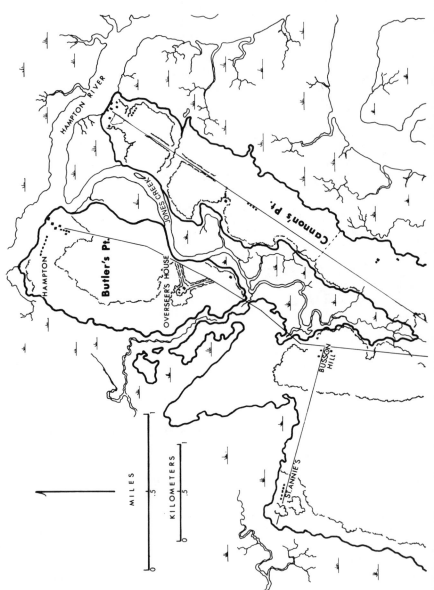

Figure 1.2. The settlement patterns of Butler's Point and Cannon's Point plantations. (Adapted from Kemble 1961:198; U.S. Coast Survey 1869.)

MATERIAL LIVING CONDITIONS OF OLD SOUTH SLAVES

A long-standing controversy in American history has been the treatment of slaves in the Old South. The traditional interpretations, offered by Ulrich B. Phillips, emphasized the southern slaveholders' paternalistic concern for their slaves (Phillips 1918, 1929). In reaction, postwar historians such as Kenneth Stampp and Stanley Elkins stressed the harshness of Old South slavery (Davis 1974; Elkins 1959; Stampp 1956). In 1974 Robert Fogel and Stanley Engerman, authors of the controversial *Time on the Cross*, portrayed Old South slavery as an economically efficient institution, wherein slaves enjoyed living conditions comparable to those of many free white people. Following the publication of *Time on the Cross*, dozens of studies have criticized or defended the book's thesis as historians have intensively reexamined the treatment of Old South slaves (e.g., David *et al.* 1976; Genovese 1974; Gutman 1975a; Holt 1976; Ransom 1974).

The problem of slave treatment, however, is multifaceted, involving at least three distinct topics: the legal status of slaves, the social consequences of slavery, and the daily living conditions of slaves (Genovese in Foner and Genovese 1969:203). Since scholars have long been concerned with the legal aspects of slavery, several works have compared New World slaves' access to freedom and citizenship. And since slavery affected the family, religious, and recreational life of blacks, a number of studies have considered the social and psychic effects of slavery (e.g., Blassingame 1972; Elkins 1959; Gutman 1976; Tannenbaum 1947). But until the publication of *Time on the Cross*, comparatively less research had been devoted to the daily living conditions—the quantity and quality of food, housing, clothing, working conditions, and the availability of leisure time (Genovese in Foner and Genovese 1969:203).

In researching the living conditions of slaves, historians have used an impressive array of sources. Most commonly they have researched plantation records, account books listing purchases for slave provisions, plantation day books describing slave work, planters' letters mentioning slave life, and even planters' diaries revealing their private views of slave treatment. Historians have also favored travelogues, written by visitors to the Old South, for these contain descriptions of slave material life. Agricultural journals have proved especially valuable, since planters often detailed their treatment of slaves in articles, presenting their plantation regimes as examples to be followed by others. Even newspapers that advertised the apparel of runaway slaves have been used as historical sources (see Stampp 1956:34–85, 279–321).

But in spite of their obvious worth, these sources have the same inherent limitations. They are ethnohistorical sources, which record the often biased observations of outsiders who were only partly aware of another social reality (Sturtevant in Clifton 1968:454). Not only were travelers superficial observers of the world around them, but their perceptions of slave life were shaped by preconceived notions. Whether they defended or denigrated slavery, most travelers saw what they had come to see.

Even plantation whites were unaware of the totality of black slave life. In addition to their negative views of black people, their daily contacts with blacks were limited: Although they supervised field slaves in the daytime, plantation whites did not live in the slave quarters and many never even ventured inside the slave cabins (see Bonner 1944:663; French 1862:164). The planters may have furnished their slaves with housing, food, clothing, and leisure time, but they knew little of how the slaves themselves evaluated their living conditions or how they worked to improve their quality of life. For within their slave cabins, slaves created their own social and cultural world—a black world that whites rarely penetrated (Osofsky 1969:21; Rawick 1972:xix-xx).

In order to enter the slaves' quarters and discover their private world, it is necessary to turn to the slave-authored sources. North America is unique in having a sizable body of slave testimonies: autobiographies, narratives, letters, speeches, and interviews. These are folk historical sources, containing the insiders' own perceptions and evaluations of their social reality (Hudson 1966:52–54; Otto 1981a:169–170)—in this case, the slaves' own view of their treatment. Only the slave testimonies permit us "a measure of access to the privacy of the mind of a slave and the conversations that took place in the slave cabin" (Osofsky 1969:21). And during the past decade, awakened interest in the slave testimonies has represented a major turning point in slave historiography (Davis 1974:7).

Some of antebellum free blacks wrote their own narratives, while others dictated their experiences to editors who published them as antislavery propaganda (Blassingame 1975:474–479). Unfortunately, the few dozen antebellum narrators included few women, field hands, or Deep South slaves such as those from the Georgia coast. Consequently, no one knows how accurately these antebellum narratives portrayed the living conditions of all slaves in the Old South (Blassingame 1975:480; Brown 1972:xii–xiii; Hedin 1981).

Postbellum ex-slave narratives, however, are far more plentiful and comprehensive. In addition to the postbellum ex-slave autobiographies and biographies, there are hundreds of transcribed interviews with former slaves. During the 1920s black scholars from Fisk and Southern universities interviewed dozens of surviving ex-slaves, and during the following decade, hundreds of elderly former slaves told Works Progress Administration (WPA) interviewers of their lives before and after emancipation. Though the WPA Slave Narrative Collection contained testimonies from women, field hands, and Deep South blacks among others, their reminiscences were often marred by lapses of memory, colored by life experiences in the postbellum South, or misinterpreted by WPA interviewers (Blassingame 1975:483; Rawick 1972:xvi, xviii; Yetman, 1970:2–3, 353, 359). Over 2000 ex-slave interviews were collected, yet not all geographic areas in the South were equally represented. In Georgia, for example, the majority of interviews were conducted with ex-slaves living near Athens, deep within the Georgia Piedmont; few ex-slaves from the Georgia coast ever testified for the WPA Slave Narrative Collection. Although some interviews with coastal Georgia ex-slaves appeared in the Georgia Writers' Project *Drums and Shadows* (1940), a study of the African cultural heritage of Georgia's coastal blacks, the interviewers were far more concerned with African cultural survival than with the subject of slave treatment (Georgia Writers' Project 1940; Rawick, ed., 1972:Vols. 12–13).

Despite these limitations, however, the slave testimonies are valuable because they are the only sources that allow the slaves to speak for themselves. Historians have begun to use the slave narratives in conjunction with white-authored sources to achieve a more complete and balanced view of slave life. Perhaps the most ambitious synthesis to date has been Eugene Genovese's *Roll, Jordan, Roll: The World the Slaves Made* (1974), which depicts the slaves' material, social, and psychic struggles with paternalistic planters who sought to achieve and maintain dominion over their chattels. In addition to such familiar ethnohistorical sources as plantation records, diaries, and travelogues, Genovese drew from the ex-slave testimonies, particularly the WPA interviews, to present the slaves' side of history. One reviewer of the book wrote that Genovese's synthesis successfully evoked "the feel and texture of plantation life" (Fredrickson 1975:131). Another reviewer, however, charged that

Genovese failed to penetrate the minds of slaves to tell us how they resisted or modified the rule of the slaveholders. The critic claimed that Genovese continued to view slave life and treatment through the planters' eyes, ignoring pertinent slave testimonies that challenged his model of planter paternalism (Anderson 1976:99, 101, 105, 113).

Rather than subordinating the unique body of slave testimonies to preexisting models and problems, George Rawick, the editor of the Fisk and WPA interviews, has suggested that slave testimonies should lead to fresh questions, insights, and new interpretations of slave life (Rawick, ed., 1972:Vol. 1, xxxix). For years, historians viewed slave life through the eyes of the elite, so blacks appeared as shadowy, background figures in a white-dominated world. The slave testimonies, however, have presented another view of past reality, one also clouded by preconceived ideas and attitudes, but one looking up the social hierarchy instead of down. In the slave-authored sources, the blacks appeared as sharply focused individuals, and it was the whites who were the hazy, background figures.

By using both white- and slave-authored sources, we may view slavery from two perspectives. Yet, even then, the picture is incomplete. Much of human behavior is so patterned that it lies below the level of consciousness and cannot be readily brought to mind. This is particularly true for the mundane, monotonous household tasks that are overlooked by outsiders and participants alike. People take much of their own behavior for granted; in turn, they are not fully aware of the significance of others' behavior. Consequently, the written and oral descriptions of the past are always incomplete (Hall 1977:42–43, 153–167; Schuyler 1970:86).

In the case of slaves, these household tasks were not trival; rather, they were the foundation of an autonomous black life in the quarters. In and around their cabins, slaves raised gardens, kept livestock, cooked and ate their meals, fashioned handicrafts, raised their children, worshipped, slept, and just relaxed. In their cabins, between sundown and sunup, the slaves created the Afro-American way of life, America's most distinctive subculture (Rawick 1972: xix–xx; Thorpe in Gilmore 1978:59). Since slave household life is not fully documented in the written record, Charles Fairbanks initiated slave cabin archaeology at Kingsley and Rayfield plantations. By excavating ruined slave cabins, Fairbanks hoped to recover tangible evidence about the housing, foods, utensils, crafts, and recreation of slaves—aspects of black household life often overlooked in the written record but which were present in the archaeological record (Ascher and Fairbanks 1971:3–17; Fairbanks 1974:63).

The archaeological record can furnish both quantitative and qualitative evidence about the slaves' living conditions, especially their housing, diet, and household furnishings. By excavating slave cabins, one can determine cabin construction materials and techniques as well as the available living space, the expected durability, and the amenities available to the occupants. Refuse areas, on the other hand, should contain the discarded remains of foods (the bones of domestic and wild animals as well as traces of domestic and wild plant foods) and household artifacts, including tools used in work (hoes, for example), food collecting equipment (fishing tackle, possibly), household utensils (such as ceramics), and items used in recreation and status consumption (beverage bottles and tobacco pipes).

The archaeological record, nevertheless, is not omniscient. Archaeological evidence is selective and incomplete because of decay, corrosion, and disturbance. Certain classes of artifacts, such as clothing, furniture, and plants, usually decay, whereas buttons, ceramics, and food bones usually survive. Although archaeological remains themselves are not falsified, since no one ever expected an archaeologist to excavate their trash (Ascher and Fairbanks 1971:3), archaeological data become susceptible to both error and bias once they are excavated and interpreted. Perhaps the greatest problem with slave cabin archaeology, however, is that fewer than a dozen slave dwellings have been excavated and described (Ascher and Fairbanks 1971; Fairbanks 1974; MacFarlane 1975; Smith 1975, 1976). These represent a mere handful of the tens of thousands of Old South slave cabins.

Fortunately, most of the excavated slave cabins come from plantations located in the "tidewater"—the offshore islands and contiguous coastline of South Carolina, Georgia, and Florida, which formed a distinctive environmental zone, cash crop region, and cultural area of the Old South. In the tidewater, long-staple cotton and rice planting predominated; and here the plantation system flourished, since only the larger planters could successfully grow these labor-intensive crops (Phillips 1929:125–128). Thus, the excavation of a single tidewater slave cabin could draw upon a larger comparative body of slave cabin reports, ethnohistorical accounts, and slave testimonies. Because of this abundance of comparative data it should be possible to determine whether the archaeological remains left by slave occupants were unique or whether they were part of a wider pattern of slave lifestyles on the tidewater.

All too often the living conditions of slaves have been viewed in isolation. Occasionally scholars have compared the treatment of slaves in various regions, countries, or times. Yet few have compared the lives of slave and free people in order to delineate the similarities as well as the differences in their living conditions. Over a decade ago Eugene Genovese noted the futility of judging the quality of slave life without considering the lives of lower- and upper-status free people (Genovese in Foner and Genovese 1969:203).

On sea island plantations, however, black slaves, white overseers, and white planters could often be found living on the same estate. Such a situation existed on Cannon's Point, a sea island cotton plantation. The abandoned plantation contained the ruins of at least eight slave cabins and their associated refuse middens. Equally important, the plantation contained the ruins of an overseer's house and its refuse area and the ruins of a planter's house, kitchen, and refuse dump. Therefore, Cannon's Point offered a unique opportunity to compare the living conditions of sea island slaves with those of plantation whites.

As in the case of sea island slaves, there is a body of ethnohistories and personal testimonies to aid in reconstructing the material, social, and ideological worlds of plantation whites. By using archaeology, travelers' accounts, and personal documents, we can better evaluate the planters' living conditions, especially their conspicuous consumption of housing, foods, possessions, and slave labor. It is often believed that planter families diverted much of their wealth to ostentatious living in order to impress visitors, peers, poorer whites, and slaves (Pease 1969:380–389).

In the case of overseers, however, the written record is strangely silent about their living conditions. Travelers and planters rarely described the overseers' lifestyles for posterity. The overseers themselves left few letters and fewer diaries. Slaves, of course, mentioned overseers in their testimonies, but they rarely described the overseers' private lives. And only occasionally did overseers describe their lifestyles, in articles which they submitted to the regional agricultural journal, *The Southern Agriculturist*. Thus the excavation of an overseers' house site could provide a rare glimpse into the daily lives of the middling white men who lived among white planters and black slaves.

STATUS PATTERNING IN THE
ARCHAEOLOGICAL RECORD OF MATERIAL
LIVING CONDITIONS

The presence of black slave and free white house sites on Cannon's Point Plantation offered the investigators an opportunity to explore the problem of status patterning in the archaeological record. For several decades, archaeologists who have excavated sites in complex societies have confronted the same problem: How are status differences reflected in the archaeological remains? Traditionally, archaeologists have routinely inferred the status of past site inhabitants from the quality and quantity of archaeological evidence, even though the true status of the inhabitants was unknown (e.g., Trigger in Chang 1968). Many archaeologists have assumed that there was a perfect correlation between the archaeological remains they found and the status of the former site inhabitants. They assumed that high status was always associated with higher quality and quantities of housing, possessions, and foods; in turn, they assumed that low status was always associated with lower quality and quantities of material goods.

In complex societies there are a great variety of status differences that may produce patterning in the archaeological record. In addition to age and sex differences, there are racial, ethnic, linguistic, legal, occupational, and political differences. These various status positions are ranked in hierarchies and offer differing access to symbolic and material rewards. These rewards include power or the legal right to coerce others; psychological rewards such as prestige, dignity, security, and a sense of independence; and property or access to material wealth and labor (Tumin 1967:39–46; Warner in Tumin 1970:233, 241). Yet evidence of these symbolic and material rewards may be difficult to recover at archaeological sites. Symbolic rewards such as power and prestige—which may have been of greater concern to site inhabitants than material rewards—will be lost or only partially described in incomplete written records. And because so much of material culture is perishable, the material rewards such as housing, possessions, and foods consumed will be only partially preserved in an archaeological record.

In analyzing these sites, it is significant to recognize that status positions and access to symbolic and material rewards are not perfectly associated in complex societies (Laumann et al. 1970:63–65).

People may occupy high-status positions that have only symbolic rewards or minor material rewards that are not appropriate to their social standing. On the other hand, people may occupy low-status positions but may accumulate material rewards that are not commensurate with their true economic status. Given this imperfect association between status and material rewards, the living conditions of former site inhabitants may not accurately reflect their actual status positions. It is quite possible that the archaeological evidence of living conditions at many sites will not reflect any status patterning.

In Old South society (1789–1861), for example, access to power, prestige, and material rewards was not perfectly associated with status in racial, economic, and social status hierarchies. Frequently there were similarities in the housing, foods, clothing, daily tasks, and recreation of white farmers, white laborers, and black slaves (Craven 1930:16–18; Otto 1981b). Although free southern whites enjoyed a higher racial and legal status than black slaves, their higher status was not always associated with superior material rewards. Surprisingly, some black slaves may have had better housing, foods, and possessions than some of the poor whites (see Genovese 1974: 24, 63, 533). Given our present limited knowledge of Old South sites, archaeologists should attempt to identify the true status of former site inhabitants rather than simply inferring status from the archaeological evidence alone.

Often representatives of the three major groups of the Old South—white planters, white overseers (who were usually the sons of white farmers), and black slaves—could be found living on the same plantation (Bonner in Link and Patrick 1965:158; Wall in Link and Patrick 1965:177). Fortunately, historic site archaeologists often have an independent set of data—written documents and oral testimonies—that may be used to identify the racial, economic, and social status of the people who once occupied the houses, who acquired and used the artifacts, and who consumed the foods that appear at Old South archaeological sites. With documentary controls, correlations can be established between the status of former site inhabitants and the archaeological remains they left behind (South 1977:231–232).

Such a situation existed at Cannon's Point Plantation, where documents attested to the presence of a white planter family (the Coupers), white overseers, and black slaves. The dwelling sites once occupied by the planters, overseers, and slaves were identified from documents as well as from analogies with the settlement patterns of other coastal cotton plantations (Otto 1975b). On Cannon's Point, the planter's house, kitchen, and refuse midden were located on the banks of the Hampton River and were part of the "administrative and technical nucleus" that included cotton houses and store-houses. The northern set of four slave cabins was located near the planter's complex; in turn, the second set of four slave cabins lay at the southern end of the plantation. The overseer's house was placed in a central location, so presumably the overseer could police both slave quarters (Figure 1.3).

At the planter's site, investigators mapped the standing ruins, conducted test excavations inside the ruins, and sampled the refuse midden associated with the planter's kitchen. They also cleared and mapped the ruins of the overseer's house and sampled its refuse disposal area. And at the third slave cabin in the northern set of cabins, they excavated a cabin and sampled its associated refuse midden. From documents, the investigators knew that the dwellings had been constructed during the antebellum years (U.S. Coast Survey 1869). The excavations also yielded antebellum refuse contexts at all three sites. Three refuse zones in the planter's kitchen midden contained no artifacts whose beginning date c. manufacture was later than 1860; the ceramics from these zones provided mean ceramic dates of circa 1815, 1818, and 1824 (see South 1972 for a discussion of the mean ceramic date formula). Two refuse zones in the overseer's house midden contained only antebellum artifacts; the ceramics in these zones dated to circa 1821. Finally, a refuse zone in the slave cabin midden, which contained only antebellum artifacts, yielded a mean ceramic date of circa 1817 (see Tables 3.4, 3.12, 4.1, 5.1).

With chronological controls, it was possible to compare house ruins, household artifacts, and food remains that dated to the ante-bellum period of occupation (1794–1861). With documentary controls, it was possible to identify the status of the plantation inhabitants. Since status and chronology could be held as constants, the differences as well as the similarities in the archaeological remains at all three sites could be explained by differences and similarities in known status (South 1972:100, 1977:231).

In addition to differing in status, the Cannon's Point inhabitants had differing access to the plantation surplus—the cash crops, the food crops, and the livestock produced on the plantation, or their equivalent value in cash. The Couper family, who owned and managed Cannon's Point, monopolized the surplus: They sold crops on the market, they reinvested the profits, and they spent sums on

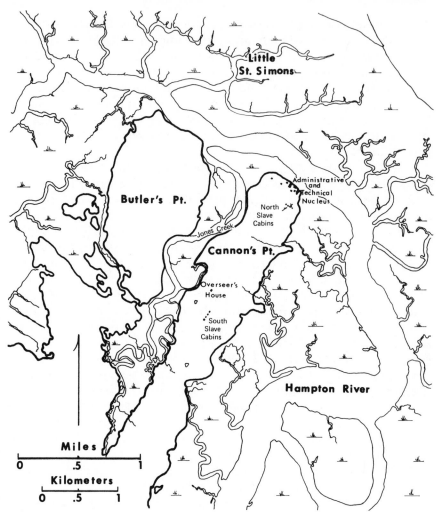

Figure 1.3. Cannon's Point Plantation. (Adapted from U.S. Geological Survey, 1954.)

household necessities and luxuries. Although the slaves produced the plantation crops under the supervision of hired overseers, the slaves and overseers had only limited access to the plantation surplus. In return for their daily labor, the slaves received only rations of food and clothing, occasional gifts, and the use of cabins. And in return for long hours of supervision, the overseer received only the use of a house and a yearly income ranging from $200 to $400. Using credit on their yearly salaries, many overseers had to purchase their own food, clothing, and many of their household utensils (Couper 1826–1852, 1839–1854; Wolf 1959:136–138).

The higher status of the planters and their monopoly of plantation surpluses and the lower status of overseers and slaves and their more limited access to plantation surpluses should have been reflected in their material living conditions—the quality and quantity of housing, foods, and possessions. Yet the archaeological remains of their living conditions could have reflected several kinds of status differences—racial, legal, social, and economic.

Obviously the Cannon's Point inhabitants differed in racial and legal status—the plantation occupants included both free whites and black slaves. Since the planters and overseers both belonged to the free white caste, qualitative and quantitative similarities may have appeared in housing, foods, and artifacts at the planter and overseer sites. If so, the archaeological remains at these sites would reflect the racial–legal similarities existing between the free white planters and overseers.

The plantation inhabitants differed in social and occupational status. The planters were owners and managers, the overseers were hired supervisors, and most of the slaves were agricultural laborers. If qualitative and quantitative differences appeared in the archaeological remains at the three dwelling sites, then the archaeological remains would reflect the social differences existing among the plantation inhabitants.

It was possible that the overseers and slaves had a similar economic status and a restricted access to plantation surpluses. In contrast to the planters, who owned the plantation and monopolized the plantation surplus, most Cannon's Point overseers had little job security, and they received only a few hundred dollars as a yearly reward for their services. And unlike the slaves, the overseers had to provide their own food and clothing by drawing on their small yearly salaries (Couper 1839–1854). Thus, despite their higher racial and social status, the low economic status (or poverty) of overseers may have approximated that of the slaves. And if qualitative and quantitative similarities appeared in the archaeological evidence, their material living conditions would reflect the poverty of both overseers and slaves.

In conclusion, comparisons of housing, artifacts, and food remains from the Cannon's Point dwelling sites could reveal three different kinds of status patterning. If similarities appeared in the archaeological remains at the planter and overseer sites, and if these remains were superior to those at the slave sites, this would reveal a "white dominance pattern" reflecting the higher racial–legal status of the plantation whites. In turn, if differences appeared in the archaeological remains at all three sites, this would reveal a "hierarchical pattern" reflecting the known social or occupational differences among the planters, hired overseers, and slave laborers. Finally, if similarities appeared in the archaeological remains at the overseer and slave sites, and if these remains were inferior to those at the planter's site, this would reveal the "wealth–poverty pattern" reflecting the wealth of planters and the poverty of overseers and slaves.

If the archaeological evidence of material living conditions reveals any of the three status patterns, it should be possible to determine which kinds of evidence are the most sensitive indicators of status on antebellum plantations. It is also possible, however, that whole categories of archaeological evidence—or even the entire archaeological record—may not reveal any status patterning. Although status differences existing between officers and enlisted men have been demonstrated in the archaeological remains of several military sites (e.g., Ferguson 1975; South 1974), Stanley South and many others believe that archaeologists "have yet to demonstrate clearly that there is status related patterning in material culture in civilian situations" (South 1974:213). The Cannon's Point project thus offered a chance to test the hypothesis that status patterning appears in the archaeological remains of plantations (Ferguson 1979; Mathewson 1973; Otto 1975a).

CHAPTER 2

Cannon's Point: The History of a Long-Staple Cotton Plantation (1794–1890)

Although we were primarily concerned with delineating the differences and similarities in the material living conditions of the plantation inhabitants, we found that Cannon's Point was one of the most historically significant plantations in the tidewater culture area of the Old South. John Couper, the owner of Cannon's Point Plantation from 1794 to 1850, hosted such notable visitors as Aaron Burr, Fanny Kemble Butler, and Basil and Margaret Hall (Burr in Jones 1957; Hall 1829, 1931; Kemble 1961; Van Doren 1929). After John Couper's death in 1850, his son James Hamilton Couper used Cannon's Point as his summer home until the Civil War, entertaining Charles Lyell, Frederika Bremer, and Amelia Murray (Bremer 1853; Lyell 1849; Murray 1857).

The visitors to Cannon's Point Plantation left detailed descriptions of the Couper household, but they generally overlooked the slaves and overseers who resided on the plantation. Only Basil Hall left a detailed description of slave life on Cannon's Point, and all of the visitors neglected the overseers, mentioning them only in passing. The Cannon's Point Plantation daybooks and account books, which should have contained information about the slaves and overseers, were missing. Possibly these books were lost in 1861 when James Hamilton Couper abandoned the island plantation to live in comparative safety on the mainland. A Union naval officer from the blockading fleet visited Cannon's Point in 1863 and noted "large amounts of books and manuscripts strewn around the rooms of the main mansion" (Barnes and Barnes 1963:57). Fortunately, James kept some of the Cannon's Point accounts in the books of the Hopeton Plantation, where he served as hired manager from 1816 to 1852. Though the Cannon's Point accounts did not begin until 1846, and they ended abruptly in 1854, these accounts listed the provisions purchased for the slaves as well as the overseers' household accounts (Couper 1826–1852, 1839–1854).

Many of the Couper family's letters survived the Civil War and were available in archives and libraries (Couper Family Papers [1775–1960]; Fraser–Couper Family Papers [1850–1884]; John Couper Collection [1775–1963]; James Hamilton Couper Plantation Records [1826–1854]; William Audley Couper Papers [1795–1930]; Mac Hazelhurst Burroughs Scrapbooks). These letters, nonetheless, dealt almost exclusively with the planter family and their kinspeople and friends. The Couper family correspondence rarely touched upon the lives of the Cannon's Point slaves or overseers.

The U.S. Census Manuscripts (1820–1860) for Glynn County, Georgia, the community in which Cannon's Point was located, contained some information about the plantation inhabitants. The 1850–1860 Census Schedules were especially valuable because they listed the names, ages, occupations, and wealth of the white plantation inhabitants, including several of the Cannon's Point overseers. In both Census years, however, slaves were listed anonymously, and the Cannon's Point slaves could not be differentiated from the slaves living on James Hamilton Couper's other plantations (U.S. Bureau of the Census, Glynn County 1820–1860).

The Couper family and their lives were rather well documented in the written record, but the slaves and overseers received little attention because few outsiders thought to describe their social and material living conditions. And apparently no Cannon's Point slaves or overseers left written or oral testimonies. Although Ryna Johnson, an informant for the Works Progress Administration (WPA) Slave Narrative Collection, had been one of the Couper slaves, it is not known if she lived at Cannon's Point or at another of James

Hamilton Couper's plantations (Georgia Writers' Project 1940: 175–176).

There was, however, a wealth of indirect historical evidence about the material, social, and psychic lives of black slaves living on the sea islands and the tidewater coastal fringe of Georgia, South Carolina, and Florida. In addition to the plantation records left by tidewater planters, numerous visitors toured this area before the Civil War and described the lives of the tidewater slaves. During the war, northern missionaries and cotton agents—the so-called Gideonites—lived among the newly liberated sea island blacks. Their letters, diaries, and published reminiscences contain details about black life that are not found elsewhere. Coastal planters also often portrayed the lives of slaves and even overseers in the articles they penned for the regional agricultural journal, *The Southern Agriculturist*. Despite their biases and selectivity, these ethnohistorical accounts are relatively numerous, and they have been synthesized by several historians. Such ethnohistorical generalizations are useful in determining whether material and social situations at Cannon's Point were unique and noteworthy or whether they were part of a wider pattern (e.g., Ames 1969; Botume 1968; French 1862; Holland 1969; Johnson 1930; Pearson 1969; Rose 1964; Russell 1954; Woofter 1930).

In addition to these ethnohistorical accounts left by outsiders, a few tidewater slaves managed to leave accounts of their lives in bondage. Newspaper correspondents interviewed some tidewater black refugees during the Civil War, but most ex-slave testimonies dated to the 1930s, when WPA interviewers interrogated the last generation of ex-slaves. Despite lapses in memory and biases introduced by white WPA interviewers, these testimonies contained unique evidence about slave behavior and thought as well as African cultural survivals (e.g., Blassingame 1977:358–363, 369–384, 449–454; Georgia Writers' Project 1940; Rawick, ed., 1972:Vols. 2–3, 13, 17). In addition to these slave folk histories, a few white overseers wrote articles for *The Southern Agriculturist* describing their working and living conditions on tidewater plantations. Although few in number, these overseer-authored articles are the only sources that present the overseers' perceptions and evaluations of their social and material lives (e.g., Anonymous 1836; An Overseer 1836; P. C. 1838).

Thus, despite the gaps that exist in the written record for Cannon's Point Plantation, the surviving documents from the plantation as well as the ethnohistorical and folk historical sources from the tidewater culture area permitted us to partially reconstruct the history of Cannon's Point, its operation through time, and the lives of its white and black inhabitants.

THE SETTLEMENT OF THE CANNON'S POINT REGION

The area known as Cannon's Point was originally granted in the 1730s by the Trustees of Georgia to Daniel Cannon, a carpenter and an early settler of Frederica (Figure 2.1). Cannon constructed a "modest story-and-a half house" on the tract, and he ranged his livestock on the peninsula. Cannon and his two sons built many of the houses in Frederica, but in 1741 they left Cannon's Point to move to Charleston, South Carolina (Wightman and Cate 1955:43, 55; Cate n.d.a).

Portions of the Cannon's Point tract were redistributed as Royal Provincial Grants in the mid-eighteenth century. Nicholas Nielson obtained 350 acres of the Cannon's Point peninsula in 1768 (Glynn County Courthouse, n.d.:Deed Book D, 79–81) but later transferred the title of this land to David and Jane Mitchell of Chatham County, Georgia. On December 11, 1793, they sold Nielson's old section of Cannon's Point to John Couper and James Hamilton (Cate 1930:75; Glynn County Courthouse n.d.:Deed Book ABEF, 117–120).

John Couper, born in 1759, immigrated to Georgia from Scotland. Serving as a clerk with Lundy and Co. (Savannah merchants), Couper fled to St. Augustine with his loyalist employers in 1775. In 1783 Couper returned to Georgia and opened a store at Sunbury (Liberty County) in partnership with James Hamilton (White 1854: 496; Wylly 1916:53). After his marriage to Rebecca Maxwell in 1792, Couper sealed his partnership by naming his first son James Hamilton and by naming his first daughter Isabella after Hamilton's wife (Wylly 1914; Cate n.d.c).

In the 1790s Couper and his partner began purchasing plantations on the Georgia coast because the price of long-staple cotton—used for thread and lace—was generally high. One of the tracts they bought in 1793 was 350 acres on Cannon's Point peninsula. Covered with live oak hammocks, the Cannon's point tract contained prime cotton lands. In 1796, Couper moved his family to Cannon's Point to begin his new career as a long-staple cotton planter (Editor

1833:249–252; Glynn County Courthouse n.d.:Deed Book CD, 79–81, Deed Book ABEF, 117–120; Gray 1941:Vol. 2, 737; Wightman and Cate 1955:55).

Cannon's Point was located in sparsely settled Glynn County. Created in 1777 when the First Constitution of Georgia called for the replacement of parishes with counties, the community was named for John Glynn, a member of the British Parliament who was sympathetic to the American cause. To encourage the settlement of Glynn and other new counties, the state constitution provided headrights for prospective settlers: each household head could receive 200 acres, and the state would provide 50 acres for each additional free person or slave. But despite these incentives, Glynn attracted few settlers. By 1790, only 193 free whites and 215 slaves resided in the county. Many of these early settlers were cattle herders who ranged their stock in the long-leaf pine forests that covered most of the county. Owning few slaves, the herders rarely cleared more than a few acres for growing corn (Campbell and Keller 1973:12; Coleman 1958:82–83; Hazzard 1825; Otto 1979:462).

Although it was located in the coastal flatwoods of Georgia—an area of poor sandy soils—Glynn also contained tracts of fertile bottomland along the Altamaha and Little Satilla rivers, which formed the northern and southern boundaries of the county (Figure 2.1). Covered with swampy cypress forests, these river bottomlands could be cultivated only after clearing and draining—onerous tasks requiring much labor. In addition to these river bottoms, Glynn's territory also included two large sea islands—St. Simons and Jekyll—whose live oak–magnolia forests covered fertile sandy loam soils (Gray 1941:Vol. 2, 641, 721–722, 733; Hart 1978:516–517; Shelford 1963:75, 86) These pockets of fertile soil began attracting rice and cotton planters after 1790. In the river valleys, the tidal fluctuations in the river levels allowed planters to flood and drain their rice fields. After clearing and draining the bottomlands, planters constructed a series of banks, levees, and sluice gates. Given these initial labors, slaves were indispensable to rice planting (Gray 1941:Vol. 2, 721–722; Hilliard 1972:36). One former slave recalled the contribution of black labor to rice growing: "All dem rice-field been nothing but swamp. Slavery people cut kennel (canal) and dig ditch and cut down woods-and dig ditch through the raw woods. All been clear up for plant rice by slavery people" (Rawick, ed., 1972: Vol. 3, Pt. 3, 92).

On the sea islands, the planters found the sandy loams were ideal for cultivating long-staple or black-seed cotton—a West Indian

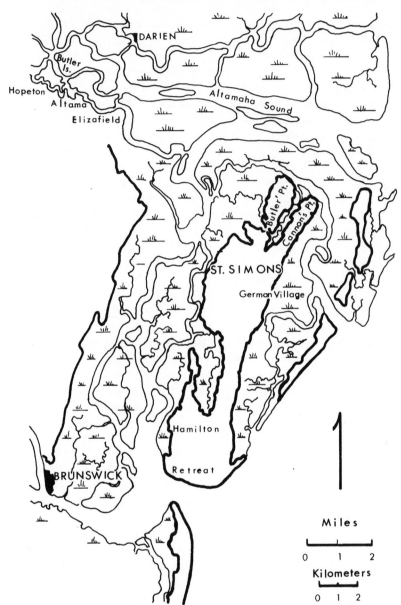

Figure 2.1. Glynn County plantations mentioned in the text. (Kemble 1961:xl.)

hybrid that possessed a longer fiber ($1\frac{1}{2}$–$1\frac{3}{4}$ inches) than the short-staple ($\frac{3}{8}$–1 inch) or green-seed cotton that was grown elsewhere in the Old South. Since long-staple cotton required a much longer growing season than short-staple, it could be grown only in the tidewater fringe of Georgia, South Carolina, and Florida where there were up to 260 frost-free days a year. Furthermore, it required much greater care in cultivation and ginning than other cottons. Being a more labor-intensive crop than short-staple, long-staple cotton was generally grown on the larger slave-based plantations (Couper 1831:243–244; Elliot 1828:151–163; Gray 1941:Vol. 2, 731–739; Hilliard 1972:30; Spalding 1831:131–133; Stephens 1976:399).

ECONOMIC INSTABILITY OF CANNON'S POINT CROPS

Given these opportunities for rice and long-staple cotton growing in Glynn County, dozens of planters with hundreds of slaves settled in the county during the 1790s. Among these planters was John Couper who prospered during his first decade on Cannon's Point, buying additional lands on credit, clearing fields, and accumulating over 200 slaves. He also began a regimen to preserve the fields' fertility by spreading crushed oyster shells and marsh mud on the cotton fields in alternate years. By 1804 Couper had built two cotton gin houses on Cannon's Point, each containing three ox-powered Eve's roller gins (Editor 1804, 1833:159–160; Johnson 1930:58). But after 1806, trade embargos and the War of 1812 disrupted the cotton trade, and long-staple prices plummeted. In 1807 Couper mortgaged his 290 slaves by borrowing $100,000 from James Hamilton. And during the war, British raiders carried off "60 prime and effective Negroes," which lessened Couper's capital by $15,000. To rebuild his labor force and his agricultural prosperity after the war, Couper purchased 120 slaves on credit at an average price of $450 each (Couper 1828; Glynn County Courthouse n.d.:Deed Book G, 12–16; Gray 1941:Vol. 2, 738; Wylly 1914).

Couper's agricultural fortunes, nevertheless, faltered; cotton prices recovered in the late 1810s but fell again in the 1820s. Even nature conspired against Couper. In September 1804 a hurricane devastated the cotton crop, then valued at $100,000, and in 1824 another hurricane struck, destroying a cotton crop valued at $90,000. In 1825 another crop was almost lost to caterpillars, and in that same year cotton prices collapsed. Furthermore, when the price of cotton fell, it also depressed the value of land and slaves (Couper 1828; Gray 1941:Vol. 2, 738; Ludlum 1963:116–117; Van Doren 1929:176). Couper described the repercussions in a letter to his brother living in Scotland: "Cotton then sunk in price [after 1826] without any hope of improvement. Lands were reduced to 1/3 their value to [$] 250 or 200" (Couper 1828).

Declaring bankruptcy in 1827, Couper reviewed his financial disaster:

> You know I commenced planting without capital. Of course I got into debt and 8 percent compound interest [seems?] to be the real perpetual motion. . . . In short I saw no hopes of paying my debts and retaining my property . . . . Mr. Hamilton being my principal creditor, on his agreeing to pay what other debts I owed, I surrendered to him all my property debts, and dues of every description, except my lands on St. Simons [Cannon's Point] and one hundred slaves. So on the 1st day of January 1827, I was thrown on the world without a dollar to support my people and family. And glad to be off so well. (Couper 1828)

Having sold his share of the Hamilton–Couper properties to his ex-partner James Hamilton and to his own son James Hamilton Couper, John turned his attention to Cannon's Point, continuing his agricultural experiments and contributing to *The Southern Agriculturist* (Couper 1831, 1832, 1835). Although he experimented with olives, dates, oranges, sugar cane, and even silkworms as possible cash crops (Kemble 1961:266; Sitterson 1953:32; White 1849:276; Wightman and Cate 1955:276), long-staple cotton remained his main source of income. As an example, Cannon's Point slaves planted 200 acres of cotton in 1828, but they cultivated a total of only 25 acres of corn, peas, and sweet potatoes (Hall 1829:Vol. 3, 218–219).

When Basil Hall visited Cannon's Point in 1828, he found the plantation's life revolved about the growing of long-staple cotton. In January and February, the slaves manured the fields with marsh mud, grass, and oyster shells. After pulling down the old cotton beds, they created new beds with plows and hoes. In March, the slaves used hoes to plant the cotton seeds—usually a bushel of seed per acre was sufficient. After the clusters of plants sprouted, the slaves thinned them with hoes. Surviving plants were then weeded six to eight times during the summer. Often the grass near the plants was pulled by hand to protect the delicate cotton stalks. The slaves "topped" the cotton in August to limit its upward growth.

They began picking the ripe bolls in late August, continuing as the bolls ripened through October. In early November, slaves began cleaning the seed cotton with roller gins. The wooden rollers separated the oily black seeds from the long-staple lint without injuring the fiber. On Cannon's Point and other St. Simons plantations, the gins were animal-powered Eve's roller gins which cleaned up to 600 pounds of cotton per day. Ginning often lasted into the next year. After "moting"—picking out the trash—slaves laboriously hand-packed the clean cotton lint into bags, using wooden or iron pestles (Hall 1829:Vol. 3, 218–220).

Since long-staple cotton required a lengthy growing season, it was confined to the sea islands and the coastal fringe. Elsewhere in the Old South, planters grew short-staple cotton, which was cultivated wherever there were 200 or more frost-free days a year. Faced with a shorter growing season, a hardier crop, and the need to maximize their slave labor force during the warm months, short-staple cotton planters lavishly used plows to make the beds, to seed, and to weed the cotton plants. To clean the short-staple lint, they used the Whitney saw gin which pulled the staple from the tufted seeds. Slaves then packed the cleaned short-staple into bales, using a screw press to compact the cotton. Since they used plows in cultivating, short-staple cotton planters grew up to 10 acres per field hand; conversely, long-staple planters grew fewer than 4 acres per hand (Thorpe 1854:452–457; Bonner 1964:52–53; Seabrook 1831:344).

Given a low-volume that required careful weeding and numerous pickings, long-staple planters adapted their labor system to suit their crop. Rather than working their slaves in plow- and hoe-gangs (as was the custom among short-staple planters), they assigned daily tasks to each slave. With this task system, they could adapt the tasks to meet the physical capabilities of individual slaves. On Cannon's Point in 1828, a "full hand" cultivated between one-half and three-quarters of an acre per day. Other slaves, rated as "partial hands," performed less than a full task. "Active hands" on Cannon's Point finished their work by the "middle of the day, others in two-thirds of the day" (Hall 1829:Vol. 3, 218–223). Thus, despite the long and laborious preparation of long-staple for market, the slaves working under the task system had more daily leisure time than slaves working under the gang system who labored from dawn to dusk during the briefer short-staple cotton season.

Successful long-staple cotton cropping, nonetheless, often had less to do with labor systems or the weather than with market prices. After cotton prices fell to a low of $.18 per pound in 1832, the

Compromise Tariff stimulated trade and long-staple prices began to recover, peaking at $.45 to $.50 per pound by 1837. But the Panic of 1837 touched off another decline in cotton prices, so by 1842 cotton sold at only $.18 per pound. Since it cost planters about $75.00 to produce a 350-pound bag of common long-staple cotton, a bag selling at $.18 per pound would have garnered less than $63.00. These prices made it difficult for planters to repay the legal interest on the capital they had borrowed. Understandably, Thomas Spalding, a noted Sapelo Island planter (Figure 1.1), declared that long-staple cotton growing was "one of the most profitless pursuits within the limits of the United States" (Coulter 1940:72–73; Gray 1941:Vol. 2, 738–739).

The low cotton prices of the 1840s struck at the heart of Glynn County's slave-based plantation economy. In 1840 Glynn's population was composed of white planter families and thousands of black slaves with a scattering of white farmers and herders—there were six slaves for each free white. But during the 1840s, Glynn's huge slave population began a decline that accelerated in the 1850s—a loss of slave population that was created by the decline of long-staple cotton planting in the county (Otto 1979).

After years of struggling with the fluctuating cotton market, John Couper retired as the Cannon's Point administrator in 1845. He was then 86. His eldest son James became manager of Cannon's Point and John moved to Hopeton, a rice plantation on the Altamaha River that James managed for the Hamilton family (Figure 2.1). After 1845 the Coupers used Cannon's Point only as a summer home, residing there during the malarial season in the Altamaha valley. John Couper died at Hopeton on March 24, 1850 (Bremer 1853:488; Cate n.d.c; Kemble 1961:391).

Despite financial reverses during his career as a planter, John Couper remained one of the largest slave owners in Glynn County. Couper was one of only 10 people in Glynn who still owned over 100 slaves in 1830 (Otto 1979:468). In addition to his fame as an agricultural experimenter, Couper held several public offices, serving as Justice of the Glynn County Inferior Court from 1796 to 1811 and as Glynn County's representative to the 1798 Georgia Constitutional Convention (Anonymous n.d.b; U.S. Bureau of the Census 1830). On John's death, Cannon's Point passed to his son James. Although researchers could not locate a formal will, they found an informal inventory of the Cannon's Point estate (1850) which James kept in the account books of Hopeton Plantation. In 1850 the Cannon's Point estate was valued at a total of $43,830. The realty, valued at

$8,500, included lands at Cannon's Point (circa 800 acres) as well as unoccupied Long (Sea) Island which served as a livestock range. The livestock, boats, carriages, and household furnishings were rated at only $830. The bulk of the estate consisted of 90 slaves who were valued at $31,500 (Couper 1839–1854).

James Couper recorded the Cannon's Point accounts (1846–1854) in his Hopeton Plantation books while he served as manager of Hopeton estate, a post he had held since 1816. Having turned the Hamilton-owned Hopeton Plantation into an agricultural show-place, James purchased the southern portion of Hopeton and created his own plantation called Altama. He also acquired Hamilton Plantation on the southern end of St. Simons Island (Figure 2.1). In addition to operating these plantations, Couper continued as manager of Hopeton until 1852. Couper even found time to serve on the Glynn County Inferior Court from 1821 to 1825 and 1833 to 1841. And finally, he acted as executor of the Hamilton estate from 1828 to 1852. But in 1852 Richard Corbin, the son of James Hamilton's daughter, came of age, assumed the administrator's role, and Couper ended 40 years of service with the Hamilton family (Anonymous n.d.a; Couper 1851; Kemble 1961:391, 395, 405; Wightman and Cate 1955:115; Wylly 1914).

When his father John died in 1850, the 56-year-old James already owned two plantations (Altama and Hamilton), managed a third (Hopeton), and inherited a fourth (Cannon's Point). Burdened with overwork and weakened by malaria, James discussed his future with his own son James:

> Disgusted with the constantly recurring sickness of a rice planta-
> tion and warned by my age to withdraw in time from labors and
> exhaustion now becoming beyond my waning powers, I have deter-
> mined to sell Altama Plantation, and have advertised it in the
> Charleston and Savannah papers. If I sell I shall bring the Altama
> gang to St. Simons and divide them between Hamilton and Can-
> non's Point. The arrangement will place the Negroes in a healthy
> climate, and under my immediate management. At which ever of
> the places I may reside, the other is within daily reach, and I shall
> avoid the dangerous and laborious expense of my present summer
> trips up the river. I may make a smaller amount of saleable crops,
> but I shall gain in the [?] and health of the Negroes, and in the
> reduced plantation expenses. (Couper 1851)

Couper, however, failed to sell Altama. And when he advertised to sell Hamilton Plantation in 1855, he apparently found no buyers. He still owned Hamilton in 1860, when he offered the position of overseer to his son (Couper 1855, 1860, 1861). James did not attempt to sell Cannon's Point, and he continued to use his father's old estate as a summer home. Although malaria was endemic in the river valleys, the sea islands were subject to fevers only in very wet seasons (White 1849:282–283). On Cannon's Point, James Hamilton Couper's family could escape the "malarial miasmas" that plagued the low country planters.

When James assumed control of Cannon's Point in 1845, the plantation was operating at a loss. Given the poor cotton prices of the 1840s, Cannon's Point was not a profitable concern. In 1846, for example, the sale of Cannon's Point cotton netted only $2405.76, while plantation expenses totalled $3027.80. But after 1850, cotton prices began to recover. Although long-staple sold for $.29 a pound in 1851, the same cotton brought $.45 per pound 2 years later. After deducting service charges, the 1851 Cannon's Point crop brought in $1993.03, while expenses were $1818.66. Two years later, the cotton crop realized $2566.12, and expenses were $2006.24 (Couper 1839–1854:200–247, 376, 425, 464, passim). The same plantation that once produced cotton crops valued at $90,000 now yielded crops averaging less than $3000. Cannon's Point, however, was not an isolated example; many Glynn County planters reduced their cotton acreage during the 1850s. Despite prices that averaged $.30 per pound during the 1850s, long-staple planting had become moribund in the county (Couper 1828, Couper 1839–1854: 229, 297, 314, 320, 247, 376, 425, 464; Gray 1941:Vol. 2, 739). Cotton production fell from 1036 bales in 1850 to 688 bales in 1860. There were corresponding decreases in the production of plantation food crops—corn, peas, potatoes, and molasses. Only the production of rice increased from 3,829,875 pounds in 1850 to 4,842,755 pounds in 1860. Even with increased rice production, however, over 2600 acres went out of cultivation in the county, and the value of land fell by almost $150,000 (U.S. Bureau of the Census 1853:377–383, 1864:22–25). Apparently the poor cotton prices of the 1840s had so weakened the county's cotton planters that the decline continued into the 1850s (Gray 1941:Vol. 2, 738; Otto 1979:464). Struggling cotton planters cut back the acreage devoted to cotton and food crops; in addition, they sold excess slaves in order to reduce their operating costs. Glynn's slave population fell from 4232 in 1850 to 2839 slaves in 1860 (Otto 1979:464–466).

No other tidewater Georgia county suffered the losses in cotton production, improved acreage, and slaves that Glynn experienced. Only in Camden County—where cotton yields fell by 219 bales, where 5774 acres went out of cultivation, and where the slave population fell by 103—did the losses approximate those of Glynn. Yet, in every tidewater Georgia county except Bryan, the coastal counties registered huge gains in rice production between 1850 and 1860. Liberty and McIntosh counties literally doubled their rice output (U.S. Bureau of the Census, 1853:377–383, 1864:22–25). Rice, a more dependable high-yield crop, had gained in favor over long-staple cotton, a risky crop even in the best of years.

By the late 1850s, Florida had supplanted tidewater Georgia as the second leading producer of long-staple cotton. Since they freely used plows in cultivation, Florida planters grew twice as many acres per field hand as the tidewater Georgia growers. Furthermore, Florida planters adopted the more efficient McCarthy roller gin to process their larger crops (Gray 1941:Vol. 2, 733–734; Shofner and Rogers 1962:373, 377–379; Smith 1973:153–154). Slow to adopt either plows or McCarthy gins, the tidewater Georgia cotton planters lagged behind in production and profits (Gray 1941:Vol. 2, 737; A Practical Planter 1831:393–402; Shofner and Rogers 1962:379).

Although James Hamilton Couper continued to grow long-staple cotton at Cannon's Point at only a small margin of profit during the 1850s, he remained one of the wealthiest men in Glynn County. By 1860 his total realty was valued at $176,000, and his personal assets were estimated at $131,000 including 210 slaves. In Glynn County as a whole, only five planters held over 100 slaves in 1860. And throughout the Old South, fewer than 3000 planters owned over 100 slaves (Owens 1976:9; U.S. Bureau of Census 1860b: Schedules I and II). But 4 years later, in 1864, Couper was living on a 490-acre farm in Ware County, deep within the Georgia pine barrens. Though he managed to evacuate his slaves and some of his livestock before Union troops invaded St. Simons Island in March 1862, he lost his coastal plantations of Altama, Hamilton, and Cannon's Point. In his 1864 Confederate tax returns, Couper listed the 812-acre Cannon's Point Plantation as valued at $10,000 in 1860, but it was "now in the possession of the enemy and worth nothing" (Couper 1864).

THE ABANDONMENT OF CANNON'S POINT

When Union troops landed on St. Simons Island, they found it deserted. Even the Confederate garrison had fled. Union officers, however, established a contraband colony for refugee blacks at Hamilton and Retreat plantations on the southern end of the island. Operating from this colony, newly freed blacks and Union soldiers visited neighboring plantations to salvage farm implements, wagons, and livestock. On one occasion a Union landing party traveled up the Hampton tidal river to Cannon's Point, where they found a "quantity of cattle." But in November 1862, most of the blacks on St. Simons departed for Hilton Head, South Carolina, and Fernandina, Florida. Thomas Wentworth Higginson, commander of the black First South Carolina Volunteers, landed on St. Simons to transfer the remaining black families to Fernandina and to remove salvaged equipment and livestock. Finally, government cotton agents arrived to strip the plantations of window sashes, panes, and "old iron." They left behind "deserted fields and ruined empty houses" (Barnes and Barnes 1963:50–51; Heard 1938:252–254, 265; Higginson 1962:xv; Official Records 1901:Series I, Vol. 12, 663). Two years after Couper abandoned Cannon's Point, a Union naval surgeon visiting the plantation described the Couper mansion: "In the basement, large quantities of [fossil] bones and minerals of all sizes and kinds are scattered around the floor [Couper's geological collection]. Broken furniture, dilapidated paintings, and broken crockery by the boatload are strewn around the rooms" (Barnes and Barnes 1963:57).

After the war Couper returned to find a destitute plantation. He mortgaged Cannon's Point to James Couper Lord of New York for $6000. And in March 1866, Couper sold Cannon's Point to John Griswold of Newport, Rhode Island, for $9000. Four months later, Couper died of apoplexy and was buried in Christ Church cemetery on St. Simons (Glynn County Courthouse n.d.: Deed Book C, 370–377, Deed Book N, 364–365; Leigh 1883:45).

When Frances Butler Leigh, Fanny Kemble's daughter, visited Cannon's Point in 1873, the only inhabitant was Old Rina, a former house servant. The old mansion lacked furnishings and the gardens were overgrown. Three years later, Col. W. R. Shadman, owner of a nearby sawmill, purchased Cannon's Point from the Coupers; and his son William and his daughter-in-law Emma moved into the old Couper house (Cate 1930:132; Engel and Stebbins 1974:1; Glynn County Courthouse n.d.: Deed Book BB, 194–195; Leigh 1883: 280). The Shadmans eschewed long-staple cotton planting, preferring to grow rye, oats, sugar cane, and sweet potatoes. They even marketed olives and oranges from John Couper's old groves. Shadman also claimed to own the largest "hogpen" in Glynn County, fencing in 350 acres for his 100 hogs. In 1886, however, a hard freeze killed the groves, and in 1890 a fire swept the old mansion. The plantation was abandoned, ending almost a century of operation (Engel and Stebbins 1974:1–2, 38, 51; Wightman and Cate 1955:43, 55; Wylly 1914).

CHAPTER 3

The Slaves' Living Conditions

$20 Reward

Ranaway from the subscriber, living in Glynn County sometime since, a negro man named *Jacob*, commonly called Gold, 25 or 26 years of age, about 5 feet ten inches high—He has a down look, and stutters considerably when spoken to quickly, and particularly when telling a lie. . . . The above reward will be paid for his apprehension and lodgement in jail, so that I can get him; or fifty dollars for his apprehension and proof to conviction, of his having been harbored by a white person.

Brunswick *Advocate*, 22 November 1838

As we saw in Chapter 2, the rising and falling fortunes of the Couper family were documented in letters, account books, travelogues, and public records. From these scattered written sources, we observed the Coupers as they operated in the white planter-dominated world of tidewater Georgia. The white planter minority was sustained by the labor of the black majority—the thousands of slaves who grew cotton, rice, and foodstuffs, raised the livestock, and cared for the planter families.

On Cannon's Point, the vast majority of the Plantation's antebellum inhabitants were black slaves. At times, they outnumbered the plantation whites over 10 to 1. For most of the antebellum period, the Cannon's Point slave force averaged over 100. It was one of the largest slave holdings in the tidewater region where the median slave force was an impressive 64. In 1820 the Cannon's Point slaves numbered 132, including 30 males and 39 females over 14 years of age. Ten years later, the 113 slaves included 30 males and 43 females over 10 years of age, and the 1840 census enumerated 127 slaves—the 49 females outnumbered the 35 males who were over 10 years old. The informal 1850 inventory of Cannon's Point listed only 90 slaves. The size and composition of the 1860 slave population is unknown, however, since the Cannon's Point slaves were not differentiated from the other slaves that the Coupers owned at Altama and Hamilton plantations (Couper 1839–1854; Gray 1941:Vol. 1, 531; U.S. Bureau of the Census 1820–1860).

THE HIERARCHY OF LABOR

Most of the Cannon's Point slaves spent their lives as field hands, growing the cash and food crops that supported the plantation. When Basil Hall visited the plantation in 1828, at least 128 slaves lived on Cannon's Point. Of these, 70 were adult men and women between the ages of 14 and 50—the rest being children and the elderly. Of the 70 adults there were only 39 "full hands" who could perform a full day's task—usually the cultivation of between $\frac{1}{4}$ to $\frac{3}{4}$ of an acre. In addition there were 16 "three-quarter hands," 11 "half hands," and 4 "quarter hands," all performing less than a full day's work. Thus, the 70 adults actually yielded a total of $57\frac{1}{2}$ "taskable hands," of whom only 44 "taskables" worked in the fields.

The field hands cultivated 200 acres of cotton and 25 acres of corn, peas, and sweet potatoes. These 225 acres were subdivided into square patches measuring 105-feet on a side, making each patch equal to one-quarter of an acre—the units in which tasks were assigned. Each field hand cultivated one or more patches a day as a task (Hall 1829:Vol. 3, 218–219).

Cotton dominated the slaves' lives on a year-round basis. Cotton season actually began in late winter when the slaves listed, manured, and bedded the cotton fields. (*Listing* was hoeing down the old cotton beds or ridges.) A full hand listed $\frac{1}{2}$ acre per day. Then using plows and hoes, the slaves created new beds set 5 feet apart. This was easier work than listing, so a full hand bedded $\frac{3}{4}$ of an acre. Cotton planting began in March: Two hands walked down a bed, hoeing open holes about 18 inches apart; another slave followed dropping about 50 seeds into each hole. As soon as planting ended the slaves began weeding. Generally, a full hand weeded $\frac{1}{2}$ an acre per day. At this rate, the slaves hoed all the fields every 2 weeks. During the second round of hoeing, they thinned out the cotton clusters, leaving only seven or so plants. On the third round, they left only one or two of the best cotton plants per hole. Then in late August or early September, when the cotton began to open in "good blow," the slaves began the long process of picking. A typical hand picked about 100 pounds a day, although women usually picked more than men. After ginning, groups of slaves—usually women and invalid men—sorted the cotton lint according to quality: "first quality," "second quality white," and "yellow." Slaves also "moted" the cotton lint, picking out leaves, stems, and seeds that remained after ginning. After moting, they hand-packed the cotton into bags using iron or wooden pestles (see Figure 5.7). Picking, ginning, moting, and packing often continued into January, completing the yearly work cycle (Hall 1829:Vol. 3, 219–220; Phillips 1969:Vol. 1, 196–203).

Despite the long growing season, the slaves had some leisure time during the daylight hours. On Cannon's Point, the "active hands" finished their tasks by "the middle of the day," after which they were left "to employ the balance, as it is rather well called, or what remains of daylight, in their own fields [gardens], in fishing, or in dancing—in short as they please." This was typical of tidewater plantations, where the task system prevailed. Tidewater slaves enjoyed more daily leisure time than slaves elsewhere in the Old South, but during the late spring when cotton had to be hoed at crucial stages, and again during the fall picking time, tidewater slaves had to work longer hours (Hall 1829:Vol. 3, 223; Johnson 1930:124).

Each morning, with the exception of Sundays and holidays, the slave drivers roused the field hands and escorted them to the fields. Drivers assigned the slaves their tasks and inspected their work in the afternoons. The drivers punished any slaves who failed to complete their work. Each driver wore the badge of his office—the "cotton planter"—a short whip with a heavy handle and a plaited, tapering thong (Hall 1829:Vol. 3, 223; Mallard 1892:40–41). The threat of the whip was always there. Few ex-slave testimonies failed to mention whippings (see Rawick, ed., 1972:Vol. 2, 281, Vol. 3, 201, 273, Vol. 13, 229, Vol. 17, 160–161). As an example, one former tidewater slave testified:

> If slabe don't do tas', de get licking wid lash on naked back. Driver nigger gib licking, but maussa most always been dere. Sometime maybe nigger steal hawg or run 'way to de wood, den he git licking too. Can's be no trouble 'tween white folks and nigger in slabery time for dey do as dey choose wid you. But maussa good to slave if dey done day's tas' and don't be up to no meanness. (Rawick, ed., 1972:Vol. 3, 273)

Some tidewater planters eschewed the whip, preferring other modes of punishment such as extra work, reduced rations, or confinement (King 1828:524; Hazzard 1831:352). The plantation regime, however, was always based on the threat of coercion. As Basil Hall wrote, "It is very disagreeable to speak of the punishments inflicted on these Negroes, but a slaveholder must be more or less a despot in spite of himself, for the laws neither do, nor can they, effectually interfere in the details of discipline" (Hall 1829:Vol. 3, 225).

The drivers meting out these punishments were the agents of the planters' authority. To enhance their stature as authority figures, planters often furnished their drivers with better housing, food, and clothing in order to set them apart from other slaves (King 1828:524–525; Hazzard 1831:351). One overseer claimed, "The more the driver is kept aloof from the [other] negroes, the better" (An Overseer 1836:227). At times the ranks of drivers included such well-respected blacks as African-born slaves, conjurers, and preachers. On Cannon's Point, for example, John Couper's best known driver was "Tom" or Salih Bilali, a Muslim Fullah from the Kingdom of Massina in the Niger Valley of West Africa. Couper purchased Salih Bilali in the Bahamas in 1800 and he later became the head driver at Hopeton (Curtin 1967:145–151; White 1849:228; Lyell, 1849:Vol. 1, 266; Wightman and Cate 1955:153). In a letter to his grandson, Couper also mentioned a slave driver who was a preacher: "I staggered out this forenoon to give old Harry not old Nick but old Parson Harry-directions to prepare land for melons" (Couper 1839).

In addition to drivers, the Cannon's Point slaves included a staff of skilled and service workers. In 1828 Basil Hall enumerated $13\frac{1}{2}$ taskable hands who did not work in the fields, including "cart-drivers, nurses, cooks . . . , carpenters, gardeners, house servants, and stock minders. . . (Hall 1829:Vol. 3, 218). White observers believed that drivers, servants, and skilled workers stood at the top of the tidewater slave hierarchy. These were the "swonga" slaves who were most acquainted with the ways of the "buckras"—the plantation whites. Recent studies of ex-slave narratives, however, have suggested that slaves had their own ingroup social ranking based on their own values system. At the top of the slaves' own hierarchy were the conjurers, root doctors, and preachers. Below them were the craftspeople, exceptional field hands, and the just drivers. Below them were the temporary house servants who lived in the slave quarters as well as the common field hands. And at the bottom of the slave hierarchy were the harsh drivers and the permanent house servants—those slaves who were accorded the highest status in the white social world (Blassingame 1976:150–151; Johnson 1930: 130).

The plantation reward system, nonetheless, was designed to reward those slaves who were most valued by the whites. Often it was the slave drivers who could lay claim to the best housing, food, and clothing (Fairbanks 1974:91; An Overseer 1836:227). Therefore, unless the slaves' own elite—conjurers, root doctors, and preachers—were also drivers, their living conditions would have approximated those of the field hands. Suzanne MacFarlane located a superior slave cabin on Cannon's Point that may have been a driver's residence. In the southern set of slave dwellings (Figure 1.3), she found the ruins of four duplex structures with clay brick chimneys. Three of the cabins measured 20 by 40 feet and their sills apparently rested on the ground or on wooden piers. The cabins were presumably dirt-floored. Each duplex once housed two families—perhaps two generations of the same family. The fourth cabin, however, was larger than the others, measuring 20 by 45 feet. Furthermore, it rested on brick piers, and it surely possessed a plank floor. Since it was the finest slave dwelling on the plantation, this cabin may have housed drivers and their families (MacFarlane 1975:Chap. V).

LIVING QUARTERS AND CONDITIONS

In the northern set of slave dwellings, there were only four one-room cabins whose inhabitants were presumably field hands or skilled slaves. Excavation of the third cabin revealed the ruins of a single-room frame structure which had once housed a slave family—possibly seven or eight persons given the slave population of 90 in

1850 (Otto 1975b:134). When extant, the slave cabin was of frame construction and rested on piers. The frame itself was secured with spikes and bolts such as those recovered from the cabin site (Table 3.1). The walls were clad with hand-sawn boards or clapboards split from logs. The boards were secured to the frame with machine-cut iron nails with machine-made heads—a nail type used since the 1820s (Table 3.2). Shingles split from logs were nailed to the roof rafters and purlins; but the scarcity of shingle nails at the third cabin site (Table 3.1) suggested that the builders fastened shingles by laying down poles over each course of shingles and then nailing the poles to the rafters and purlins (see Parsons 1970:108).

The cabin possessed a single exterior chimney. The chimney was constructed of tabby brick, a kind of concrete made from crushed shells, sand, and lime (see Spalding 1830); the hearth itself was partly lined with fire-resistant clay bricks. The wing-shaped hearth that rested on a crushed shell footing had a fire-baked dirt floor. Since there was a small refuse pit in what would have been the floor area (Figure 3.1), the cabin apparently had a dirt floor. The floor area was a well-packed, sandy soil with crushed shells, food bones, and some artifacts.

The dimensions of the slave cabin were rather difficult to determine. A tabby block and clay brick bats presumably supported the southwestern corner of the cabin (Figure 3.1): this possible pier was 8.5 feet (2.6 m) from the center of the hearth. In addition, a brick bat pier may have supported the sills of the western wall of the cabin: this edge of the cabin wall was about 19.7 feet (6.0 m) from the interior edge of the hearth. Given this evidence, the approximate dimensions of the one-room cabin would have been 17 by 20 feet (5.2 by 6.0 m), providing about 340 square feet of living space for a slave family (Otto 1975:112).

Although offering relatively little floor space, the cabin was outfitted with at least one glazed and shuttered window as well as with a door that could be locked. Fragments of glazed window glass appeared at the third cabin site and in the household refuse (Table 3.3). A small pintle (3.6 inches [9 cm] in length) driven into a window frame to support a swinging window shutter was found near the pier that once supported the western wall. Finally, a bolt from a plate stock lock (Noël Hume 1969a:247–248) and a hinge was found west of the hearth along with a large pintle (5.6 inches [14 cm] in length) that had once been driven into the door frame to support a door. The slave cabin door apparently faced southwest toward the area where the household rubbish was dumped (Figure 3.1).

TABLE 3.1

Hardware Fastenings from the Plantation Sites: Nails

Identifiable fastenings: whole nails[a]	Possible function[b]	Slave cabin		Overseer's house		Planter's kitchen	
		Number	%	Number	%	Number	%
2d	Laths and shingles?	2	1.2	9	12.0	7	2.9
3d	Laths and shingles?	3	1.9	7	9.3	22	9.1
4d	Shingles?	4	2.5	17	22.7	51	21.0
5d	Shingles?	8	5.1	5	6.7	11	4.5
6d	Clapboarding?	12	7.6	7	9.3	41	16.9
7d	Clapboarding?	24	15.2	8	10.7	44	18.1
8d	Boarding and Flooring?	11	7.0	4	5.3	12	5.0
9d	Boarding and Flooring?	12	7.6	5	6.7	19	7.8
10d	Boarding and Flooring?	17	10.8	4	5.3	9	3.7
12d	Rafters and Framing?	22	14.0	6	8.0	17	7.0
16d	Rafters and Framing?	28	17.7	2	2.7	9	3.7
20d and larger	Heavy framing	15	9.5	1	1.3	1	0.4
		158		75		243	

[a]From Fontana (1965) and J. Walker (1971).
[b]From Dunton (1972), Fontana (1965), and J. Walker (1971).

TABLE 3.2

Nail Types from the Plantation Sites (Identifiable Whole and Partial Nails)

Identifiable specimens—whole and partial nail types	Dates of manufacture	Slave cabin		Overseer's house		Planter's kitchen	
		Number	%	Number	%	Number	%
Wrought nails—rose head	Into the early 1800s	1	0.1	1	0.4	5	0.5
Machine-cut, hand-made heads	1790s–1820s	6	0.8	7	3.1	181	19.4
Machine-cut, early machine-made heads	1815–1830s	—	—	—	—	1	0.1
Machine-cut, machine-made heads	1820s to present	717	99.0	217	96.4	746	79.8
Machine-cut sprig	1810s to present	—	—	—	—	2	0.2
		724		225		935	

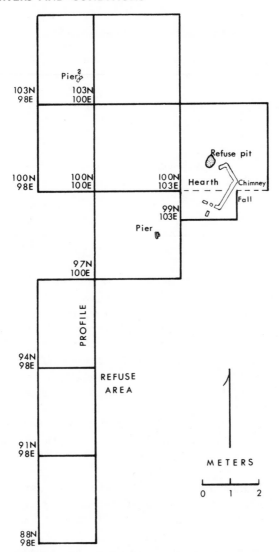

Figure 3.1. Cannon's Point third slave cabin site. Transit station is 7.86 m north of stake 103N 98E.

The third cabin and the remaining three cabin sites in the northern slave quarters were associated with a pit-dug well located about 25 feet (7.6 m) east of the fourth slave cabin site (Figure 1.3). Within the pit a rectangular well casing, measuring about 31 by 36 inches (0.8 by 0.9 m), had been built from posts and discarded

TABLE 3.3
Artifacts from the Plantation Sites

Slave cabin	Overseer's house	Planter's kitchen
Building hardware		
1 eye spike	3 hinge fragments	—
3 hinge fragments		
1 key		
Window glass		
49 fragments	36 fragments	243 fragments
Household furnishings		
—	—	10 stove? fragments
		1 grill fragment from a Franklin stove?

planks. Barrels without bottoms were stacked inside the casing and the space between the casing and barrels was filled with building rubble. This rubble packed between the barrels and casing yielded a "Peter Dorni" pipestem, indicating that the well had been dug during the 1850s—the decade that Dorni pipes began to appear at American sites (Humphrey 1969:15; Omwake 1961). The well fill contained a fired, three-banded, standard Union-issue Minie bullet (Collins 1966:22), indicating the well was abandoned after 1862 when Union troops briefly occupied St. Simons Island (Heard 1938).

The third slave cabin on Cannon's Point closely resembled the one-room frame slave cabin on Rayfield Plantation (Cumberland Island, Georgia). The Rayfield cabin, measuring about 18 by 18 feet (324 square feet) was just slightly smaller than the third cabin (340 square feet). The Rayfield cabin also had a dirt floor because ashes from the hearth covered much of the living area. Moreover, the Rayfield cabin possessed a tabby brick chimney and a clay brick hearth as did the third cabin, although the Rayfield cabin apparently lacked the glazed windows of the third cabin (see Ascher and Fairbanks 1971:5–8).

Since most tidewater slave cabins were "comfortless little . . . puncheon [clapboard] cabins about twenty-five feet square [12 by 12 feet] with wooden [stick and clay] chimneys, and without glass in the windows" (Rose 1964:121), the Cannon's Point third cabin and the Rayfield cabin belonged to the better class of slave dwellings, although they were not considered superior slave cabins.

On Kingsley Plantation in Ft. George Island, Florida, Charles

Fairbanks excavated the largest cabin in a series of tabby hall-and-parlor cabins—it was possibly a driver's residence. Measuring 18.6 by 24.5 feet (455.7 square feet), the Kingsley cabin was far more spacious than the Cannon's Point third cabin, but was about the same size as one unit (450 square feet) of the largest duplex cabin at Cannon's Point which MacFarlane excavated—also possibly a driver's residence. The larger room (the hall) of the Kingsley cabin had a poured tabby floor, but the smaller room (the parlor or bedroom) had a dirt floor. And like the Cannon's Point and Rayfield cabins, the Kingsley cabin had a tabby brick chimney and a clay brick firebox, though it lacked glazed windows (Fairbanks 1974:67–75).

The large, multiroom tabby structures such as the Kingsley cabin were among the best slave dwellings in the Old South. But most tidewater planters furnished their slaves with more modest frame dwellings that resembled the houses of poor whites in terms of construction materials, building techniques, and dimensions. Frame construction, brick chimneys, and such building units as 18 by 18 feet (Rayfield cabin) were familiar features of Anglo-American architecture. Yet, other features of tidewater slave cabins—dirt floors, thatched reed roofs, and such building units as 12 by 12 feet (most tidewater slave cabins) recalled the West African past. African-born slaves often insisted on dirt floors reminiscent of the bare floors of traditional African dwellings. Some tidewater slave cabins even had the thatched roofs that were so commonly found on African structures. And the smaller tidewater slave cabins, measuring 12 by 12 feet, provided slaves with a familiar unit of space, closely resembling the 10-by-10-foot West African norm (Vlach 1978:132–136; Rose 1964:120).

Despite the apparent persistence of certain African architectural traits, most planters openly discouraged African-style huts on their plantations. For example, when Okra, one of James Hamilton Couper's Altama slaves, tried to build an African-style wattle-and-daub hut, Couper forced him to tear it down. In the words of Ben Sullivan, the son of Couper's slave butler, Couper announced "he aihn wahn no African hut on he place." Sullivan, however, heard rumors of another slave who built a house "wid cawn stalks on mud an wid a straw filluh." And on Thomas Spalding's Sapelo Island plantation, some slaves were allowed to build African-style dwellings (Georgia Writers' Project 1940:178–182; Lovell 1932:99–101). Yet, such huts were a rarity. The vast majority of tidewater slaves lived in one-room frame cabins that had stick-and-clay chimneys and lacked glass windows (Forten 1864:589–592).

On the larger tidewater plantations, the individual slave cabins were arranged in rows—single or double rows—facing a street. Often each "street" had its own well, a "sick house," and a mill house where the slaves ground their corn. In turn, each slave cabin typically had its own garden patch, poultry coop or pigpen and a refuse midden (Olmsted 1861:233).

A journalist visiting a tidewater plantation left a graphic description of a typical slave quarters:

> The huts stand in a row, like a street, each detatched, with a poultry-house of rude planks behind it. . . . No attempt at any drainage or any convenience [privy] existed near them, and the same remark applies to very good houses of white people in the South. Heaps of oyster shells, broken crockery, old shoes, rags, and feathers were found near each hut. (Russell 1954:77)

Few white visitors, however, stepped inside the cabins. Even plantation whites rarely entered the cabins. As one of the Northern "Gideonites" living on the sea islands during the Civil War wrote: "They [the slaves] seem to have not the least idea that any one will enter, and it is evident and proven, that, in the time of their masters no white person ever did" (French 1862:164). Consequently, there are few written descriptions of the interiors of the slave cabins where slave families passed the hours between sundown and sunup.

Although planters provided slave families with their cabins, the slaves themselves furnished the interiors. The planter might give a slave family an iron pot or a skillet, but the slaves accumulated the rest (Flanders 1933:156; A Planter 1836:580–584). As an example, one former slave recalled the furnishings in his family's cabin: "De master don't gib you nutting for yo' house—you hab to get dat de best you can. In our house was bed, table, and bench to sit on. My father mek dem. My mother had fourteen children—us sleep on floor" (Rawick, ed., 1972:Vol. 3, Part 3, 200).

Slave men may have fashioned the furniture for the cabins, but the cabin itself was the domain of the slave women. The tidewater slave family was decidedly matrifocal. Among the coastal blacks, who were colloquially known as the "Gullah" or "Geechee" (Crum 1940), it was believed that a person was more closely related to his or her mother than father. A common explanation was the same one offered in many West African societies: a person is fed on his mother's milk (Bascom 1941:48).

The matrilineal emphasis of the Gullah family, nevertheless, was reinforced by the white planters. Cabins were assigned to the slave women not the men. Children were listed as belonging to their mothers not their fathers. It was the woman who received the family's weekly food rations. And on plantations where textiles were issued by the yard, the women fashioned the clothing for their families. The women even tended the garden patches and cared for the family's livestock with the "casual assistance" of their husbands and children. And when women sold the garden truck and livestock, they pocketed the money, using the funds to purchase luxury clothing, household furnishings, and supplementary foods (Johnson 1930: 137; Woofter 1930:35). Slave fathers, nonetheless, made a great contribution to their families' diets by hunting and fishing. While the women tended to their many household chores, slave men devoted their leisure hours to food collecting (Johnson 1930:142; Woofter 1930:35).

Tangible evidence of the women's household labors and the men's food collecting efforts could be found in the refuse midden that lay just outside the door of the third cabin (Figure 3.1). During the antebellum years, this refuse midden was a noisome heap of ashes, bones, shells, feathers, broken crockery, smashed bottles, buttons, and rags—the mundane bits and pieces of artifacts and foods that had once been functioning elements in slave household activities such as food procuring, preparation, and consumption, clothing manufacture and repair, and relaxation (see Schiffer 1972; South 1979). In this refuse midden field crews excavated three squares with trowels. In order to maximize recovery of artifacts and food remains, the excavators screened all the refuse materials with $\frac{1}{8}$-inch mesh. Zone I(A) of the refuse midden, which contained no artifacts whose known beginning date of manufacture was later than 1860 (Table 3.4), overlay several zones containing prehistoric materials (B-D) (Figure 3.2). Therefore, only Zone I of the midden could be reliably dated to the antebellum years (Table 3.4).

HUNTING AND FISHING FOR FOOD

Perhaps the most fascinating artifacts recovered from the slaves' refuse midden were those once used by slave men in hunting and fishing. Surprisingly, lead shot, a percussion cap, and a dark-grey gunflint were found in the antebellum refuse (Table 3.5). Apparently Cannon's Point slaves had access to both percussion-lock and flintlock firearms. Yet, indirect evidence for slave-owned firearms has appeared at other slave cabins excavated in the Geor-

TABLE 3.4
Dating the Northern Third Slave Cabin Refuse (Zone I)

Ceramic hallmarks	1790	1800	1810	1820	1830	1840	1850	1860	1870
Japan Flowers[a]									
KMW & Co						├——┤			
(1835–1842)									
Archipelago—[b]									
J. Ridgway & Co.						├———┤			
(1841–1853)									
Glass hallmarks									
None									
Clay pipes									
McDougall/							├———————┤		
Glasgow[c]									
(post-1846)									
Peter Dorni[d]							├——————┤		
(post-1850)									
Buttons									
Treble Stan'd Ex-									
tra Rich[e] (1850s)							├——┤		
Scovill Double									
Gilt[f] (post-1840)							├———————┤		
U.S. Navy Button[g]									
(1800–1830s)			├——————————┤					

[a]Godden (1971:89).
[b]Godden (1971:88).
[c]l. Walker (1971:25), Walker and Walker (1969:132); Humphrey (1969:17–18).
[d]Humphrey (1969:15); Omwake (1961:12–15).
[e]Luscomb (1972:161).
[f]Luscomb (1972:174).
[g]Luscomb (1972:11).

gia and Florida tidewater. At Rayfield Plantation the slave cabin site yielded a gunflint, lead shot, a chunk of lead for molding bullets. In turn, the cabin site on Kingsley Plantation produced a "gunflint and several spherical lead balls . . . representing shot for hunting." Planters may have encouraged slaves to hunt in order to enhance their diets, in spite of lingering fears of armed slave revolt. And by using their firearms or traps, the slaves in the Cannon's Point third cabin collected opossums, raccoons, rabbits, wood rats, and mink (Tables 3.6, 3.7), though they preferred possum meat to other wild flesh

97 N
100 E

94 N
100 E

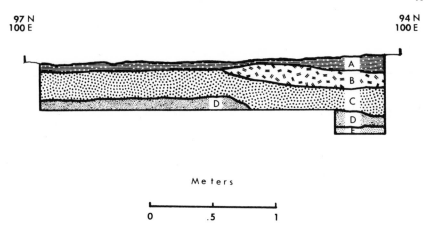

Me ters

0   .5   1

100 N
106 E

100 N
103 E

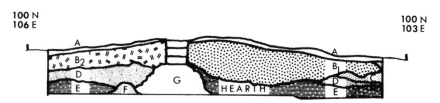

Figure 3.2. Northern third slave cabin profiles.

(top) East wall profile of square 94N 98E—slave cabin refuse. (A) humus and dark-grey sandy soil with loosely compact whole and crushed shell (Zone I); (B) compact grey sandy soil with crushed and whole shell; (C) compact greyish-brown sandy soil with scattered shell; (D) stained brown sandy soil with infrequent whole and crushed shell; (E) orange sterile sandy soil. The surface at stake 94N 100E is 1.85 m below datum.

(bottom) South wall profile of square 100N 103E—slave cabin hearth. (A) duff and humus; (B_1) ash with whole shell and refuse; (B_2) chimney fall rubble (C) dark-grey sandy soil; (D) compact dark-grey sandy soil with crushed shell—former ground surface (Zone II); (E) dark-grey sandy soil with some whole shell (burned reddish-brown in hearth area); (F) mottled dark-grey and orange sandy soil; (G) shell footing for hearth bricks. The surface at stake 100N 103E is 1.75 m below datum.

(Table 3.8). All of these small mammals could have been collected in the forests and marsh fringes of Cannon's Point. The clapper rail whose bones also appeared in the refuse was probably shot in the marsh (see Cahalane 1947:482, 489).

Fishing, however, supplied far more wild flesh than hunting (Table 3.8). At the third cabin, the antebellum refuse yielded a slip-

TABLE 3.5
Material Items Used in Occupations, Food Collecting,
and Food Processing

Slave cabin	Overseer's house	Planter's kitchen
Occupational items		
—	1 partial sickle[a]	1 piece of carpenter's marking chalk[b]
Food-collecting items		
1 dark-grey gunflint	1 dark-grey gunflint	1 flintlock plate
1 percussion cap	1 percussion cap	1 amber gunflint
1 banded slip-sinker fishing weight	1 slip-sinker	1 calcined gunflint
3 bird? shot	1 net weight	11 percussion caps
1 buck? shot	1 bird? shot	1 slip-sinker
		8 bird? shot
		6 swan? shot
		2 buck? shot
Food-processing items		
11 cooking pot fragments	6 cooking pot fragments	1 partial cooking-pot handle
	1 partial cooking-pot handle	
	1 "Dutch oven" fragment	
	1 skewer	

[a]The sickle was probably used by one of the overseer's servants to collect marsh grasses for fodder.

[b]Possibly used by one of the slave carpenters.

sinker weight—used in hook-and-line fishing—as well as a weight from a cast net. With hooks and lines, the slaves could have caught most fish except mullet. And with cast nets, they could have collected mullet and shrimp (see Larson 1969:166–172). It is not known if the Cannon's Point slaves possessed boats for fishing. On neighboring Butler's Point Plantation (Figure 1.2), the slaves fashioned and sold dugout canoes (King 1828:524). Along the tidewater, slave-owned boats were common. Yet, even if Cannon's Point slaves had access to boats, it "was seldom that a master permitted his people to go at will in boats upon the creeks, and only with special permission could they go upon the Sound for one of the most exciting of all water sports, drum fishing" (Johnson 1930:142). Even if they received permission to visit the rich fishing spots in the sounds

TABLE 3.6
Northern Third Slave Cabin Faunal Remains[a]

Taxa (genus and species)	Specimens		Weight		Minimum individuals	
	Number	%	gm	%	Number	%
Didelphis marsupialis (opossum)	32	3.4	23.0	4.9	2	2.9
Sylvilagus sp. (rabbit)	12	1.3	2.2	0.5	1	1.4
Oryctolagus cuniculus (domestic rabbit)	4	0.4	0.7	0.2	1	1.4
Neotoma floridana (Florida wood rat)	3	0.3	0.3	0.1	1	1.4
Procyon lotor (raccoon)	14	1.5	7.4	1.6	2	2.9
Mustela vison (mink)	3	0.3	0.4	0.1	1	1.4
Sus scrofa (domestic pig)	60	6.4	86.5	18.2	3	4.4
Bos taurus (domestic cattle)	16	1.7	157.4	33.2	3	4.4
cf *Ovis aries*[b] (domestic sheep)	10	1.1	43.0	9.1	2	2.9
Gallus gallus (domestic fowl)	5	0.5	8.8	1.9	3	4.4
Rallus longirostris (clapper rail)	1	>0.1	0.3	0.1	1	1.4
Malaclemys terrapin (diamondback terrapin)	137	14.6	58.9	12.4	3	4.4
Trionyx cf *ferox* (softshell turtle)	2	0.2	0.3	0.1	1	1.4
Hyla sp. (tree frog)	2	0.2	0.1	<0.1	1	1.4
cf *Rana pipens* (leopard frog)	1	>0.1	0.1	<0.1	1	1.4
cf *Dasyatis* sp. (stingray)	2	0.2	0.2	<0.1	1	1.4
Acipenser oxyrhynchus (sturgeon)	4	0.4	0.3	0.1	1	1.4
Lepisosteus osseus (longnosed gar)	92	9.8	6.7	1.4	3	4.4
Arius felis (marine catfish)	75	8.0	10.5	2.2	6	8.7
Bagre marinus (gafftopsail catfish)	93	9.9	13.4	2.8	4	5.6
Archosargus probatocephalus (sheepshead)	6	0.6	1.3	0.3	2	2.9
Bairdiella chrysura (silver perch)	24	2.6	0.6	0.1	2	2.9
Cynoscion nebulosus (spotted sea trout)	1	>0.1	0.4	0.1	1	1.4

(*continued*)

TABLE 3.6 (Continued)

Taxa (genus and species)	Specimens		Weight		Minimum individuals	
	Number	%	gm	%	Number	%
Cynoscion sp. (sea trout)	9	1.0	0.8	0.2	3	4.4
Menticirrhus sp. (kingfish)	7	0.8	0.2	<0.1	2	2.9
Micropogon undulatus (Atlantic croaker)	15	1.6	1.1	0.2	3	4.4
Pogonias cromis (black drum)	147	15.7	41.9	8.8	3	4.4
Sciaenops ocellatus (red drum)	6	0.6	3.1	0.7	2	2.9
Mugil sp. (mullet)	138	14.7	3.7	0.8	7	10.2
Paralichthys sp. (flounder)	15	1.6	0.8	0.2	3	4.4
	936		474.4		69	
Other taxa						
Unidentified small mammal	65		4.5		—	
Unidentified medium mammal	217		42.6		—	
Unidentified large mammal	661		526.3		—	
Unidentified mammal	635		71.4		—	
Unidentified Aves (bird)	137		25.0		—	
Unidentified Chelonia (turtle)	250		41.7		—	
Lacertilia (lizard)	1		0.1		1	
cf Salientia (toads and frogs)	7		0.3		—	
cf Sciaenidae (drums)	61		20.8		—	
Ariidae (marine catfish)	229		49.6		25	
Unidentified Osteichthyes (bony fish)	576		56.5		—	
cf Myliobatidae (eagle rays)	1		0.1		1	
Unidentified bone	229		30.3		—	
	3069		869.2		27	
Totals	4005		1343.6		96	

[a]Format based on Wing (1965).

[b]See Hole, Flannery, and Neely (1969) for formula to distinguish sheep and goat metapodial condyles.

TABLE 3.7
Estimated Edible-Meat Weight[a] of Domestic Animal Bones
at the Plantation Sites

Domestic	Skeletal weight (gm)	Conversion[b] factor	Total weight (gm)	Conversion factor	Edible-meat weight (gm)	%
Slave cabin						
Rabbit	0.7	(×11.6)	—	—	8.1	1
Hog	86.5	(÷.070)	1235.7	(×.70)	865.0	37
Cattle	157.4	(÷.077)	2044.2	(×.50)	1022.1	44
Sheep	43.0	(÷.073)	589.0	(×.50)	294.5	13
Chicken	8.8	(×15.6)	—	—	137.3	6
	296.4				2327.0	
Overseer's house						
Cat?	1.9	(×9.7)	—	—	18.4	2
Hog	49.2	(÷.070)	702.9	(×0.70)	492.0	55
Cattle	58.4	(÷.077)	758.4	(×0.50)	379.2	42
Chicken	0.7	(×15.6)	—	—	10.9	1
	110.2				900.5	
Planter's kitchen						
Hog	170.7	(÷0.070)	2438.6	(×0.70)	1707.0	19
Cattle	893.5	(÷0.077)	11603.9	(×0.50)	5802.0	65
Sheep	200.7	(÷0.073)	2749.3	(×0.50)	1374.7	15
Chicken	5.5	(×15.6)	—	—	85.8	1
	1270.4				8969.5	

[a]See Chaplin (1971:67–69) and Daly (1969:150) for criticisms of various techniques for converting dry skeletal weights to edible-meat weight.
[b]Conversion factors derived from Ziegler (1973:28–31).

(Figure 3.3), the Cannon's Point slaves would have faced a long trip down the Hampton River, taking the tides into account. Given the travel restrictions as well as their limited leisure time, most slaves probably fished along the banks of tidal streams (Woofter 1930:35).

The coastal salt marshes are drained by a network of tidal streams, ranging in size from small creeks that are dry during low tide to large rivers up to 2 miles wide (3.2 km). The problem is gaining access to the tidal streams. Only rarely do the tidal creeks and rivers cut into the high ground, creating a convenient bank. Usually the high ground is separated from the streams by a morass of salt marsh. Only the "high marsh" near the land is firm enough to

TABLE 3.8

Estimated Edible-Meat Weights of Wild Animal Bones at the Plantation Sites

	Skeletal wt. (gm)	Conversion factor	Total wt. (gm)	Conversion factor	Edible meat (gm)	%
Slave cabin						
Opossum	23.0	(× 12.2)[c]	—	—	280.6	15
Woodrat	0.3	(× 18.8)[c]	—	—	5.6	<1
Raccoon	7.4	(× 12.6)[c]	—	—	93.2	5
Other wild mammals	2.6	(÷ 0.060)[c]	43.3	× .60[b]	26.0	1
Clapper rail	0.3	(÷ 0.060)[c]	5.0	× .70[c]	3.5	<1
Diamondback terrapins	58.9	(× 1.9)[a]	—	—	111.9	6
Other turtles	0.3	(× 3.0)[a]	—	—	0.9	<1
Frogs	0.1	(× ?)	—	—	?	—
Chondrichthyes (rays)	0.2	(× 20.0?)[a]	—	—	4.0	<1
Osteichthyes (catfish)	23.9	(× 15.4)[a]	—	—	368.1	20
Other bony fish	60.9	(× 16.0)[a]	—	—	974.4	52
	177.9				>1868.2	
Overseer's house						
Opossum	6.9	(× 12.2)[c]	—	—	84.2	17
Squirrel	0.1	(× 14.2)[c]	—	—	1.4	<1
Wood rat	0.2	(18.8)[c]	—	—	3.8	<1
Raccoon	6.5	(× 12.6)[c]	—	—	81.9	16
Other wild mammals	0.7	(÷ 0.060)[c]	11.7	× .60[c]	7.0	1
Diamondback terrapins	50.8	(× 1.9)[a]	—	—	96.5	19
Other turtles	9.0	(× 3.0)[a]	—	—	27.0	5
Chondrichthyes (rays)	0.1	(× 20.0)[a]	—	—	2.0	<1

(continued)

walk on. The marsh banks along the creeks are simply too soft to support the weight of a person during low tide (Dahlberg 1972:327; Larson 1969:24–25; Teal 1958:185–187; Ursin 1972). When the marshes are flooded by high tides, only a few species of fish regularly feed in the high marshes firm enough to support a fisherman. Most

TABLE 3.8 (*Continued*)

	Skeletal wt. (gm)	Conversion factor	Total wt. (gm)	Conversion factor	Edible meat (gm)	%
Overseer's house						
Osteichthyes (cat-fish)	7.3	(× 15.4)[a]	—	—	112.4	22
Other bony fish	5.8	(× 16.0)[a]	—	—	92.8	18
	87.4				509.0	
Planter's kitchen						
Opossum	3.0	(× 12.2)[c]	—	—	36.6	1
Wood rat	0.2	(× 18.8)[c]	—	—	3.8	<1
Raccoon	16.0	(× 12.6)[c]	—	—	201.6	3
Deer	23.4	(× 13.7)[a]	—	—	320.6	5
Other wild mammals	3.9	(÷ .060)[d]	65.0	× .60[b]	39.0	1
Diamondback terrapins	410.8	(× 1.9)[a]	—	—	780.5	13
Pond turtles	40.1	(× 1.8)[a]	—	—	72.2	1
Other turtles	83.7	(× 3.0)[a]	—	—	251.1	4
Alligators	23.8	(× 16.0)[a]	—	—	380.8	6
Frogs	0.2	(× ?)	—	—	?	—
Chondrichthyes (rays) (sharks)	18.0	(× 20.0?)[a]	—	—	360.0	6
Osteichthyes (cat-fish)	98.9	(× 15.4)[a]	—	—	1523.1	26
Other bony fish	120.4	(× 16.0)[a]	—	—	1926.4	33
	842.4				>5895.7	

[a]Cumbaa (n.d.) Cumbaa (1974, personal communication).
[b]Cumbaa (1975b:55).
[c]Ziegler (1973:28–31).

fish, including marine catfish, do not enter the high marsh. Since they are sand- and mud-bottom feeders, catfish remain in the creek and river channels, even during high tide (Dahlberg 1972:Table 2; Larson 1969:167; Miller and Jorgenson 1969:10).

According to an 1869 map which depicted Cannon's Point Plantation (U.S. Coast Survey 1869), Jones Creek cut into the high ground along the western edge of the peninsula—directly opposite the northern set of slave cabins (Figure 1.3). Here slaves could have

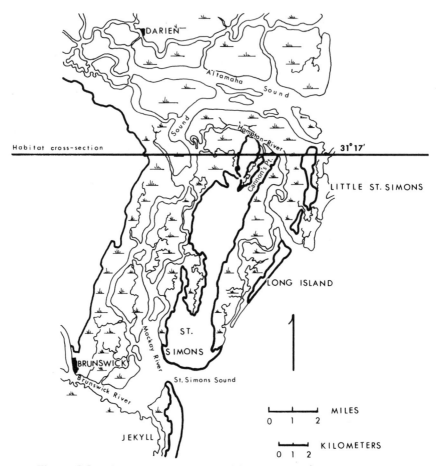

Figure 3.3. Cannon's Point and outlying habitats. (Adapted from Kemble 1961:xl; U.S. Geological Survey 1954.)

fished with lines and nets during the high tides that brought in game fish. By fishing in Jones Creek, the slaves caught a rather limited range of common fish species from among the dozens of species available in the sounds and the Altamaha estuary (Dahlberg 1972, 1975:Table 3.9). Identifiable fish taxa appearing in the slave cabin refuse included stingrays, sturgeon, gar, sheepshead, silver perch, sea trout, kingfish, croaker, mullet, flounder, and marine catfish (Table 3.6). Catfish, in particular, supplied much of the usable meat obtained from fish (Table 3.8). Yet, the slave refuse also yielded the bones of red and black drum which are commonly found

TABLE 3.9
Habitats Used by the Field Slaves for Food Collecting[a]

Aquatic	Terrestrial
Sounds	Cannon's Point forests and secondary
croakers?	growth
black drums?	Opossums
red drums?	Rabbits
Sounds, tidal rivers, and creeks	Woodrats
(lower reaches of the estuary)	Raccoons
diamondback terrapins	Minks
Stingrays	Salt marsh
Sturgeons	Clapper rails
Gars	Raccoons?
Marine catfish	Minks?
Gafftop-sail catfish	
Sheepshead	
Silver perch	
Spotted sea trout	
Sea trout	
Kingfish	
Croakers?	
Black drums?	
Red drums?	
Mullet	
Flounders	
Streamside salt marsh	
Diamondback terrapins	
Landward marsh	
Soft-shell turtles?	
Freshwater ponds	
Leopard frogs	
Soft-shell turtles?	
Freshwater rivers	
Sturgeons?	

[a]Sources: Dahlberg (1972); Fairbanks (1974); Goldman (1910); Hazzard (1825); Larson (1969); Shelford (1963); Teal (1962); Ursin (1972).

in the deeper sounds. Perhaps the slaves caught drums on rare visits to the sounds, or perhaps these fish were gifts from the planter's fishermen (see Dahlberg 1972:342–343). Turtles—both diamondbacks and soft-shells—were far less important food sources than fish. Fish, not turtles and game, were the most important wild food animals for the slaves living in the third cabin (Table 18), corroborating Basil Hall's claim that the Cannon's Point slaves spent most of their leisure time fishing (Hall 1829:Vol. 3, 223).

At the Kingsley slave cabin, Fairbanks also found that fish, turtles, and game were a "significant supplement" to slave diets. Moreover, he noted: "The absence of forest game such as deer suggest that the adjacent tidal streams were the major hunting [and fishing] areas" (Fairbanks 1974:87). But at the Rayfield slave cabin, there was less evidence of the wild foods the slaves collected. Although the bones of wild birds and mammals were present, the fragments were too small to permit naming the animals. No turtle remains could be identified and the only identifiable fish were catfish and shad (Ascher and Fairbanks 1971:11).

Slaves at Kingsley, Rayfield, and Cannon's Point collected wild animals in order to supplement their weekly food rations. On Cannon's Point in 1828, slaves over 14 years of age received 9 quarts of corn per week, and the children received from 5 to 8 quarts. Slaves could also substitute a bushel of sweet potatoes or two pecks of "paddy"—unhusked rice—for the corn (Hall 1829:Vol. 3, 224). In addition, the Coupers cultivated a special patch of cabbage and cauliflower for their slaves who also had their pick of the turnips and rutabagas from the fodder crop (Editor 1833:252; Couper 1835: 350–352). And during the 1840s, the time of the extant Cannon's Point accounts, the slave rations included rice flour, molasses, and "2nd quality and small" rice (Couper 1839–1854). The weekly peck of corn was a near universal feature of tidewater slave life. Moreover, most slaves received regular issues of salt, molasses, and vegetables in season. But in the tidewater area, not all slaves received the weekly 3 pounds of "bacon" (salt pork), a standard feature of Old South slave diets. Some tidewater planters periodically butchered cattle, hogs, and even sheep, issuing fresh meat to their slaves. Other planters issued rations of salt fish—a curious custom that may have been adopted from the West Indies (Handler and Lange 1978:87; Hilliard 1972:59; Rose 1964:122–123; Woofter 1930:30). On a few tidewater plantations, there was no meat ration. One former slave, for example, claimed that slaves on her plantation received only corn and potatoes: "No meat whatsoever was issued." These slaves had to furnish their own protein by fishing (Rawick, ed., 1972:Vol. 13, Part 3, 229).

On Cannon's Point, the food bones from the third slave cabin refuse demonstrated that the Coupers' slaves supplied much of their own protein by hunting and fishing. By translating bone weights of food animals into their equivalent meat weights, one finds that the slave men who lived in the third cabin supplied almost half of their family's meat diet by collecting game and fish (Table 3.10).

For Cannon's Point slaves, food collecting was a necessity, not a luxury, because the slaves did not receive regular meat rations during much of the plantation's history. In 1828 the slaves received only salt fish and occasional issues of salt beef. The fish could have been salted on the plantation, but it was probably commercial salt fish such as the "No. 3, Mackerel," which the Butler's Point slaves received. The salt beef ration, which was a favor and could "never be claimed as a right," was probably salted on the plantation (Hall

TABLE 3.10
Domestic and Wild Food Animals from the Plantation Sites

	Slave cabin		Overseer's house		Planter's kitchen	
	Number	%	Number	%	Number	%
Minimum number of individuals (MNI)						
Wild	56	82.4	36	87.8	154	90.1
Domestic	12	17.6	5	12.2	17	9.9
	68		41		171	
Identifiable bone fragments						
Wild	839	89.8	257	82.9	2506	93.4
Domestic	95	10.2	53	17.1	178	66
	934		310		2684	
Bone weights (gm)						
	Weight (gm)		Weight (gm)		Weight (gm)	
Wild	177.9	37.5	87.4	44.2	842.4	39.9
Domestic	296.4	62.5	110.2	55.8	1270.4	60.1
	474.3		197.6		2112.8	
Estimated edible-meat weights (gm)						
Wild	>1868.2	44.5	509.0	36.1	>5895.7	39.7
Domestic	2327.0	55.5	900.5	63.9	8969.5	60.3
	4195.2		1409.5		>14865.2	

1829:Vol. 3, 224; also see King 1828:526). John Couper left a document telling how "To Salt Meat in Hot Weather" (Couper n.d.c). Surprisingly, no references to a "bacon" ration appeared in any travelogues or in the Cannon's Point accounts until 1853 when in June James H. Couper purchased a 732-pound hogshead of bacon sides. The November accounts listed two more hogsheads (1500 pounds) of bacon sides (Couper 1839–1854:472, 479–480). If there were about 90 slaves living on Cannon's Point in 1853, these three hogsheads would have furnished a little less than three pounds a week for each slave for half the year. Thus until 1853 the Cannon's Point slaves received only occasional issues of beef, mutton, and pork (Table 3.6). The slaves had to supplement their meager meat rations through their own efforts. Meat hunger was not a trivial matter for slaves. More tidewater slaves claimed that food shortages—not cruel treatment—drove them to run away (see Blassingame 1977:359).

In addition to collecting wild animals, slaves could supplement their rations by raising small livestock. On Cannon's Point, slaves used surplus corn and vegetables from their rations to feed their hogs, which they were always "allowed to rear on their own account." Marked slave hogs could have foraged in the plantation's forests, visiting the slave cabins for handouts; or, the hogs could have been penned behind the cabins, fattening on surplus food and offal. Since hogs converted one-fifth of what they ate into meat, and since they had large, frequent litters, hogs were ideal domestic stock for slaves. Although slaves sold many of their hogs to planters or local shopkeepers, they ate some of their stock (Hall 1829: Vol. 3, 224; Leeds and Vayda 1965:233; Olmsted 1968:422; Woofter 1930:30–31). The high ratio of pork bones to identifiable individual pigs (Table 3.11) in the third cabin refuse strongly suggested that the slave family occasionally enjoyed fresh pork (see Chaplin 1971:67), since locally killed animals can be identified by a high ratio of bones to individual animals.

Domestic fowl provided another source of protein and money. In 1828 the Couper family bought slave-grown poultry at the following rates: Eggs at $12\frac{1}{2}$ cents [per dozen]; chickens, $12\frac{1}{2}$ cents [each]; fowls [guinea?], 20 to 25 cents, . . . ; ducks, twice as much" (Hall 1829:Vol. 3, 224). In addition, slaves ate eggs and chickens from their own flocks since shell fragments and bones appeared in the refuse midden. Even domestic rabbit bones appeared in the slave refuse (Table 3.6). Behind their cabin, the slave family built a rabbit

TABLE 3.11
Fresh and Commercial Meats: Ratios of Bone
Fragments to Individuals

	Slave cabin	Overseer's house	Planter's kitchen
Cattle	16/3 = 5.3	8/1 = 8	48/4 = 12.2
Hogs	60/3 = 20	33/2 = 16.5	61/5 = 12.2

hutch, a poultry house, and possibly a pigpen. A posthole from one of these structures appeared in the refuse midden.

THE SLAVE DIET

Near their cabin, the slaves often cleared a patch for a garden. Although the Cannon's Point slaves were free to plant as much land as they chose, most slave gardens were less than an acre in size. Commonly, tidewater slaves planted a few rows of corn and the rest in sweet potatoes, cowpeas, and greens. A few African-born slaves, however, grew sesame (an Afro-Asian plant) which they pounded in mortars to make sesame oil and candy (Georgia Writers' Project 1940:70–71, 162; Hall 1829:Vol. 3, 224; Hilliard 1972:183; Johnson 1930:136; Wightman and Cate 1955:163). Slave women usually tended the gardens and sold the surplus truck. Some of the garden produce was fed to the stock; the rest went into the cooking pots (Johnson 1930:136–137).

Each woman—with the aid of her children—prepared her family's meals. One evening each week, usually on Mondays, the slave women met at the corn house to receive the weekly rations from the drivers. After the women shelled the corn cobs by rubbing them together, the drivers poured the corn kernels onto a large hide or blanket and measured each slave's allotment into baskets. Each woman ground her family's corn rations on small hand-powered mill stones, if they were available; or, she pounded the corn in wooden mortars—artifacts with probable African antecedents (Pearson 1969:52–53; Glassie 1968:116). After milling, the woman separated the meal by shaking it in pinestraw baskets, using coarse meal, or grits, to boil as hominy and using the finest meal, corn flour, to bake as pone. If a Dutch oven was available, wet meal could have been baked in it with coals heaped on the top lid to bake the meal thoroughly. Pone could even be baked in a skillet such as the one that turned up at the Kingsley slave cabin (Fairbanks 1974:87; Johnson 1930:136; Pearson 1969:53). But even if such utensils as "ovens" and skillets were missing as they seem to have been at the third cabin (Table 14) and the Rayfield cabin (Ascher and Fairbanks 1971), slaves could bake corn pone on hoe blades placed directly in the ashes (Carawan, Carawan, and Yellin 1967:34). If they received no rice flour, they beat wet rice into a paste, mixing it with honey, brown sugar, and salt to make flatcakes—"sarakas" (Georgia Writers' Project 1940:70–71, 162, 193–194). Possibly, the Cannon's Point slaves used their rations of rice flour and sweetening to make sarakas.

In addition to breads, tidewater slaves cooked grain-based pottages. Corn kernels or grits could be boiled in iron pots as hominy—a favorite food of tidewater slaves and poorer whites. Often the ubiquitous hominy pot was the only cooking utensil in a slave cabin (French 1862:163). At both the third cabin and the Rayfield cabin, only fragments of iron cooking pots could be identified. Yet, even if slaves possessed only a pot or two, they could have cooked a variety of stews and pottages: Vegetables and meats could be added to hominy; sweet potatoes, turnips, cowpeas, and other truck could be cooked with cured or wild meats. "Hopping John," a concoction eaten by poorer whites as well as slaves, included cowpeas, rice, and salt meat. Rice, a common slave food, could be cooked in rice-based stews, *pileaus*. These one-pot meals were a convenient way of combining many different foods—grains, vegetables, and meats (see Ames 1969:27; Fairbanks 1976:172; Genovese 1974:548; Hilliard 1972:51; Holland 1969; Pearson 1969:53; A Planter 1836:582–583; Towne 1901:399).

Stewing seems to have been a rather common means of preparing foods at the third cabin. The food bones from the third cabin refuse offered indirect proof of one-pot meals. There were no saw marks on the beef, mutton, and pork bones, suggesting the meat was not divided into regular cuts for roasting. Rather, many of the large mammal bones had been cleaved open with axes or cleavers. This would have offered a way of gaining more nourishment from a limited meat supply. A former slave from South Carolina described this practice in his description of a one-pot meal: "The whole [stew] had been boiled . . . until the flesh had disappeared from the bones, which were broken in small pieces—a flitch of bacon, some green corn, squashes, tomatoes, and onions had been added" (Ball 1859:139).

THE USE OF CERAMICS

Ceramics, which are found in plenitude on most historic sites, are among the most useful artifacts in studying the past, offering insights into the "foodways" of site inhabitants—"the system of food conceptualization, procurement, distribution, preservation, preparation, and consumption" (Anderson 1971:xl; Deetz 1973:16)—as well as providing useful tools for dating sites (South 1972). Stanley South has devised a *mean ceramic dating formula* based on the frequency of ceramic types with known timespans of manufacture. But when we applied the South mean ceramic dating formula to the sample of ceramic sherds from the antebellum refuse at the third cabin, we received a mean ceramic date of 1816.5 (Table 3.12)—a date that is earlier than the probable span of occupation at the slave cabin. The profusion of machine-cut nails with machine-made heads indicated the cabin was built during or after the 1820s (Table 3.2). In addition, the presence of Peter Dorni pipestems and a "treble Stan'd Extra Rich" button in the antebellum refuse (Table 3.4) indicated that the cabin was occupied in the 1850s.

Charles Fairbanks, who used the South mean ceramic data formula to date the ceramic assemblage from the Kingsley cabin, also received earlier dates than he expected. Possibly, this discrepancy can be explained by a lag between the date of manufacture of ceramics and the date of acquisition by the slaves. Perhaps slaves used chipped, outmoded ceramics that had been discarded by the planter family. If so, these older, discarded ceramics would have produced an earlier ceramic date than the median date of occupation as derived from nonceramic artifacts (Fairbanks 1974:79, 82). But when we compared the ceramics from the slave cabin refuse with the ceramics from the planter's kitchen refuse (Chapter 5), we found that the slaves in the third cabin used a few ceramic discards from the planter family. Only four ceramic items out of a total of 126 ceramic vessels in the slave refuse matched the surface decorations of ceramic items from the planter's refuse (Otto in South 1977:97). Since the slaves rarely used the planter family's discards, they acquired their ceramics in other ways. Possibly, the planter family furnished their slaves and hired overseers with a "special class of wares" that was "judged more durable and 'suitable' for laborers" [and super-

TABLE 3.12
Applications of the Mean Ceramic Data Formula[a]

Ceramic type	Type median	Count	Product
Slave cabin site—refuse (Zone I)			
13	05	97	485
8	05	26	130
20	05	67	335
17	0	19	0
12	05	7	35
10	18	9	162
11	18	105	1890
20	05	86	430
2	60	74	4440
1	60	4	240
5	15	6	90
		500	$(8237 \div 500) + 1800 = 1816.5$
Overseer's house site—refuse (Zones II–III)			
13	05	18	90
8	05	2	10
6	43	13	559
15	−2	3	(−6)
19	05	9	45
12	05	8	40
10	18	3	54
11	18	16	288
20	05	52	260
2	60	36	2160
3	57	1	57
1	60	1	60
27	−15	7	(−105)
5	15	2	30
		171	$(3653 \div 171) + 1800 = 1820.7$

(continued)

TABLE 3.12 (*Continued*)

Ceramic type	Type median	Count	Product
Couper kitchen—refuse (Zones II–IV)			
13	05	3	15
8	05	6	30
15	−2	28	(−56)
19	05	26	130
17	0	41	0
10	18	20	360
11	18	900	16,200
12	05	10	50
30	05	61	305
2	60	56	3,360
3	57	10	570
27	−15	1	(−15)
1	60	2	120
5	15	13	195
		1177	(21,264 ÷ 1177) + 1800 = 1818.1

Ceramics used in mean ceramic dating

Ceramic type number	Ceramic type	Date range
1	Brown stoneware bottles	(c. 1820–1900)
2	Whiteware	(c. 1820–1900+)
3	Ironstone and granite china	(c. 1813–1900)
5	Canton porcelain	(c. 1800–1830)
6	Mocha	(c. 1795–1890)
8	Finger-painted wares	(c. 1790–1820)
10	Willow transfer on pearlware	(c. 1795–1840)
11	Transfer-printed pearlware	(c. 1795–1840)
12	Underglaze polychrome pearlware	(c. 1795–1815)
13	Annular wares pearlware	(c. 1790–1820)
15	Lighter yellow creamware	(c. 1775–1820)
17	Underglaze blue pearlware	(c. 1780–1820)
19	Blue-and-green-edge pearlware	(c. 1780–1830)
20	Undecorated pearlware	(c. 1780–1830)
27	Black basaltes stoneware	(c. 1750–1820)

[a]See South (1972).

visors] (Fairbanks 1974:78–79). If so, there should be similar ceramic types at the slave and overseer sites, and the slaves' and overseers' ceramics should differ significantly from those of the planters. It is also possible that the slaves and overseers purchased their own ceramic vessels from local dealers. If so, there should be significantly different ceramic types at the slave and overseer sites.

At the slave cabin and planter's kitchen, lead-glazed earthenwares were predominantly pearlware and whiteware sherds that had been decorated with underglaze hand-painting, underglaze slip or liquid clay, and underglaze transfer-printing. Such decorative techniques as hand-painting and slip-decorating were time-honored means of adorning utilitarian earthenwares. Underglaze hand-painting—usually in cobalt blue—decorated the molded rims of the edge flatware that appeared at both the slave and planter's sites (Tables 3.12, 3.24). In addition, underglaze hand-painted blue and polychrome floral designs decorated some utilitarian items at both sites (Table 3.24) (see Miller 1980:4) Slip-decoration—the application of slip bands and panels to earthen hollowware items (see Godden 1963:108–109; J. Walker 1971:132–134; Fleming 1923: 57–59—appeared on many of the slaves' ceramics but few of the planter's (Table 3.13). Finally, transfer-printing—a technique perfected in the late eighteenth century—involved the transfer of inked designs from engraved copper plates to earthenware biscuit (see Coysh 1970; Whiter 1970). The vast majority of the planter's earthenwares were transfer-printed, but only a minority of the slaves' ceramics were transfer-printed (Table 3.13).

TABLE 3.13
Surface Decorations of Ceramic Types

Types	Slave cabin (%)	Overseer's house (%)	Planter's kitchen (%)
Banded	25	30	1
Blue and green edge	12	5	2
Underglaze hand-painted	5	5	4
Transfer-printed	21	14	77
Undecorated (creamware, pearlware, and whiteware)	29	36	9
Others	7	11	7
	543	179	1242

During the 1800s, hand-painted decorations appeared on a variety of utilitarian shapes such as bowls, pitchers, mugs, and flatware (Noël Hume 1969c:395, 1973:245; J. Walker 1971:129). In turn, banded decorations appeared on such shapes as pitchers, mugs, cups, and "common bowls" (Van Rensselaer 1966). Common bowls—serving vessels with carinated, flaring sides and with foot rings—were particularly long-lived shapes (Figure 3.4). For example, one British potter, T. G. Green & Co., which operated in the late 1800s, was still turning out banded whiteware "common bowls" that closely resembled banded creamware examples that were made a century earlier (Godden 1966:133; Van Rensselaer 1966).

Banded wares and hand-painted wares were less sensitive to changes in popular fashion (see Noël Hume 1969c:395; Watkins 1970:22) than transfer-printed wares (Whiter 1970). Banded ware, in particular, was an inexpensive utilitarian ware that did "not meet later, more sophisticated standards of taste" (Van Rensselaer 1966:340). Yet, quantities of banded ware were produced for the "cottages" of Britain and for export to Africa and the United States (Godden 1963:108–109; Noël Hume 1969a:131). Thus, the folklike, slip-decorated banded ware appears to have appealed to people who were still participating in folk subcultures. By definition, *folk subcultures* are the traditional sectors of preindustrial and industrial societies that retain many behaviors and artifacts that are "old and acceptable" to their members (Foster 1953:170–171; Glassie 1968:3–4). The banded wares with long-lived utilitarian shapes were produced by British potters because they appealed to a smaller but steady group of customers: rural Britons; African agriculturalists; and black slaves.

A   B

Figure 3.4. "Common bowl" shape. (A) reconstructed finger-painted pearlware bowl from the northern third slave cabin refuse; (B) partial slip-decorated bowl from southern third slave cabin site.

In contrast, people who participated more fully in the popular culture of western Europe and North America preferred the transfer-printed wares which were sensitive to changing fashions (Whiter 1970). Transfer-printed wares reached their height of popularity in the United States from 1790 to 1850. In the earlier decades, Oriental patterns predominated; but in later decades, there was a plethora of English, American, and Near Eastern scenes (see Figure 3.5). Scenic designs remained popular into the 1840s, when floral designs superseded them (Godden 1963:113). With their evolving design motifs, "Staffordshire printed wares became the most popular form of tableware for the [British and American] middle classes during the nineteenth century" (Kingsbury 1974:169, 172). During 1800–1825 over half of all the earthenware produced in Great Britain was transfer-printed blue on white (Godden 1963:11).

On Cannon's Point, the planter family far preferred the popular transfer-printed wares to other types (Table 3.13). They acquired large, matched sets of transfer-printed tablewares, teawares, and chamberwares. At the planter's kitchen, 185 transfer-printed forms, representing 60 different patterns, could be recognized from a total of 1520 transfer-printed sherds (Otto 1977:Appendix C).

In contrast, the planter family furnished the slaves with heterogeneous collections of ceramics. At the slave cabin, 33 transfer-printed forms, representing 30 different patterns, could be recognized from a total of 154 transfer-printed sherds (Otto 1977:Appendix C). Possibly the planter family purchased crates of mixed lots of transfer-printed wares to issue to their slaves, or slaves purchased lots from local shop-keepers. As an example, Sawyer & Herring, shop-keepers in nearby Darien, advertised "30 crates [of] blue and printed Crockery, assorted expressly for country stores" (Darien *Gazette*, 8 February 1819).

A comparison of ceramic types from the slave, overseer, and planter refuse revealed that slaves and overseers used remarkably similar ceramics. Banded, edge, and undecorated wares composed about 70% of the ceramics at the slave and overseer sites, but these wares composed only 12% of the ceramics at the planter's kitchen. In turn, transfer-printed wares were far more common at the planters' kitchen than at the overseer and slave sites (Table 3.13). Apparently the planter family purchased transfer-printed wares for their own use; and they purchased banded, edge, and undecorated wares to issue to slaves and overseers.

But a comparison of the ceramic shapes from the plantation sites revealed that the slaves, overseers, and planter family also used

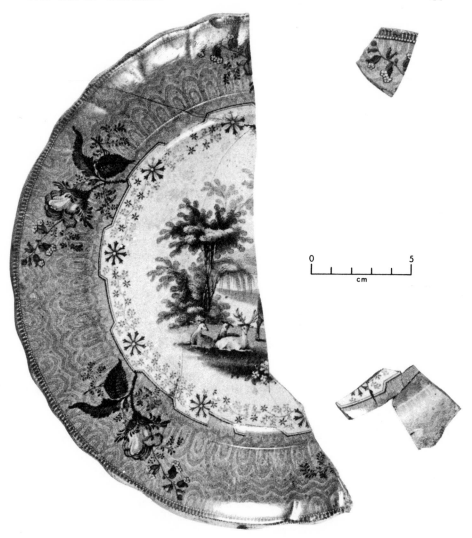

Figure 3.5. Transfer-printed serving flatware from the planter's site.

rather different shapes of ceramics (Tables 3.14, 3.15). In particular, there were striking differences in the tableware shapes—serving bowls, plates, and platters. Serving bowls composed 44% of the slaves' tableware shapes, 24% of the overseers' tableware, and only 8% of the planter's tableware. In turn, serving flatwares (plates and platters) were most common at the planter's site, composing over 80% of the tableware, but were less common at the overseer's site,

TABLE 3.14
Shape and Function of Ceramic Items from the Plantation Sites
(Site Totals)[a]

Shapes	Slave cabin (%)	Overseer's house (%)	Planter's kitchen (%)
Tableware	64	58	52
Tea and coffeeware	21	31	27
Storage vessels (excluding bottles)	4	2	11
Dairy ware	0	1	1
Chamberware	3	2	3
Others and unidentified	8	6	6
	126	135	309

[a]Adapted from Table 5.2 in Otto in South (1977:98).

and least common at the slave cabin (Table 3.16). Apparently the planter family purchased serving flatware for their own use, and they issued more serving bowls to the slaves than the overseers.

Although utilitarian tablewares predominated among the slave family's ceramics, some teawares and storage wares were also present (Table 3.14). Even chamberwares—washing bowls, pitchers, and chamber pots—could be identified among the slaves' ceramics; chamberwares were regarded as luxury items for slaves. As an example, J. Hume Simons, a noted tidewater physician, urged planters to provide a "seat with a hole and cover for the calls of nature" in each slave cabin, "because there are seldom or never any conveniences in the way of chamber [pots]; and if they [the slaves] had them, they would immediately break them." He claimed that it was "almost a universal practice among negroes to go into the open air for the calls of nature, in all kinds of weather" (Simons 1849:208).

TABLE 3.15
Ceramic Bottles from the Plantation Sites

Bottle types	Slave cabin	Overseer's house	Planter's kitchen
Brown stoneware	4	1	2
Slip-coated stoneware	—	1	—
	4	2	2

TABLE 3.16
Shape and Function of Tableware Items from the Plantation Sites
(Site Totals)[a]

	Slave cabin (%)	Overseer's house (%)	Planter's kitchen (%)
Shapes			
Serving bowls	44	24	8
Serving flatware (plates, platters, and soup plates)	49	72	84
Other tableware shapes	7	4	8
	80	78	161

[a]Adapted from Table 5.3 in Otto in South (1977:99).

HEALTH CARE ON THE PLANTATION

Exposure to the elements, crowding in cabins, and possible dietary deficiencies created health problems for tidewater slaves: fevers, typhoid, cholera, and infants' diseases took their toll. Most articles on "raising negroes" in *The Southern Agriculturist* mentioned the topic of slave health. One planter wrote a typical admonition: "Let us compel our negroes to take care of themselves and their young; they will be the happier, and we the richer for it" (A.S.D. 1838:80). Some plantation whites insisted that slaves accumulate their rubbish in middens (P. C. 1838:345). Others encouraged slaves to sweep out their cabins, air their bedding, launder their clothes, and clean their cooking pots so that "no 'caked hominy' or sweet potatoes is suffered to remain about them" (A Planter 1836: 580–584).

Plantation whites were, of course, unaware of pathogens, but they attributed diseases to "humoural imbalances" and "morbific matter." Claudius Galen's theory—that imbalances in bodily humours (blood, phlegm, yellow and black bile) caused illness—still had its adherents. Others believed in Thomas Sydenham's theory that diseases were caused by decaying materials—"morbific matter," released by decay, infected the air and entered the body through the respiratory tract. But whether one subscribed to the excess humours or the infection by "morbific matter" theory, it was agreed that the body must be regulated or cleansed by bleeding, blistering, sweating, vomiting, and purging. Consequently, lancets, blister compounds, emetics, purgatives, and enema pipes were common on plantations. Moreover, drugs such as calomel (a mercury compound) and quinine were regarded as panaceas: they were prescribed for practically any illness (Duffy 1959:54–56; Simons 1849). Quinine, first isolated from cinchona bark in 1822, was especially popular since malaria was endemic in much of the Old South (Shyrock 1930:163).

Given the widespread belief in Galen's and Sydenham's theories, planters stocked their shelves with "plantation medicines" such as "castor oil, spirits of turpentine, blue mass, quinine, laudanum, paregoric, liniment, vermifuge, and epsom salts" (Flanders 1933:163–164). Purchases of such nostrums frequently appeared in the Cannon's Point accounts (Couper 1839–1854:285, 300, 355, 378, 417). Although some planters themselves administered these bromides to their slaves, others called on physicians, but more commonly the overseers were expected to "physick" the slaves. Overseers diagnosed the slaves' illnesses and doled out the necessary medicines (Scarborough 1966:86–87; Shyrock 1930:172). The bottles and vials that once held these "plantation medicines" were plentiful in the third slave cabin refuse, composing almost one-third of the total glass containers (Table 3.21). Medicine bottles also appeared at the Kingsley slave cabin (Fairbanks 1974:86), although none were reported from Rayfield (Ascher and Fairbanks 1971).

The bottles of harsh medicines administered by the plantation whites left an indelible impression in the memories of slaves. Almost a century later, a former slave recalled: "If been berry sick, doctor gib you calomus (calomel) or castor oil. Sometimes he gib you Dead-Shot for worms, or puke (powder) to make you heave. If I just hab a pain in muh stummick, my mother gib me Juse-e-moke [root] w'at she git outen de wood" (Rawick, ed., 1972:Vol. 3, Part 3, 201).

In addition to home remedies fashioned from roots, berries, and leaves, the slaves turned to the "conjure doctors" in the quarters. Many slaves attributed sickness to sorcery, a probable survival from their African past (see Georgia Writers' Project 1940). While plantation whites, fearing "morbific matter," forced slaves to clean up the refuse near their cabins in order to conform with antebellum standards of sanitation, some slaves may have been more concerned with finding the conjure devices that enemies had planted. Such charms, roots, and herbs, however, were perishable and left no archaeological traces.

CLOTHING

The clothing worn by the slaves was decidedly perishable, yet, this aspect of slave culture was rather well documented in the written record. In 1828 Basil Hall noted that the Cannon's Point slaves received clothing twice a year. The winter textiles were Welsh plains: each man received seven yards, each woman six yards, the children in proportion. Although the textiles were white, the slaves dyed them purple, probably using indigo. The winter issue also included a cap for the men, kerchiefs for the women, and a pair of brogans for each. Every second year, an adult received a blanket: two children received one blanket. In the summer, the textiles were coarse cottons called Osnaburgs (Hall 1829:Vol. 3, 225). During the 1840s, the Cannon's Point accounts listed two large textile purchases each year, the slaves' biannual clothing rations. As an example, when warm weather began in April, 1841, John Couper bought $58\frac{1}{4}$ yards of "Jeans," $313\frac{1}{4}$ yards of Osnaburgs, 4 pounds of thread, 4 gross of buttons, and 4 papers of needles from Anderson & Co., a Savannah dry goods dealer. In November the winter textile issue from Anderson & Co. included $351\frac{1}{2}$ yards of plains, $66\frac{1}{2}$ yards of cotton shirting, $64\frac{1}{2}$ yards of blue cotton plaids, 3 pounds of blue thread, and 3 gross of buttons. One month later, Couper purchased 43 pairs of brogans from S. L. Collins, a general merchandiser in Darien. In other years the clothing purchases included blankets as well as red flannel for underwear (Couper 1839–1854:72, 91, 96, passim; House 1954: 299, 301).

Most tidewater plantations issued clothing by the yard. Usually, each male slave received enough textiles for two shirts, two pairs of pants, and two pairs of underwear. Women had the equivalent of two dresses, two petticoats, and two pairs of drawers. Children generally received only two long shirts, though many went nude during the warmer months. Some plantations had seamstresses who fashioned the field slaves' apparel, but no slave seamstresses were known from Cannon's Point. On Cannon's Point, each slave woman apparently sewed her own family's clothing—a common practice in the tidewater (Flanders 1933:160–162; Hall 1829:Vol. 3, 218; Johnson 1930:132–133, 139; Rose 1964:123). The third cabin site yielded a pair of iron scissors (Otto 1975:247) and a thimble (Table 3.17) which a slave woman used for sewing.

The yearly clothing issues, however, were rarely adequate, consequently many escaped slaves claimed to have deserted their masters because of inadequate clothing (Blassingame 1977:359). Understandably many tidewater slaves purchased extra clothing, especially Sunday finery, and Basil Hall claimed that the Cannon's Point slaves devoted most of their income to "dress and trinkets" (Hall 1829:Vol. 3, 225; Johnson 1930:140–141).

Fasteners from the slaves' Sunday finery appeared in the third cabin refuse. The shell buttons came from fancy shirts, whereas the brass buttons once adorned coats and waistcoats (see House 1954:268; South 1964:132, 1974:190), and the brass and iron hooks and eyes may have once fastened dresses (Table 3.18). Most of the buttons in the slave refuse, nevertheless, came from work clothes. These were the four- and five-hole bone buttons; four-hole porcelain buttons; and four-hole iron buttons that also appeared at the Rayfield and Kingsley cabins. These buttons were presumably included as part of the yearly clothing issues. The bone buttons probably fastened trousers and underwear; the porcelain buttons fastened shirts; and the iron buttons probably fastened trousers and outergarments. Furthermore the third cabin, as well as the Rayfield and Kingsley cabins, yielded antebellum military buttons that probably came from surplus coats given to the slaves (see Ascher and Fairbanks 1971:13; Fairbanks 1974:88–89; South 1964:121–123; Watkins 1970:74–75; Table 3.18).

Even field slaves were aware of the latest fashions. Whenever James Hamilton Couper's wife, Caroline, visited Savannah, the Hopeton slave women instructed her to buy the latest styles for them. And Charlotte Forten, a black "Gideonite," was impressed with the Sunday garb of recently liberated tidewater blacks:

> They were neatly dressed in their Sunday attire, the women mostly wearing clean, dark frocks, with white aprons and bright-colored head-handkerchiefs. . . . We noticed that the people had much

TABLE 3.17
Clothing Items and Sewing Equipment from the Plantation Sites

Slave cabin	Overseer's house	Planter's kitchen
Clothing items		
1 partial iron buckle	—	—
Sewing equipment		
1 brass thimble	1 needle fragment	1 needle
	1 straight pin	14 straight pins

better taste in selecting materials for dresses than we had supposed. They do not generally like gaudy colors, but prefer neat, quiet patterns. They are, however, very fond of all kinds of jewelry. (Forten 1864:589–592)

To enhance their Sunday clothes and to relieve the drabness of their work clothes, slaves often wore beads (Table 3.19). Faceted, hexagonal beads were found at the third cabin as well as the Rayfield and Kingsley cabins. Although Robert Ascher believed the faceted blue bead from the Rayfield cabin had once been worn by an

TABLE 3.18
Clothing Fasteners

Fastener types[a]	Slave cabin refuse		Overseer's house refuse Zones II–III		Couper kitchen refuse Zones II–IV	
	Frequency	%	Frequency	%	Frequency	%
Bone						
One-hole disc (type 15)	1	2.4	—	—	5	20.8
Four-hole button, type 20	3	7.3	—	—	—	—
Five-hole button, type J and type 19	8	19.5	—	—	3	12.5
Shell						
One-hole disc	—	—	—	—	1	4.2
Two-hole button	1	2.4	—	—	—	—
Four-hole button, type 22	1	2.4	—	—	3	12.5
Blank	1	2.4	—	—	—	—
White Porcelain						
Four-hole, type 23	3	7.3	1	16.7	3	12.5
Glass						
Glass front, brass set holder (sleeve link?)	1	2.4	—	—	—	—
Iron						
One-hole disc	—	—	—	—	1	4.2
Four-hole button, type 21	2	4.9	2	33.3	—	—
Eye	1	2.4	—	—	—	—

(continued)

TABLE 3.18 (Continued)

Fastener types[a]	Slave cabin refuse Frequency	%	Overseer's house refuse Zones II–III Frequency	%	Couper kitchen refuse Zones II–IV Frequency	%
Brass						
Type D and type 7	3	7.3	—	—	—	—
Type F	—	—	—	—	1	4.2
Type I	1	2.4	—	—	—	—
Type 18	2	4.9	—	—	3	12.5
Type 18, U.S. Navy	1	2.4	—	—	—	—
Type 25	—	—	—	—	1	4.2
Type 32	1	2.4	—	—	—	—
Hook	3	7.3	1	16.7	—	—
Eye	6	14.6	1	16.7	2	8.3
Grommet	—	—	1	16.7	—	—
Trouser fastening or grommet	1	2.4	—	—	—	—
Elliptical front with gilt	—	—	—	—	1	4.2
White metal						
Type C and type 8	1	2.4	—	—	—	—
	41	100.0	6	100.0	24	100.0

[a]Types based on Olsen (1963); South (1964).

enslaved African who was smuggled into Georgia (Ascher and Fairbanks 1971:8–9), these "faceted [hexagonal] beads, usually in a pale blue metal [turquoise] are quite common in the New World, occuring in large quantities in Seminole graves from about 1780 to well into the nineteenth century" (Fairbanks 1974:90). Virtually every slave cabin that has been excavated in the South has yielded faceted beads, and they may prove to be reliable indicators of slave status on Old South plantation and farm sites (see Smith 1977).

"LUXURY" ITEMS

In addition to beads and Sunday finery, some slaves acquired tobacco and pipes. Although planters occasionally rewarded their

TABLE 3.19

Glass Beads from the Plantation Sites[a]

	Turquoise	Brite navy	Black	Dark palm-green
Slave cabin refuse				
Cornerless, hexagonal, monochrome beads similar to type 10 (van der Sleen nd: Figure 5)	2 whole (4 × 5 mm) (5 × 5 mm)	1 whole (4 × 5 mm) 2 fragments	3 whole (4 × 5 mm)	—
Overseer's refuse (Zones II–III)				
Monochrome tube bead similar to type Ia^2 (Kidd and Kidd 1970: 54, 67)	—	—	1 (7 mm)	—
Couper's kitchen refuse (Zones II–IV)				
Cornerless, hexagonal, monochrome beads similar to type 10	1 (5 × 6 mm)	1 (5 × 5 mm)	—	—
Wire-wound monochrome bead similar to type WIb9 (Kidd and Kidd 1970: 62, 84)	—	—	—	1 (4 × 6 mm)

[a] Color categories from Kidd and Kidd (1970).

slaves with tobacco, most masters expected slaves to purchase their own (Johnson 1930:141). This seems to have been the case at Cannon's Point because only one tobacco purchase appeared in the accounts: The plantation bought one box of tobacco (104 pounds) in November 1853 from Robert Mure, the Coupers' cotton merchant in Charleston, South Carolina (Couper 1839–1854:479–480). In spite of this, the third cabin refuse yielded numerous clay pipe fragments (Table 3.20), attesting to the slaves' penchant for pipe-smoking. Pipes were far more plentiful at the third slave cabin than at the white overseer and planter sites (Table 3.20). In fact, clay pipes were called "Negro Pipes" in newspaper advertisements such as the one appearing in the Savannah Georgian: "150 Boxes, Negro Pipes, best sizes, landing from brig. Wm. Taylor, and for sale. . . ." (Savannah, Georgian, 14 November 1832). Fragments from such "Negro pipes" have appeared at all excavated slave cabins (Ascher and Fairbanks 1971; Fairbanks 1974; MacFarlane 1975; Smith 1977).

Slaves also purchased liquors, although some tidewater slaves received "grog" rations. Overseer Roswell King, for instance, regularly issued rum to the Butler's Point slaves (Johnson 1930:141; King 1828:526). But on Cannon's Point the slaves received whiskey only during the Christmas holidays (Hall 1829:Vol. 3, 224); slaves apparently purchased their own liquor during the remainder of the year.

In the third slave cabin refuse, most of the liquor bottle fragments were from cylindrical olive-green bottles, though some sherds also came from squarish "case" bottles which usually held gin or from light-green and clear wine bottles (Tables 3.21, 3.22). These ubiquitous olive-green cylindrical bottles once held a variety of beverages including "Wine, Porter, Beer, or Cyder" (Jones 1971:73). The darkest olive-green bottles, commonly called "black bottles," were light-repelling. The black bottles usually held brewed beverages such as porter—a dark, bitter beer—and the medium-hued olive-green bottles generally held wines (Noël Hume 1974:197–198). Assuming there was a correlation between the hue of the olive-green bottles and their contents, the higher frequencies of the black bottle fragments in the slave refuse suggested the slaves drank more brewed beverages; conversely, the higher frequencies of medium-green fragments at the overseer and planter sites suggested that plantation whites drank more wine (Table 3.23).

Other luxuries appeared in the well associated with the slave cabins in the northern quarters. A brass pulley, probably from a clock, was found in the well pit fill. By 1860 serviceable clocks could

TABLE 3.20
Clay Tobacco Pipe Fragments from the Plantation Sites

Pipes	Slave cabin		Overseer's house		Planter's kitchen	
	Number	%	Number	%	Number	%
"Peter Dorni" (Omwake 1961)	3	4	—	—	—	—
"McDougall/Glasgow" (Humphrey 1969:17–18)	1	1	1	6	1	5
Ribbed pipes, variety E (Hanson 1971:94)	5	6	—	—	—	—
Type 23 with raised tobacco-leaf design (Noël Hume 1969a:302–303)	—		1	6	—	—
Type 30 detachable stem bowls	1	1	3	17	1	5
Unidentified decorated or marked pipe fragments	14	17	5	28	8	36
Undecorated "apple" bowl pipes (Wilson 1961:121, 124, 1966:34)	1	1	2	11	—	—
Undecorated bowl with mushroom spur (Wilson 1966:34)	—		1	6	—	—
Undecorated pipe fragments	58	70	5	28	12	55
	83		18		22	

be purchased for as little as $3.00 (Martin 1942:102). A partial doll's head of white earthenware, covered with a translucent greenish glaze, also appeared in the well fill as did a brass handle from a fan (Otto 1975b:276). The fan may have been a discard from the planter family or a purchase to complement the Sunday finery of a slave woman. Finally, fragments of cut-and-molded glass tableware appeared in the slave cabin refuse (Table 3.21). Again, these glass tableware items may have been discarded by the planter, or they may have been purchased from local shop-keepers. Several Darien shop-

TABLE 3.21
Fragments of Glass Containers

Glass containers	Slave cabin refuse		Overseer's house refuse Zones II–III		Couper kitchen refuse Zones II–IV	
	Frequency	%	Frequency	%	Frequency	%
Olive-green bottles for ale, wine, beer, cider, porter, etc. (Switzer 1974:17–18; Olsen 1965:105–107; Noël Hume 1974:196–197)	313	48.8	43	38.7	247	52.9
Light-green "Champagne" bottles (Switzer 1974:24–26; J. Walker 1971:149)	41	6.4	9	8.1	32	6.9
Other imported (i.e., Bordeaux) bottles identified from shoulder seals	4	0.6	—	—	—	—
Case bottles for gin, bitters, etc. (Toulouse 1970:61–62; Noël Hume 1969b:62; J. Walker 1971:171–173, 178)	13	2.0	6	5.4	58	12.4
Pale green cylindrical bottles with embossed lettering, unknown function	—	—	—	—	20	4.3

(continued)

keepers offered to sell "Plain and Cut Glass" and "Elegant cut glass Decanters, Tumblers" (Darien *Gazette*, 4 October 1819, 27 October 1821).

Such luxuries as clocks, toys, glassware, liquors, tobacco, and fancy clothes did much to relieve the drabness of bondage, though

TABLE 3.21 (*Continued*)

Glass containers	Slave cabin refuse		Overseer's house refuse Zones II–III		Couper kitchen refuse Zones II–IV	
	Frequency	%	Frequency	%	Frequency	%
Medicine vials and bottles (Watkins 1970:51–56, 63–67; J. Walker 1971:151–178)	200	31.2	48	43.2	80	17.1
Cut-and-pressed glass bowls and covered dishes, etc. (Durrenberger 1965:40–46; Watkins 1968:154)	14	2.2	1	0.9	4	0.9
Decanters, carafes, and cruets (Watkins 1970:51–59)	27	4.2	—	—	—	—
Stemmed goblets and wine glasses (Watkins 1968:151–152)	1	0.2	—	—	1	0.2
Cut-and-pressed glass tumblers (Watkins 1970:55; Watkins 1968:154)	1	0.2	4	3.6	20	4.3
Culinary bottles (Switzer 1974:50–58; J. Walker 1971:149; Berge 1968:186)	27	4.2	—	—	5	1.1
	641		111		467	

plantation whites often belittled these indulgences. And some planters and overseers who feared that slaves would raid storehouses and fields in order to obtain trading stock, forbade their bondsmen to trade for luxuries (Anonymous 1833:284; Johnson 1930:141). A typical advertisement appeared in a local paper: "All persons are

TABLE 3.22
Liquor Bottle Fragments from the Plantation Sites

Bottle types	Slave cabin		Overseer's house		Planter's kitchen	
	Number	%	Number	%	Number	%
Olive-green	313	84	43	74	247	73
Light-green ("champagne")	41	11	9	16	32	10
Other imported wine bottles	4	1	—	—	—	—
Case (gin, etc.)	13	4	6	10	58	17
	371		58		337	

hereby cautioned against trading for any articles whatever, particularly corn, from any of the Col. Island negroes without permission, as the law will be rigidly enforced against such" (Brunswick *Advocate*, 21 December 1837). To prevent illicit trade, one overseer urged that planters provide plantation stores where slaves could purchase luxuries without leaving the estates (An Overseer 1836:230).

On Cannon's Point, slaves could sell their produce to the Couper family for cash, or they were free to carry their goods to a better market if they could find one (Hall 1829:Vol. 3, 225). In addition to selling poultry, hogs, and garden truck, slaves also offered handicrafts for sale. In 1842, for example, Anna King of Retreat Plantation on St. Simons Island purchased "two straw hats from Mr. Couper's Man." She also bought cedar pails and piggins [buckets] from her own slaves, offering money or "Old Whiskey" in exchange (King 1854–1864).

TABLE 3.23
Hues of Olive-Green Bottle Fragments

Bottle hues	Slave cabin (%)	Overseer's house (%)	Planter's kitchen (%)
Dark-green or "black" (porter, ale, etc.?)	57	33	36
Medium-green (wines)	43	67	64
	313	43	247

CULTURAL CHANGES AMONG TIDEWATER
SLAVES

The Africans who came to the tidewater region of Georgia, South Carolina and Florida were highly atypical immigrants. White immigrants to the tidewater often came as family or kin groups; the African slaves came as isolated individuals, forcibly removed from their families and kinspeople. While European immigrants could import artifacts, foods, and building materials in order to partially reproduce familiar surroundings, African slaves brought nothing but their shackles. While European immigrants settled in urban areas where they attempted to reproduce their old ways of living, the African slaves were settled on plantations that contained slaves from many different linguistic and cultural groups. Given such circumstances, the African immigrants could not fully reproduce their old ways of life, including their familiar houses, artifacts, and diets.

The African immigrants coming to the tidewater had been uprooted from their African communities, agricultural villages, and commercial cities. As former members of their old communities, the individuals who later became slaves possessed a "private culture" or a personal organization of experience. This private culture included a knowledge of the rules and principles that allowed individuals to make their speech and behavior meaningful to others. Though each individual's manifest speech and behavior varied slightly, knowledge of accepted standards of speech and behavior allowed for interaction and cooperation among individuals. But the standards of appropriate speech and behavior varied among social contexts. Since the contexts of social interaction differed with age, sex, and occupation, the shared standards of speech and behavior or the "operating cultures" of male farmers differed somewhat from those of skilled craftsmen, women traders, or young children. In the large, socially complex societies that characterized much of West, Central, and Southwest Africa, there were many occupational specialties and operating cultures (see Davidson 1968:91−99; Goodenough 1963: 259−264).

Of the estimated 400,000 Africans who were imported into what is now the United States (Curtin 1969), a disproportionate number were young male agriculturalists (see Curtin 1967, 1969). Consequently, relatively few of the operating cultures of African societies were transmitted through the slaves that arrived. The "majority of the Negroes of the colonial Southeast (and of the Old South in the United States) were not imported from the English or other European sugar islands in the Caribbean, nor from Virginia and the older mainland colonies to the north, but from Africa directly to Charleston and the lesser ports of South Carolina" (Higgins 1971:47). Georgia planters then purchased African slaves from merchants residing in the Carolina ports (Wax 1967:73, 1973:395). Planters preferred cargoes "of slaves with a preponderance of males" and "as few females as possible." They required "nearly full-grown slaves capable of long hours of arduous field work. . . ." (Wax 1973:399–400). From 1733 to 1807 about 20% of the slaves entering South Carolina and Georgia may have come from Senegambia, and approximately 40% of the slaves may have come from the Angola hinterland (Curtin 1969:143, 158; Wax 1973:390–395).

The United States formally ended the slave trade in 1808; yet, an estimated 50,000 additional African slaves surreptitiously entered the southern states during the period 1811–1860. Slave smuggling prospered because the sea islands and the navigable tidal rivers offered havens for slaving ships (Flanders 1933:183; Georgia Writers' Project 1940:xvii–xviii). The most notorious slaver was the yacht *Wanderer* which landed 409 slaves at Jekyll Island, Georgia, on November 28, 1858 (Wells 1967:24–31). Slaves from the Congo basin and Angola were heavily represented in the illegal cargoes (Curtin 1969:234, 258, 260); frequently 300 to 400 "Prime Africans" would appear in the Savannah slave markets. Former slaves from the Georgia coast often recalled "Golla" slaves from Portuguese Angola (Georgia Writers' Project 1940:xviii, 65–66, 99). Moreover, studies of the Gullah-Geechee dialects and Afro-American art and funerary practices suggest that many slaves in tidewater Carolina and Georgia came from Angola (Thompson 1969:140–149).

If many of the imported slaves in the nineteenth century were young males from agricultural societies in Central and southern Africa, and if many imported slaves in colonial times were young males from agricultural societies in West and Central Africa (Wax 1973:399–400), this would have resulted in the simplification of the complex material cultures of African societies because of the biased selection of immigrants (see Foster 1960:10). Since other age, sex, and occupational categories were poorly represented in the samples of newly imported slaves, the slaves could not have reproduced the full range of sex- and age-specific material items that were found in various African social contexts. In the case of the antebellum tidewater South, this may account for the prominence that carved wooden items achieved in the oral testimonies of former tidewater slaves since wood-carving was a skill generally associated with males (Georgia Writers' Project 1940; Vlach 1978:27–32). Ex-slaves and their sons and daughters living on the Georgia coast often recalled the wooden artifacts fashioned by African slaves. Elderly residents of Tatemville, a settlement near Savannah, recollected African slaves who made the following: "spoons, trays, buckets. Dey made . . . mawtuh an pestle from a lawg uh wood. Dey would make wooden cuttuhs fuh meat an vegetubble an would dress some uh dem wid pretty figyuhs" (Georgia Writers' Project 1940:66–67).

It is known from documents and oral testimonies that tidewater slaves produced an impressive array of handicrafts for sale and home use, including coopers' ware, baskets, bowls, spoons, trays, and mortars and pestles. Frequently, these handicraft items were based on West African models (Georgia Writers' Project 1940; Vlach 1978). Yet at the Cannon's Point, Rayfield, and Kingsley slave cabin sites, there was no evidence of such African-style handicrafts. At the Cannon's Point slave cabins, all of the artifacts were commercial items that were based on European or Euro-American models. And at the Rayfield cabin, Fairbanks found the same types of household artifacts that would have appeared at a poor white farmer's house (Ascher and Fairbanks 1971:11). Even at the slave cabin on Kingsley Plantation, where African-born slaves were known to have lived, Fairbanks found "no surely African elements" in the archaeological record (Fairbanks 1974:90).

The lack of "surely African elements" in the archaeological record at tidewater slave cabins is rather surprising, since the African cultural heritage of southern coastal blacks has been well demonstrated. Scholars have discerned numerous African cultural survivals in the speech, behavior, folklore, and material culture of the Gullah and Geechee blacks of coastal South Carolina, Georgia, and Florida (Bascom 1941; Parsons 1923; Puckett 1968; Thompson 1969; Turner 1949; Vlach 1978). And at a variety of archaeological sites dating to the 1700s in the coastal Southeast, archaeologists have recovered an abundance of "Colono Ware"—an unglazed, low-fired earthenware that is believed to have been made by slave potters but was used by black slaves and poor whites alike (Anthony 1979; Ferguson 1980). Often found in the form of cooking pots and flat-bottomed bowls, such Colono Wares have been located at most eighteenth-century domestic and military sites in the tidewater region, yet they are virtually absent at domestic and military sites dating to the 1800s. Apparently, the flourishing Colono Ware industry died out in the early nineteenth century and no sherds of "Colono Ware" could be positively identified at the third cabin site (see Ferguson 1980:17–22).

To explain the demise of African-style Colono Ware in the antebellum coastal Southeast, archaeologist Leland Ferguson has hypothesized that the scarcity of European ceramics during the eighteenth century caused colonial whites and blacks to turn to African-style Colono Wares to meet their needs for ceramic vessels in food preparation and consumption. But when European ceramics became readily available in the nineteenth century, the need for locally produced African-style ceramics declined (Ferguson 1980:22). Therefore, the slaves living in the third cabin (built during or after the 1820s), felt little need to make or acquire African-style, unglazed, low-fired ceramics when cheap European, lead-glazed, refined ceramics were furnished by the planter family or could be easily purchased from local shop-keepers.

Yet, the explanation for the absence of Colono Ware and other African-style artifacts at the third slave cabin may be more complex than a substitution of European artifacts for African ones. The lack of "surely African" artifacts at the Cannon's Point, Rayfield, and Kingsley slave cabins may be indicative of wider processes of culture change occurring among antebellum tidewater black slaves.

The most common African-style wooden utensils appear to have been the mortars and pestles used for preparing maize, rice, and sesame. Katie Brown, daughter of Thomas Spalding's driver, reminisced about her grandmother beating wet rice into a paste in a mortar in order to make "sarakas," flat rice cakes. Shad Rudolf's grandmother on Woodbine Plantation in Camden County also made sarakas from rice and sugar. Rosanna Williams stated that her father, a slave owned by Charles Grant of Glynn County, grew sesame and pounded it in a mortar with salt. Finally, the slave parents of Charles Wilson crushed sesame in mortars to make cakes and candy (see Georgia Writers' Project 1940:70–71, 162, 166–167, 193–194; Wightman and Cate 1955:163).

Since the slaves who arrived in the colonial and antebellum tidewater came from societies that were spread from the Gambia River in West Africa to Angola in southern Africa, it is exceedingly difficult to trace Afro-American material items to a specific African ethnic group (see Mullin 1972:174n). But in spite of the cultural diversity existing among African societies, there were some widely shared similarities in food preparation techniques and foodstuffs. For example, African peoples living in the Gambia Valley, in Nigeria, and in Angola used wooden mortars and pestles to prepare rice and maize (Ojo 1966:55, 80–81; Park 1888:11; Tams 1969:101). Maize, introduced to Africa by Iberians in the sixteenth century, was an important crop from the Gambia River to Angola (Crosby 1972:

170–171; Miracle 1965:46, 51, 55). In addition to maize, Europeans introduced such American crops as manioc, sweet potatoes, peanuts, red peppers, and sugar cane (Crosby 1972:170). Indigenous West African or Afro-Asian cultigens included rice, yams, okra, cowpeas, sesame, sorghums, and millets. In much of sub-Saharan Africa such familiar Afro-Asian domestic animals as cattle, sheep, goats, swine, and fowl were present wherever stock diseases were not endemic (see Baker 1962:229–233; Fagan 1965:28–29). Thus, even before they landed in the tidewater, Africans ate the same foods—maize, rice, sweet potatoes, and cowpeas—that appeared in their weekly slave rations.

Africans from Gambia to Angola prepared their grains, vegetables, and meats by stewing them with pepper in ceramic vessels (see Duncan 1967:59, 251; Winterbottom 1969:Vol. 1, 64–66); or they cooked the grains separately and served them with a stewed vegetable and meat relish (see Curtin 1967:73; Fagan 1965:73; Monteiro 1968:Vol. 2, 238–239, 291; Smith 1965:123–124). Africans ate their foods from ceramic bowls as among the Ibos, or from wooden bowls and calabashes as in the Gambia Valley (Basden 1966:177; Park 1888:20). Such traditional food preparation techniques may have furnished the antecedents for the stewed hominy, pottages, pileaus, and "Hopping John" that tidewater slaves cooked in iron pots and served in ceramic bowls. Thus, given the process of selection and simplification, such widely-shared characteristics as mortars and pestles and cooking techniques were more likely to survive among American slaves than more culturally-specific traits.

During the eighteenth century the tidewater planters imported hundreds of thousands of slaves from Africa; but when the legal slave trade ended in 1808, the slave force became predominantly American-born. Planters aided the increase of their American slave force by providing better housing, clothing, and food. Standards for living conditions "became part of the normal expectations of the slaves" (Genovese 1970:146). "By 1860, all but one percent of the U.S. slaves were native-born, and most of them were second, third, fourth, or fifth generation Americans" (Fogel and Engerman 1974a: 23–24).

African slaves who were smuggled into Georgia during the 1800s appeared among masses of acculturated native-born slaves. The Africans had to acquire new standards of speech and behavior that were appropriate for the agricultural and household work contexts of tidewater cotton and rice plantations. The white overseers and even the American-born slaves, however, had little knowledge of

African ways or little sympathy for the plight of newly arrived Africans. Wallace Quarterman, an ex-slave who was interviewed in the 1930s, recalled the problems that arose when his owner, Colonel Fred Waring of Skidaway Island, purchased seven or eight Africans in Savannah: The African slaves were unable to communicate with the American slaves or with Mr. Blue, the overseer: "Mr. Blue put um in duh fiel, but he couldn do nuttn wid um. Dey gabble, gabble, an nobody couldn unduhstan um an dey didn know how tuh wuk right. Mr. Blue he go down one mawnin wid a long whip fuh tuh whip um good" (Georgia Writers' Project 1940:150). The plantation whites were most concerned that slaves acquire the appropriate standards of speech and behavior that would allow them to perform their agricultural, skilled, and service roles. In the work context, there was much interaction between blacks and white supervisors, and the domestic servants, in particular, were under the close scrutiny of whites. Therefore, the slave operating cultures in the white-dominated work contexts would have shown conformity to white American standards.

The plantation whites usually provided the slave houses that were arranged in rows for easier inspection and control. Some tolerant planters such as Thomas Spalding might allow his slaves to construct African-style huts, but most planters built standardized dwellings similar to the folk houses of white Americans, though many of these dwellings might be based on African (circa 12 by 12 feet) building units, possess dirt floors, and be thatched with reeds (Vlach 1978:132–136). Planters also imposed European standards of dress and modesty, although many slave women continued to don African-style head kerchiefs and turbans (Glassie 1968:117; Georgia Writers' Project 1940:179–180). Even the slave family itself was modeled on western European standards, and polygynous unions were rare (Gutman 1976:58–59, 331; Jones 1965:75–78).

Many planters dealt harshly with public manifestations of African material culture. When the African-born slave Okra attempted to build an African-style dwelling on Altama Plantation, James Hamilton Couper forced him to destroy it, publicly stating that he wanted no African huts on his plantation. And when another Altama slave, Dembo, attempted to beat the drums at a funeral, Couper again tried to squelch an obvious African custom. One black informant recalled Couper telling the Altama slaves "he dohn wahn drums beatin round duh dead." Despite Couper's injunction, the slaves surreptitiously continued their funerary practices. Okra himself made a drum from maplewood and calf skin "about eighteen inches wide an fifteen inches deep wen he finish it" (Georgia Writers' Project 1940:178–182).

In Africa, even such prosaic items as wooden vessels and benches would be decorated with carved designs (e.g., Ojo 1966:81, 242). Although few slave furnishings have survived, some decorated spoons from the twentieth century hint at the craft that was lost (Georgia Writers' Project 1940:Plates IIa, IIc). And since planters and overseers rarely entered tidewater slave cabins, they could not monitor the slaves' household speech (Turner 1949), prevent them from telling "Anansi" stories (Georgia Writers' Project 1940:107; Thompson 1969:127), discourage beliefs in herbalism and sorcery (Georgia Writers' Project 1940:passim), or prevent them from carving small figurines in the privacy of their cabins (Georgia Writers' Project 1940:Plates I-IV). And at secret meetings in the woods, slaves continued to hold harvest dances—accompanied by African-style stringed instruments (Georgia Writers' Project 1940:186–187). Finally some slaves even secretly fashioned ritual objects:

> Duh African mens use tuh all time make lill clay images. Sometime day lak mens and sometime lak animal. Once dey make a big un. Dey put a speah in he hand an walk roun im an say he wuz duh chief. But dat clay got too much ribbuh mud in um an he ain las long. Sometime dey try tuh make duh image out uh wood, but seem lak duh tool ain right, so mos times dey's ub clay. (Georgia Writers' Project 1940:106)

Thus, the more intimate expressions of tidewater slave life—which were either overlooked by plantation whites or were hidden from their view—often contained vestiges of the African cultural past: these included cookery, speech, stories, sorcery, basketry, quilting, the carving of figurines and walking sticks, and dance forms (Georgia Writers' Project 1940; Thompson 1969:127; Vlach 1978). These Africanisms, however, tended to be intangible words, behaviors, or artifacts that were fashioned from perishable wood and fiber. At the Cannon's Point third cabin, such African-derived cultural manifestations rarely survived to become a part of the archaeological record; archaeological evidence of Africanisms appeared only indirectly in the form of culinary practices such as one-pot meals.

Tidewater slaves could have reproduced African food preparation and consumption utensils in the privacy of their cabins. Traditional African ceramic cooking pots and ceramic, wooden, and gourd serving vessels were adapted to the same range of foodstuffs that slaves ate: common African crops, such as maize, sweet potatoes, cowpeas, and okra were also basic slave foods. But at the third slave cabin, the slaves apparently substituted European utensils for their African functional equivalents. Cast iron cooking pots, probably supplied by the Couper family, replaced the traditional equivalents of unglazed, low-fired earthenware cooking pots. To replace the African ceramic, wooden, and gourd serving bowls, Cannon's Point slaves obtained European ceramic bowls and flatware from the planter family or from local shop-keepers. By the 1800s the European glazed, refined earthenwares were seemingly so plentiful and cheap that they could be easily acquired by slaves who had formerly used African-style earthenwares such as "Colono Wares" (see Ferguson 1980:22).

At the third slave cabin, we can view in microcosm this process of substituting commercial functional equivalents for traditional material things. Beginning in the eighteenth century and accelerating in the nineteenth and twentieth centuries, mass-produced commercial artifacts based on innovative models progressively replaced folk functional equivalents in the Western world (Glassie 1968: 17–18). Commercial items could be mass-produced in western Europe and the northern United States so cheaply and transported so efficiently that consumers found it easier to purchase commercial artifacts than to laboriously fashion their own folk functional equivalents.

This process of availability and substitution is best illustrated by the ceramics from the Cannon's Point slave cabin and the planter's kitchen. With the exception of some American-made earthenware dairy vessels, stoneware storage vessels, and Oriental porcelains, the bulk of the ceramics at both the slave cabin and the planter's kitchen were lead-glazed, refined earthenwares produced in Great Britain and exported to the United States (Table 3.24).

But the slaves were probably less concerned with the homogeneity and modernity of their ceramics than with their utility. Their ceramics may well have reflected a folklike world view that was characterized by traditionalism and little concern for symmetry and homogeneity in material culture. In contrast, the planter family's matched sets of transfer-printed wares may well have symbolized an innovative world view that was characterized by progressivism and concern for symmetry and homogeneity in material culture (see Deetz 1973:180).

As a result of cultural change the material culture of tidewater slaves underwent progressive alteration during the eighteenth and nineteenth centuries. Although tidewater slaves continued to fash-

TABLE 3.24
Ceramic Types from the Plantation Sites[a]

Types	Slave cabin refuse		Overseer's house refuse—Zones II–III		Couper kitchen—Zones II–IV, closed contexts	
	Frequency	%	Frequency	%	Frequency	%
Unglazed coarse earthenware	5	0.9	1	<0.6	4	0.3
Glazed coarse earthenware	3	0.6	1	<0.6	16	1.3
Banded pearlware	97	17.9	18	10.1	3	0.2
Banded whiteware	1	<0.2	21	11.7	3	0.2
Finger-painted pearlware	26	4.8	2	1.1	6	0.5
Mocha whiteware	—	—	13	7.3	—	—
Mocha drab yellow	—	—	—	—	—	—
Banded drab yellow	14	2.6	—	—	1	<0.1
"Orangeware"	—	—	—	—	1	<0.1
"Jackfield" type ware[b]	—	—	—	—	3	0.2
Undecorated creamware	—	—	3	1.7	28	2.3
Blue-and-green edge pearlware	67	12.3	9	5.0	26	2.1
Underglaze blue hand-painted pearlware	19	3.5	—	—	41	3.3
Underglaze blue on bisque	1	<0.2	—	—	—	—
Underglaze polychrome pearlware	7	1.3	8	4.5	10	0.8
Willow transfer-printed pearlware	9	1.7	3	1.7	20	1.6
Transfer-printed pearlware	105	19.3	16	8.9	900	72.5
Undecorated pearlware	86	15.8	52	29.1	61	4.9
Transfer-printed whiteware	2	0.4	6	3.4	33	2.7
Sponged whiteware	—	—	—	—	1	<0.1
Undecorated whiteware	71	13.1	9	5.0	19	1.5

(continued)

TABLE 3.24 (Continued)

Types	Slave cabin refuse		Overseer's house refuse—Zones II–III		Couper kitchen—Zones II–IV, closed contexts	
	Frequency	%	Frequency	%	Frequency	%
Ironstone and granite china	—	—	1	<0.6	10	1.5
Brown stoneware bottles	4	0.7	1	<0.6	2	0.2
Salt-glazed stoneware	2	0.4	1	<0.6	25	2.0
Lead-glazed stoneware?	1	0.2	—	—	3	0.2
Alkaline-glazed stoneware?	—	—	—	—	6	0.5
Slip-coated stoneware	1	0.2	1	<0.6	—	—
Unglazed stoneware	1	0.2	—	—	1	<0.1
Glazed black basaltes	—	—	7	3.9	1	<0.1
Glazed red stoneware	13	2.4	1	<0.6	—	—
Undecorated European porcelain	2	0.4	1	<0.6	4	0.3
Transfer-printed European porcelain	—	—	—	—	1	<0.1
Sprigged European porcelain	—	—	1	<0.6	—	—
Canton porcelain	6	1.1	2	1.1	13	1.1
Gold overglaze Oriental porcelain	—	—	1	<0.6	—	—
	543	100.0	179	100.0	1242	100.0

[a]Types based on South (1972); Noël Hume (1969a).
[b]Charles Fairbanks, personal communication (1974).

ion some African-style artifacts during the 1800s, most such material items were of perishable materials and did not survive to become a part of the archaeological record at the Cannon's Point, Rayfield, and Kingsley cabins. The durable material items recovered from the third cabin only hinted at the survival of African customs.

The archaeological record at the third cabin did not accurately reflect the African cultural heritage of the slaves, but the archaeological remains clearly demonstrated that the Cannon's Point slaves struggled to improve their living conditions within the rules established by the planter family. After work, slave men devoted their leisure hours to hunting and fishing, thereby supplying much of their family's protein diet. Slave men fashioned furniture and utensils for their cabin and for sale. Slave women, in turn, not only cooked the family's meals and sewed the garments, but they raised the livestock, tended the garden, and cared for the children. Their livestock and garden truck bought many of the "easements" of slave life—tobacco, pipes, brewed beverages, and Sunday finery. During their leisure hours, the Cannon's Point slaves wrote a "record of black achievement under adversity" (Fogel and Engerman 1974a: 264). They provided themselves with both the necessities and the luxuries that the Couper family failed to provide. Much of the credit for this achievement apparently belongs to the slave women who performed a "full task" in the fields during the day and shouldered the burden of household work during the night.

CHAPTER 4

The Overseers' Living Conditions

An Overseer Wanted
To take charge of my plantation on Colonel's Island,
near Brunswick, Glynn County. The situation is a very
healthy one—fish and oysters are very handy. A man
with a family would be preferred to a single one. Sobriety
and attention to order, will be indispensably necessary.
He must be capable of writing a plain hand, and keeping
common accounts—also, a recommendation from a respectable planter, without which, no application need
be made.

Darien *Gazette*, 30 October 1823

The black slaves who formed the majority of the Cannon's Point
inhabitants stood at the bottom of the plantation hierarchy, and the
white planter family stood at the top, but the white overseers occupied a more ambiguous position. Some of the overseers were the

sons of local planters, some may have been landless poor, but most seem to have come from the small class of middling tidewater farmers and small planters. The uncertain status of Cannon's Point overseers was rather typical for the tidewater region.

Although white overseers ostensibly belonged to the middle class of tidewater white society, the class lines were not strictly drawn. The elite among overseers were the head overseers or "general managers" who served as the proxies of absentee planters. Serving as surrogate planters, managers were responsible for selling the cotton and rice crops, purchasing the plantation provisions, and supervising the slaves and the "common overseers." And since managers were often the sons of planters, they were usually accepted as social equals by their planter employers (Johnson 1930:75–76, 107; Scarborough 1966:179, 181, 183). James Hamilton Couper, of course, served as manager of the Hamilton-owned Hopeton Plantation before he himself became the owner of Altama, Hamilton, and Cannon's Point plantations. Managers enjoyed higher standing in tidewater society than the common overseers, and this was reflected in their respective salaries. Managers often received between $1000 and $2000 a year; overseers rarely earned half that much (Johnson 1930:76). Common overseers were usually sons of farmers who owned land and slaves, though some overseers came from the landless poor. Farmers' sons became overseers in order to gain money and experience, hoping one day to establish themselves as independent farmers (Scarborough 1966:5–6).

One planter writing an article for *The Southern Agriculturist* sarcastically claimed that young men became overseers in order to avoid the rigors of farm life, but in reality the common overseer's life was a demanding one. Overseers were expected to rise with the slaves, assign them their tasks, inspect the slaves' work, police the slave quarters, dole out the slave rations, "physick" the sick slaves, punish the malingerers, and prevent slaves from sabotaging plantation property (A Well Wisher 1836:509; P. C. 1838:344–346). To ensure completion of all these duties, common overseers were often forbidden to fraternize with slaves or to entertain white guests. An overseer even required the planter's permission to leave the plantation. And since many planters regarded their overseers as social inferiors, they rarely socialized with them (Anonymous 1836: 189–190; Scarborough 1964:15). Lastly, overseers were supposed to present a model of respectable white behavior for the slaves: "Let him [the overseer] carouse and entertain his neighbors out of his employer's 'meat house,' then will the negroes supply their 'cronies' out of the [corn] 'crib.' Should he be inattentive to his person and his dress, we will see the negroes careless of theirs—like overseer like man!" (P. 1837:505).

Overseers also bore the brunt of slave resistance. Slaves were quick to exploit any discord between planters and overseers, as one contributor to *The Southern Agriculturist* noted: "The master and the overseer should always pull the same end of the rope. Negroes soon discover any little jarring between the master and overseer, and are sure to take advantage" (H. C. 1834:369). Caught between demanding planters and resisting slaves, few overseers enjoyed long tenures. Some drifted from job to job; some turned to alcohol (Johnson 1930:76; Scarborough 1964). One advertisement for overseers in the local newspaper, the Darien *Gazette*, stressed that applicants should be men of "sober, industrious habits." Another advertisement stated that "sobriety" was a necessary qualification for employment (see Darien *Gazette*, 30 October 1823, 29 March 1825).

Planters often searched in vain for men of "good moral character—able to read and write—honest—humane and observant," who would be willing to work for modest salaries (P. 1837:505). In addition to offering yearly salaries, tidewater planters usually provided their overseers with a rent-free house, some provisions, and the loan of a servant or two. Yet, even this humble remuneration consumed the equivalent of the production output of 6 to 10 field slaves. Given the expense of keeping overseers, as well as the difficulty of finding trustworthy employees, some planters simply dispensed with white overseers, relying instead on slave overseers and drivers. Thomas Spalding, for example, boasted that he ran his plantation without the interference of any white overseers (Agricola 1845:429; Coulter 1940:85–86; Johnson 1930:75).

THE CANNON'S POINT OVERSEERS

The Couper family chose to retain white overseers on the Cannon's Point Plantation. There is a reference to an overseer as early as 1804. Basil Hall, who visited the plantation in 1828, also referred to an overseer (Editor 1804; Hall 1829:Vol. 3, 223). In addition, Fanny Kemble Butler claimed that Thomas Oden, the overseer at the Butler's Island rice plantation, had once served for 14 years with John Couper at Cannon's Point. Oden was also an overseer at Hopeton Plantation from 1831 to 1836, serving the manager, James Hamilton Couper. In 1838 Oden began overseeing at Butler's Island, serving there until his death in 1841. Since the Cannon's Point accounts for the 1820s and 1830s were lost, there was no means of corroborating Kemble's claim. Yet, in the 1840 census, Oden is listed as being between 30 to 40 years of age. If he supervised slaves for 14 years at Cannon's Point prior to his Hopeton tenure, Oden would have been a mere teenager when he began overseeing at Cannon's Point in 1817 (Kemble 1961:27, 50, 72, 168, 400; Glynn County Courthouse n.d.: Wills and Appraisement Book D, 247, 298, 311, 315; U.S. Bureau of the Census 1840). Possibly, Kemble meant that Oden completed 14 years of service with both John Couper, owner of Cannon's Point, and James H. Couper, manager of Hopeton.

By 1841, William Audley Couper, the son of John Couper and manager of Hamilton Plantation at the time, was also overseeing his father's Cannon's Point Plantation. Living at Hamilton Plantation on the southern end of St. Simon's Island, William commuted to Cannon's Point to oversee his father's slaves and crops. His performance as visiting overseer, however, failed to satisfy his elderly father. Due to infirmities, John Couper rarely visited the fields; but on one occasion, he discovered the cotton was poor:

> About a month ago when William was at Cannon's Point and returning that day to Hamilton, I walked out to the cornfield leaving a request to see him as he rode home—waiting until tired, I returned and saw him, [he] said that I meddled in every way with the crop. He would have nothing more to do with it. I accepted his resignation—not a word more passed and we are friends as usual. If this event had happened sooner the cotton would have been saved. Our united exertions were required—I perceive my situation and the convenient way will be to plead dottage [sic]. Interest to the loss of the crop and blame to boot. . . . I will thank William to show a single instance of my contradicting any orders he ever gave. (Couper 1842)

The name of William Couper's successor as overseer at Cannon's Point is not known, but in 1844 James Hamilton Couper, then manager of Hopeton Plantation, began keeping the Cannon's Point accounts in the Hopeton books. In that year, Couper hired the 30-year-old John Piles, Jr.; he served as overseer from December 1844 to November 1845 at a salary of $243 (Couper 1826–1852; 1839–1854:217). Piles was listed in the 1850 Glynn County census manuscripts as an unmarried "farmer," though he was actually a landless overseer who owned 19 slaves. During the 1850s he served as postmaster and tax collector for Glynn County. By the eve of the Civil War, Piles's personal estate was valued at $5000, including seven slaves (House 1954:214, 308; Scarborough 1966;49; U.S. Bureau of the Census 1850a, 1850b, 1860a, 1860b).

After Piles left Cannon's Point in 1845, his replacement was the 44-year-old John J. Morgan, who moved to the plantation with his wife Lucy and her two young daughters. During 1846 Morgan earned $271.66 for his services. The following year, Morgan received $250 in wages as well as $15 for three cows he left behind (Couper 1826–1852:320). Following his departure from Cannon's Point, Morgan became the overseer of Hugh Fraser Grant's Elizafield Plantation from 1848 to 1859. Morgan is listed in the 1850 census as a landless, slaveless "farmer"—presumably an overseer—whose personal estate was worth $1000. Ten years later the 1860 census recorded Morgan as a "farm laborer" who owned $2000 of realty and $2500 in personalty, including a 45-year-old slave woman (House 1954:307, U.S. Bureau of the Census 1850a, 1850b, 1860a, 1860b).

Morgan's successor at Cannon's Point was the 22-year-old Elisha McDonald, who received only $200 for his work in 1848. In contrast, his brother Daniel McDonald, overseer at prestigious Hopeton Plantation, drew $800 in wages the same year. Both were the sons of William McDonald, a McIntosh County planter. In 1858 Elisha began managing the Reverend Charles Colcock Jones's plantations in Liberty County (Couper 1839–1854:295, 302; Myers 1972: 1605–1606).

Ironically, McDonald's replacement was the 32-year-old William Couper. Once fired by his father, William was rehired by his brother James to oversee the family estate of Cannon's Point. Residing at Hamilton Plantation with his wife Hannah and their children, William managed Hamilton and visited Cannon's Point to oversee the operation. Couper collected double salaries, receiving $700 a year as manager of Hamilton and $200 as visiting overseer at Cannon's Point (Couper 1826–1852:309).

William Couper spent his antebellum adulthood as a hired supervisor, serving as manager or overseer at Hamilton, Retreat, and Cannon's Point—three of the largest estates in Glynn County. Although he was the son of the planter who owned Cannon's Point, William's overseeing wages were comparable to those of the other Cannon's Point overseers. Moreover, his material wealth approximated that of the other overseers. By 1850 William owned $4100 worth of realty. Ten years later, he owned $4000 in realty and $4700 in personalty, including five slaves. In contrast, his brother James, who became a successful planter after serving as manager of Hopeton for four decades, owned $176,000 worth of land and 210 slaves in 1860 (Myers 1972:1496; Steel 1964:116–117; U.S. Bureau of the Census 1850a, 1850b, 1860a, 1860b).

Even though William was moderately successful by antebellum standards, his father had higher hopes for him. In a letter to his own brother in Scotland, John Couper discussed his plans for his youngest son in 1828:

> My son William now near 11 years is an idle boy and would sooner walk a mile to race home on a plough horse than learn his lessons. I however intend to make a philosopher of him. Next year [I] shall send him to an academy at Northampton in Massachusetts, and when he has laid in a sufficient amount of Yankee cunning, I shall send him to Berlin in order to unlearn roguery and gain honour— German principles. At about 24 he may return home to plant cowpeas and pumpkins, and eat fat meat as his father has done. (Couper 1828)

William never accomplished these goals, attending but never graduating from Franklin College in Athens, Georgia, and returning to Glynn County to spend his antebellum adulthood as a hired supervisor (Myers 1972:1496). After a 2-year tenure at Cannon's Point, William departed. His replacement was Seth R. Walker, whose yearly wages were $400. Walker also left after 2 years so his name did not appear in the Glynn County census records (Couper 1826–1852:378).

E. D. Fennell assumed the overseership of Cannon's Point in 1852 for a remuneration of $400. Perhaps Fennell was the kinsman of J. N. Fennell, a plantation overseer from Liberty County (Couper 1826–1852:378; Myers 1972:1518). E. D. Fennell, like Walker, was not listed in the Glynn County census manuscripts. Both Fennell and Walker may have belonged to the class of transient landless overseers who drifted from job to job. Fennell was the last overseer listed in James H. Couper's Cannon's Point accounts.

Although the Cannon's Point overseers came from varying backgrounds, they shared many attributes. All of them held fewer than 20 slaves and none of them had acquired more than $5000 in realty or personalty by 1860. With the possible exception of John Piles, they spent the antebellum years as hired supervisors.

Tidewater overseers allegedly enjoyed longer tenures and higher wages than other Old South overseers. Yet, this may not have been true for Cannon's Point. During the years from 1844 to 1853, the average tenure of the overseers was only 1.5 years. The average salary was only $283.40 (Couper 1826–1852; Scarborough 1964:18). Even these modest wages consumed much of the plantation's profits during a time of rather poor crop prices (see Chapter 2). Since the Coupers no longer lived year-round on Cannon's Point after 1845, a resident overseer was a necessity—a costly necessity. In 1848, Elisha McDonald's yearly salary ($200) represented 15% of the plantation's income ($1322.97). In turn, Seth Walker's 1851 salary ($400) was 21% of the plantation's yearly income ($1003.03). In addition to these salaries, the Coupers had to assign servants to the overseers and maintain the overseer's house (Couper 1839–1854)—an exceptional house by tidewater standards.

THE OVERSEER'S HOUSE SITE

When extant, the Cannon's Point overseer's house was a one-story frame dwelling. The frame had been clad with clapboards secured with machine-cut nails having machine-made heads—nails that were made during and after the 1820s (Table 3.2). The number of shingle nails suggested that wooden shingles had been individually fastened to rafters and purlins with nails (Table 3.1). The frame house had rested on clay brick pilasters which the site investigators cleared and mapped. Inside the structure were two clay-brick chimney stacks with shallow, double fireplaces (Figure 4.1).

The mapped pilasters and chimneys revealed the floor plan of a Georgian or central-hall-and-four-rooms house—a symmetrical folklike house type that possessed a broad central hall with two flanking rooms on each side (see Glassie 1968:109–112;, Historic Preservation Section 1974:71; Nichols 1957:122–123). Both rooms on each side shared a common interior chimney stack with opposing fireplaces (Figure 4.2). The exterior dimensions of the house were 34.1 by 36.1 feet (10.4 by 11.0 m). The interior dimensions of each room were about 12.5 by 15.8 feet (3.8 by 4.8 m) for a total of 790 square feet of living space, excluding the central hall. In addition to the ground story, there was a pitched loft—about 10.5 feet tall at its highest point (Figure 4.3)—which may have been used for sleeping or storage.

In addition to the house, there was a detached outbuilding with a poured tabby floor and a ruined brick chimney that may have been a kitchen (Figure 4.1). To the south of this possible kitchen lay a pit-dug well. Due to root disturbance and the salvage of the casing during the nineteenth century, the excavators were unable to distinguish between the well pit and the well fill in the badly disturbed upper portion of the well (Figure 4.4). Thus, they removed the fill in

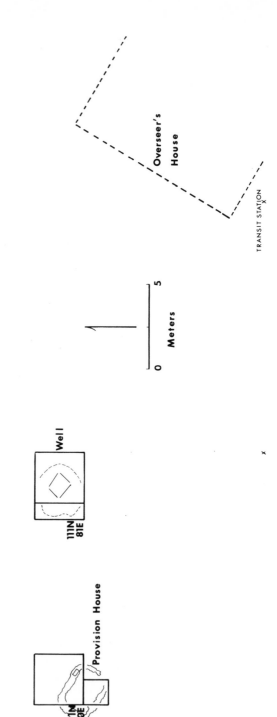

Figure 4.1. The Cannon's Point overseer's house site.

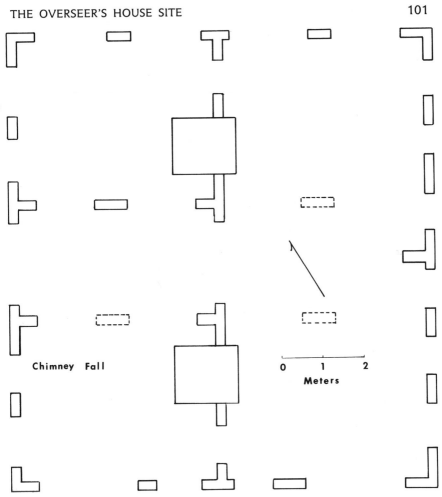

Figure 4.2. The overseer's house ruin.

10-cm levels until they located the rectangular wooden well casing which measured about 3.6 by 3.0 feet (1.1 by 0.9 m) (see Figure 4.1). The fill within the wooden well casing yielded only 12 ceramic sherds, all of whose beginning dates of manufacture fell within the antebellum years. In turn, the well pit, which was removed and screened separately, contained only seven antebellum sherds. Since several of the ceramic sherds from the well pit and well fill matched sherds from the antebellum refuse midden (Figure 4.1), this showed that workers used household refuse to fill the well pit during the well's construction and then to fill the well after its abandonment

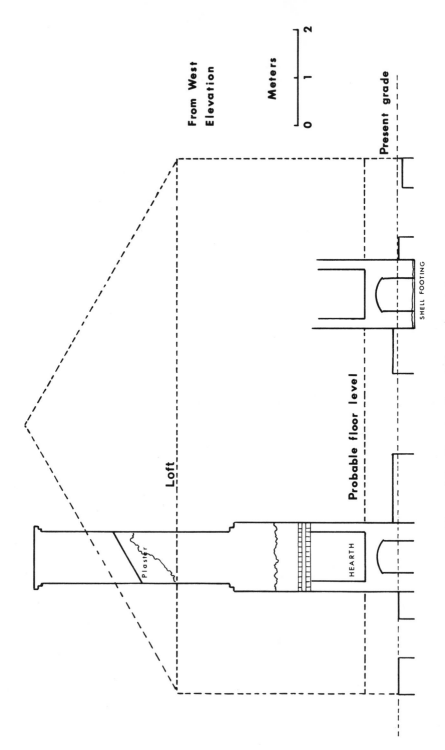

From West
Elevation

Meters

0   1   2

Present grade

SHELL FOOTING

Probable floor level

Loft

Plaster

HEARTH

Figure 4.3. Cross-section of the overseer's house.

during antebellum times (Otto 1975b:118). Another depression east of the house may have been the second well, but time did not permit its excavation.

Finally, the excavators cleared the foundation ditch of a possible provision house (Figure 4.1). The foundation ditch, which had been filled with household refuse from the midden that lay to the southwest of the possible kitchen (Figure 4.1), also contained a flattened, partial "tin can." The walls of the can had been hand-cut from tin-plated sheet iron and the seams had been soldered by hand. The archaic manufacturing techniques suggested an antebellum date of assembly (Fontana and Greenleaf 1962:68). Several tabby bricks and brickbats associated with this foundation ditch may have served as pilasters for the frame structure; tabby bricks were commonly used for foundations rather than for walls (see Coulter 1937:84).

With its detached outbuildings and its substantial central-hall-and-four-rooms house, the overseer's homestead far outranked the one-room third slave cabin with its coops and hutches. The Cannon's Point overseer's house surpassed most tidewater overseers' dwellings. Visitors to the tidewater commented on the "undesirable character" of most overseer's houses: When Fanny Kemble Butler saw the new overseer's dwelling on Butler's Point, she pronounced it a "hideous house." The Cannon's Point overseer's house, however, was comparable in quality to the houses of many small planters (Johnson 1930:109; Kemble 1961:199; Phillips and Glunt 1927: 46).

A more intimate view of an overseer's life was revealed by excavating the refuse midden that lay to the southwest of the possible kitchen (Figure 4.1). This refuse contained the discarded household artifacts and food remains left by the white overseers and servants who occupied the house. Using trowels, field crews excavated three squares in the refuse midden (Figure 4.4). In order to maximize the recovery of artifacts and food remains, excavators screened all the refuse materials with $\frac{1}{8}$-inch mesh. Zone I(A) of the overseers' refuse midden dated to the postbellum period since it contained a Davidson pipestem that postdated 1862 and a "Try Lorillard's Tobacco" pipestem that postdated 1869 (Figure 4.5) (James Heslin, written communication, 1975). The two underlying zones (Zones II–III) (B-C) however, contained no artifacts whose beginning date of manufacture was later than 1860 (Table 4.1). Thus, only Zones II–III could be reliably dated to the antebellum years, and only materials

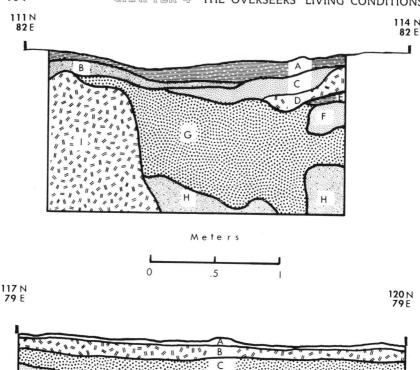

Figure 4.4.   Overseer's house profiles.

(top) West wall profile of square 111N 82E—overseer's house well. (A) modern duff; (B) grey-brown sandy soil; (C) soft, dark-brown sandy soil; (D) light-tan soil with some shell; (E) humus lime; (F) light-tan-brown mottled sand—no shell; (G) mottled tan and brown sand with shell and artifacts; (H) light-tan disturbed sand; (I) medium-tan disturbed sand with scattered shell. (A = Zone I; B and C = Zone II.) The surface at stake 111N 82E is 1.70 m below datum.

(bottom) West wall profile of square 117N 79E—overseer's house refuse. (A) modern duff and humus (Zone I); (B) loosely compact whole and crushed shell in dark-grey sandy soil (Zone II); (C) dark-brown sandy soil with some whole crushed shell (Zone III); (D) mottled tan and orange sterile sandy soil. The surface at stake 117N 79E is 1.46 m below datum.

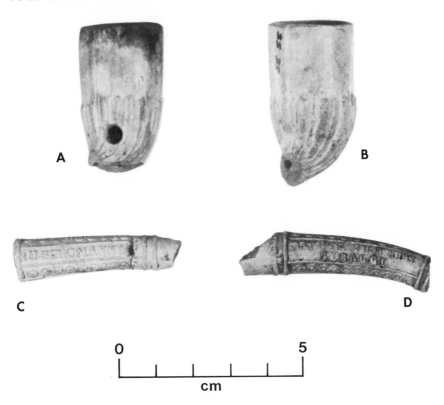

Figure 4.5. Clay tobacco pipes. (A) reused Class VII pipe from the overseer's well; (B) Class VII pipe from the southern third slave cabin site; (C) and (D) Bergmann and Lorillard pipes from the overseer's house site.

from these zones were compared with the antebellum refuse from the third slave cabin.

FOOD COLLECTION AND PREPARATION

As was the case with the slaves living in the third cabin, the overseers devoted much time to hunting and fishing. One planter claimed that overseers spent more time on food collecting than on their plantation duties (A Well Wisher 1836:509). Another planter wrote that the typical overseer kept "his dogs and his boat" and indulged "in the agreeable pastimes of the chase and the rod" (Scarborough 1964:15). But one overseer who was defending his col-

TABLE 4.1
Dating the Overseer's House Refuse (Zones II–III)

	1790	1800	1810	1820	1830	1840	1850	1860	1870
Ceramic hallmarks									
No identifiable marks									
Glass hallmarks									
"Dyottville Glassworks Phila."[a] (post-1833)						⊢———————————————⊣			
Clay pipes									
"McDougall/ Glasgow"[b] (post-1846)							⊢——————————⊣		
Buttons									
No identifiable marks									

[a]Toulouse (1971:171).
[b]I. Walker (1971:25); Walker and Walker (1969:132).

leagues claimed that for most overseers, it was "business first and amusements afterwards" (P. C. 1838:344–346). For Cannon's Point overseers, however, hunting and fishing was more than an "amusement." Wild game, turtles, and fish may have supplied over one-third of the overseer's meat diet (Table 3.10).

The antebellum refuse zones yielded archaeological evidence of the overseers' hunting equipment as well as their quarry. Lead shot, a percussion cap, and a gunflint were present in the antebellum refuse (Table 3.5). Apparently overseers used both percussion-lock and flintlock firearms. At least one overseer is known to have purchased a gun during his stay on Cannon's Point: Seth Walter bought a fowling piece, shot bag, and powder flask (Couper 1826–1852: 378). With firearms or with traps—a portion of a trap appeared in the house ruins—overseers could have collected the opossums, racoons, rabbits, squirrels, and wild rodents that appeared in the refuse. Overseers preferred opossums and raccoons to other game, eating approximately equal amounts of possum and "coon" meat (Table 3.8). All of the wild mammals eaten by overseers were small forest and marsh creatures that could have been collected on the plantation itself.

Fishing, however, was a more important source of wild flesh than hunting (Table 3.8). It is not known if the overseers possessed boats so they could visit the rich fishing grounds in the Altamaha estuary (Figure 3.3) (see Dahlberg 1972). Yet, even if the overseers had access to boats and even if they obtained permission to leave the plantation, it required a lengthy trip down the Hampton River to reach the sounds, the landward marshes, and the mainland streams (Figure 3.3). Given their daily duties and limited leisure time, overseers may have fished in Jones Creek, where that tidal stream cut into high ground creating a convenient bank (Figure 1.3). Using hooks and lines (a slip-sinker appeared in the overseers' refuse) and cast nets (a net weight was also found in the refuse), overseers could have collected such fish as stingrays, gar, menhaden, shad, sea bass, sheepshead, perch, burrfish, mullet, and marine catfish (Table 4.2). Three of the fish species (black and red drums and croakers) which could be identified in the overseers' refuse, however, rarely enter the tidal streams during high tides. Adult black and red drums and adult croakers are usually found in the deeper, more saline waters of the sounds (Table 4.3). Possibly, the drums and croakers in the overseers' refuse were caught on rare visits to the sounds, or these prize fish may have been gifts from the planter family (Dahlberg 1972:342–343; Dahlberg and Odum 1970:383, 391; Larson 1969:167; Johnson 1930:142). For example, one tidewater planter left this note: "Sent the boat on Drum fishing and caught 5 Drum. Gave a Drum to each of the overseers, and one among the Fishermen" (Phillips 1969:Vol. 1, 203).

Turtles were surprisingly important in the overseer's meat diet (Table 3.8). Diamondback terrapins were abundant in the salt marshes and tidal streams where they could have been caught with dip nets or basket traps. Snapping turtles could have been collected from the small freshwater ponds on Cannon's Point (Ursin 1972: 95). Thus, by turtling, fishing, and hunting on Cannon's Point and the nearby tidal streams, the overseers collected a limited range of the available fish, turtle, and game species (Table 4.3). They rarely ventured into the outlying habitats—the sounds, landward marshes, freshwater streams, or barrier islands—to collect a wider variety of the animals in the Altamaha estuary. Nevertheless, overseers supplied much of their own meat through the "agreeable pastimes of the chase and the rod," since game, turtles, and fish comprised over one-third of their estimated meat diet (Table 3.10).

As was the case with the slaves, the overseers collected wild foods to supplement their limited range of domestic foodstuffs. But

TABLE 4.2
Overseer's House Faunal Remains

Taxa (genus and species)	Specimens		Weight		Minimum individuals	
	Number	%	gm	%	Number	%
Didelphis marsupialis (opossum)	8	2.6	6.9	3.5	1	2.4
Sylivilagus sp. (rabbit)	3	1.0	0.4	0.2	1	2.4
cf Sciurus carolinensis (E. gray squirrel)	1	0.3	0.1	<.1	1	2.4
Neotoma floridana (Florida wood rat)	1	0.3	0.2	<.1	1	2.4
cf Oryzomys palustris (E. rice rat)	3	1.0	0.3	0.2	1	2.4
Procyon lotor (raccoon)	8	2.6	6.5	3.3	1	2.4
Felis catus (domestic cat)	11	3.5	1.9	1.0	1	2.4
Sus scrofa (domestic pig)	33	10.6	49.2	24.8	2	4.8
Bos taurus (domestic cattle)	8	2.6	58.4	29.5	1	2.4
Gallus gallus (domestic fowl)	1	0.3	0.7	0.4	1	2.4
Chelydra serpentina (snapping turtle)	34	10.9	9.0	4.5	1	2.4
Malaclemys terrapin (dia-mondback terrapin)	61	19.6	50.8	25.6	3	7.1
Masticophus flagellum (E. coachwhip)	2	0.6	0.7	0.4	1	2.4
cf Dasyatis sp. (stingrays)	2	0.6	0.1	.1	1	2.4
Lepisosteus osseus (long-nosed gar)	8	2.6	0.8	0.4	1	2.4
cf Brevoortia sp. (menhaden)	2	0.6	0.1	<.1	1	2.4
cf Dorosoma sp. (shad)	1	0.3	0.1	<.1	1	2.4
Arius felis (marine catfish)	32	10.3	4.3	2.2	5	11.9
Bagre marinus (gaff-topsail catfish)	15	4.8	3.0	1.5	2	4.8
Centropristes straitus (black seabass)	4	1.3	0.2	0.1	1	2.4

(continued)

unlike the slaves who received regular rations, the overseers had to purchase their own provisions. During the years for which the Cannon's Point overseer accounts were available, bulk purchases of corn, "2nd quality rice," rice flour, molasses, and barrels of salt meat appeared in the overseers' expense accounts. In 1846, for example, overseer J. J. Morgan purchased barrels of salt pork, salt

TABLE 4.2 (*Continued*)

Taxa (genus and species)	Specimens		Weight		Minimum individuals	
	Number	%	gm	%	Number	%
Archosarus probatocephalus (sheepshead)	14	4.5	1.4	0.7	3	7.1
Bairdiella chrysura (silver perch)	6	1.9	0.2	0.1	2	4.8
Micropogon undulatus (Atlantic croaker)	8	2.6	0.6	0.3	2	4.8
Pogonias cromis (black drum)	4	1.3	0.4	0.2	1	2.4
Sciaenops ocellatus (red drum)	3	1.0	0.8	0.4	2	4.8
Mugil sp. (mullet)	37	11.9	1.0	0.5	3	7.1
Chilomycterus schoepfi (striped burrfish)	2	0.6	0.2	0.1	1	2.4
	312		198.3		42	
Other taxa						
Unidentified small mammal	24		1.3		—	
Unidentified medium mammal	95		19.0		—	
Unidentified large mammal	219		119.8	—		
Unidentified mammal	200		14.2	—		
Unidentified *Aves* (bird)	52		11.5	3		
Unidentified *Chelonia* (turtle)	26		2.5	—		
cf *Sciaenidae* (drums)	7		2.7	—		
Ariidae (marine catfish)	23		2.1	—		
Unidentified *Osteichthyes* (bony fish)	123		9.6	—		
Unidentified bone	26		1.3	=		
	795		184.0		3	
	1107		382.3		45	

beef, and sugar from Mitchell and Mure, the Couper family's cotton merchants in Charleston, South Carolina. In addition, he bought $21\frac{1}{2}$ bushels of corn and 45 bushels of rice flour from the Cannon's Point estate. These two purchases totalled $73.85 or about one-third of Morgan's yearly salary. Since Morgan was a non-slaveholder, the foods were eaten by him, his wife, their young daughters and probably the black servants that were assigned to the Morgan family (Couper 1839–1854:226, 246, passim).

TABLE 4.3
Habitats Used by the Overseers for Food Collecting[a]

Aquatic	Terrestrial
Sounds	Cannon's Point forests and secondary
Croakers?	growth
Black drums?	opossums
Red drums?	rabbits
Sounds, tidal rivers, and creeks	gray squirrels
Snapping turtles?	wood rats
Diamondback terrapins	raccoons
Stingrays	Salt marsh
Gars	rice rats
Menhaden	raccoons?
Shad?	
Marine catfish	
Gafftop-sail catfish	
Black seabass	
Sheepshead	
Silver perch	
Croakers?	
Black drums?	
Red drums?	
Mullet	
Burrfish	
Streamside salt marsh	
Diamondback terrapins	
Landward marsh	
Snapping turtles?	
Freshwater ponds	
Snapping turtles?	

[a]Sources: Dahlberg (1972); Goldman (1910, 1918); Hazzard (1825); Larson (1969); Shelford (1963); Teal (1962); Ursin (1972).

The overseers' foodstuffs, which were so reminiscent of slave rations (see Chapter 3), were also deficient in nutritive quality. Overseers had to supplement their salt meats, starches, and sugars with fresh foods so, as was the case with slaves, overseers often raised gardens. One visitor to a plantation commented on an overseer's house nestled within a garden. Fanny Kemble Butler also mentioned that the overseer's wife on Butler's Point had cultivated "a 'sort of garden.'" And on Cannon's Point, there was indirect evidence of an overseer's garden because an iron broad hoe was found near the house (Kemble 1961:167; Olmsted 1861:233; Owens 1976:50, 54–55, 62).

Overseers also kept livestock. When J. J. Morgan left Cannon's Point in 1847, he sold three cows to the plantation (Couper 1826–1852:320). In addition, the antebellum refuse at the overseer's house yielded hog, cattle, and chicken bones (Table 4.2). Presumably the overseers raised their own chickens, but the beef and pork bones could have come either from commercial salt meats or from animals they themselves raised.

Commercial meats, however, may be identified by a low ratio of bone fragments to individual animals. In turn, a higher ratio may indicate the "fuller use" of animals slaughtered on the site (Chaplin 1971:67). The higher ratios of pork bones in the overseers' refuse suggested the overseers ate more fresh pork than salt pork. The lower ratios of beef bones hinted that they ate more salt beef than fresh beef (Table 3.11).

Using fresh meat, salt meat, garden truck, and provisions, the overseer's servants prepared the meals. Every overseer needed at least one servant—"a woman to cook and wash . . ., milk, make butter, and so on" (An Overseer 1855:340). For white overseers as well as slaves, the primary food was corn. Kernels could be boiled whole in iron kettles to make hominy—a favorite food of the "working class (white and black)" along the coast. If the corn was ground into meal, it could be cooked in kettles as gruel or pottage (A.S.D. 1838:80; A Planter 1836:582–583). Kettles were also used to prepare stews. Common garden vegetables such as turnips, greens, cowpeas, and potatoes could be simmered with salt and fresh meats. "Hopping John," a popular dish with both working class whites and blacks, combined bacon, cowpeas, and rice. The broken "2nd quality rice" the overseers bought could have been cooked as pileaus— rice stews with seafood or game and vegetables (Fairbanks 1976:172; Genovese 1974:548; Hilliard 1972:51).

White farmers and black slaves often cooked their meats, grains, and vegetables together in "seemingly incongruous mixtures" (Hilliard 1972:62). Such one-pot meals offered a convenient means of combining disparate ingredients. One-pot meals could be left to simmer for hours while cooks tended to other duties. The food bones from the overseers' refuse offered indirect proof of these one-pot meals. Beef and pork bones had been cleaved open with axes or cleavers as they had been at the slave cabin. Since none of the food bones had saw marks, carcasses were not neatly divided into cuts

TABLE 4.4
Surface Decorations of Tableware Forms at the Plantation Sites
(Site Totals)[a]

Ceramic forms	Slave cabin (%)	Overseer's house (%)	Planter's kitchen (%)
Banded serving bowls[b]	29	17	6
Blue-and-green edge			
Serving flatware	15	14	8
Other[c]	0	1	0
Underglaze hand-painted			
Serving bowls	5	3	1
Serving flatware	3	4	1
Other	1	0	1
Transfer-printed			
Bowls[d]	1	1	0
Serving flatware	19	28	62
Tureens, etc.	4	1	8
Undecorated			
Serving bowls	6	3	1
Serving flatware	11	21	6
Tureens, etc.	3	1	1
Other bowls, flatware, etc.	3	6	5
	80	78	161

[a]Adapted from Table 5.6 in Otto in South (1977:103).
[b]All banded tableware items were "common bowls."
[c]There was one blue edge tureen lid at the overseer's house.
[d]There were two transfer-printed bowls at the slave and overseer sites; these may have been tea or spill bowls.

and joints for roasting. Apparently stewing was a common way of cooking fresh as well as salt meat at the overseer's house.

THE USE OF CERAMICS AND UTENSILS

Overseers ate their one-pot meals from hemispherical ceramic serving bowls that composed one-fourth of the tableware shapes at the overseer's house (Table 3.16). Most bowls were banded "common bowls" with foot rings and carinated sides (Table 4.4)—a ceramic shape that commonly appeared at the third slave cabin. Although serving bowls were common in the overseers' refuse, serving flat-

TABLE 4.5
Cutlery from the Plantation Sites

Slave cabin	Overseer's house	Planter's kitchen
—	1 iron table knife blade	—

ware predominated (Table 3.16). Since plates and platters were not designed to hold liquid-based foods, the overseers did not always eat one-pot meals.

At the overseer's site there was also archaeological evidence of cooking utensils other than iron kettles (Tables 3.5, 4.5). Fragments of a "Dutch oven" and a skewer appeared in the overseers' antebellum refuse. In addition, the handle of an iron skillet was found in the well that was filled during antebellum times. Using a Dutch oven, servants could have baked bread made from corn meal or rice flour by placing the oven in the hearth and spreading hot coals on the top lid to thoroughly bake the dough. Dutch ovens could also be used to roast small game. Using skewers, servants could have roasted chunks of meat in the kitchen hearth and with a skillet, they could have fried eggs and meats or baked corn bread (see Booth 1971:17– 18; Hilliard 1969:7). These additional utensils would have allowed the overseer's servants to cook more foods separately and serve them on platters.

The overseers ate some of their foods from plates rather than bowls, many of which were transfer-printed (Table 4.4). Transfer-printed wares, however, were less common at the overseer's house than at the planter's kitchen where they composed 62% of the planters' tableware (Table 4.4). And unlike the planter family who used large, matched sets of transfer-printed wares, the overseer's transfer-printed wares were remarkably heterogeneous. At the planter's kitchen 185 transfer-printed forms, representing 60 different patterns, could be recognized from a total of 1520 transfer-printed sherds. But at the overseers' site, at least 33 different decorative patterns could be identified on 41 different transfer-printed items. (Otto in South 1977:Appendix C).

The ceramics from Zones II–III of the overseers' refuse produced a mean ceramic date of 1820.7 (Table 3.12), a date that was earlier than the probable occupation span of the house. The quantities of machine-cut nails with machine-made heads indicated that the house was built during or after the 1820s (Table 3.2), whereas the presence of a "McDougall/Glasgow" pipestem in the refuse (Table 4.1) showed that antebellum overseers were still living there after 1846 (Humphrey 1969:17−18). As was the case with the slaves, there was an apparent lag between the date of manufacture of ceramics and their acquisition and discard by the overseers.

The predominance of tableware forms in the overseers' ceramic assemblage also recalled the slaves' ceramics. At both the overseer and slave sites, most ceramics were used for food consumption; there were relatively few storage vessels, dairy items, or chamberwares. Teawares and coffeewares, however, were surprisingly common at the overseer's site (Table 3.14), yet, their teawares were as heterogeneous as their tablewares. Neither the overseers nor the slaves seemed particularly concerned with the homogeneity and modernity of their ceramic assemblages. The overseers' and slaves' ceramics may well have reflected a folklike world view that was characterized by assymmetry and heterogeneity in material culture. The mixed, outmoded ceramics of the overseers and slaves stood in stark contrast to the planter family's matched sets of fashionable transfer-printed wares that reflected a greater concern for symmetry and homogeneity in material culture (see Deetz 1973:18).

Although overseers could have purchased ceramics from local shop-keepers such as William Scarborough who offered to sell "30 crates [of] crockery ware, assorted expressly for this market" (Darien *Gazette*, 11 December 1823), the similarities in the overseers' and slaves' ceramics strongly suggested that the planter family furnished the overseers and slaves with most of their ceramic vessels (Otto in South 1977:100). In addition to household ceramics, the planter family probably supplied the overseers with their cooking utensils and other furnishings. For example, when James Hamilton Couper offered his son the overseership of Hamilton Plantation, the perquisites included an outfit of "plain furniture" (Couper 1860).

THE OVERSEER AS PHYSICIAN

In their role as the slaves' "physician," overseers received stocks of plantation medicines in order to "physick" the slaves, therefore medicine bottle fragments comprised 43% of the overseers' glassware (Table 3.21). When slaves became ill, overseers were expected to diagnose the illnesses and distribute the appropriate medicines (Scarborough 1966:86−87). Relying on such plantation medical manuals as *The Planter's Guide and Family Book of Medicine* (1849), overseers administered the purgatives, emetics, and opiates to restore humoural balance or purge the body of "morbific matter."

The overseers living on the sea islands usually escaped the malarial fevers that afflicted overseers living in the river valleys. Only in exceptionally wet seasons did malaria appear on St. Simons Island: "In summer and autumn, fevers and agues occur in the lower lands. The islands are regarded as desirable places of resort during the sickly season; in very wet seasons, they are occasionally subject to light cases of fever" (White 1849:282–283). Although rarely suffering from malaria, there was evidence the overseers tried to cure other illnesses. Bottle fragments with the letters "[Dyspe]psia" came from a nostrum claiming to cure gastric complaints. Another small molded bottle bore the embossed letters ". . . .E"/ . . . NCE": The original legend may have been "Genuine Essence" of Jamaican ginger, an early patent panacea (J. Walker 1971:150). Other bottle fragments had the legend "[Or]iginal/[G]enuine"—the advertising claims of another patent medicine (Otto 1975b:232). Finally, the cat bones that appeared in the overseers' refuse (Table 4.2) may have been evidence of cat soup—an alleged remedy for bronchial illness that a slave folk doctor prescribed for an overseer or his servant (Puckett 1968:370).

"LUXURY" ITEMS

Overseers presumably bought their own luxury items including liquors, but individual purchases could not be identified in the overseers' "Sundries" accounts (Couper 1826:52). Most of the glass bottles from the overseer's site once held liquors rather than medicines (Table 3.22). As at the slave cabin, most of the beverage bottle fragments in the overseers' refuse came from cylindrical olive-green bottles that once held brewed beverages and wines (Jones 1971:73). Olive-green bottles, manufactured in Great Britain or the northeastern United States, arrived in southern ports either filled with beverages or empty. Often shop-keepers and tavern-owners purchased cases of empty bottles to fill with beverages tapped from casks, barrels, and pipes (Baron 1962:242; Jones 1971:67, 73; Olsen 1965:105–107). Rice, Parker, and Co., for example, offered to sell barrels of cider "in good order for bottling" (Brunswick *Advocate*, 6 December 1838) as well as "Ale and Porter in whole and half bottles" (Brunswick *Advocate*, 25 October 1838). The darker olive-green bottles, commonly called "black" bottles generally held brewed beverages, whereas the lighter-hued olive-green bottles usually held wines Noël Hume 1974:197–198). Since two-thirds of the olive-green sherds in the overseers' refuse came from lighter-hued bottles (Table 3.23), the archaeological evidence suggested the overseers drank more wines than brewed beverages.

In addition to still wines and champagnes—a whole Class III type 2 champagne bottle was found in the well fill (Switzer 1974: 26)—overseers enjoyed gin from "case" bottles. Case bottles, blown in molds (Noël Hume 1969a:62), were more common in the over-seers' refuse than in the slaves' refuse. Containing Holland gin and other "spirits" (Noël Hume 1974:194; Toulouse 1970:61–62), case bottles were designed for shipment in wooden boxes with square compartments (Watkins 1968:150). The archaeological evidence suggested that the overseers drank more gin than the slaves (Table 3.22).

The overseers' refuse also yielded evidence of another recreational activity—pipe smoking. Clay pipes were produced in the millions from ball clay by European and American manufacturers. Pipes were fragile but cheap; smokers readily discarded them when they broke; rarely did smokers repair and reuse pipes (Ascher and Fairbanks 1971:13; I. Walker 1971:19; Wilson 1966:34). Yet, such a reused pipe was found in the overseers' refuse (Figure 4.5). After losing its original clay stem, the pipe was rebored and used with a reed stem. In addition to these clay pipes, a brass container—possibly a snuff box—was found in the well fill (Otto 1975:268). Presumably the overseers purchased their own tobacco products, though no individual entries appeared in the overseers' "Sundries" accounts (Couper 1826–1852). It is known, however, that the overseer on Hugh Fraser Grant's Elizafield Plantation purchased "Segars" and "tobacco." The tobacco he bought could have been either leaf or "twist." Twists were long ropes of tobacco leaves that were sold by the yard and could be cut into plugs for pipe smoking or chewing (Heiman 1962:117–119; House 1954:226–228).

CLOTHING AND PERSONAL POSSESSIONS

In addition to luxuries such as liquor and tobacco, overseers had to buy their own clothing. When J. J. Morgan was serving as overseer on Elizafield Plantation, he bought 28 yards of "brown lin-nen [sic] Drill"; 12 yards of "Flax Osnabergs [sic]"; 4 dozen "pearl

TABLE 4.6
Various Possessions from the Plantation Sites

Slave cabin	Overseer's house	Planter's kitchen
Personal possessions		
1 geode fragment	—	—
1 bone-handled		
pen knife		
Horse equipment and vehicle parts[a]		
1 harness ring	1 iron harness brad	1 harness buckle?
	5 brass vehicle	
	rivets[a]	
	1 copper and pewter	
	bridle ornament	

Miscellaneous items	Slave cabin	Overseer's house	Planter's kitchen
Barrel band fragments	5	1	7
Barrel nails[b]	0	0	6
Chain links	3	1	0
Flat iron fragments	37	17	45
Slag fragments	5	0	6
Wire fragments	0	2	16
Lead waste	3	0	6
Lead strips	0	1	7

[a]Watkins (1968:169–170).
[b]Fontana (1965:92).

shirt buttons"; and 25 spools of thread. The drills and Osnaburgs that Morgan purchased were very reminiscent of slave textiles (House 1954:268; Stampp 1956:290–291). The overseers' refuse yielded only a handful of buttons including one four-hole porcelain and two iron four-hole buttons—types that also appeared at the slave cabin (Table 3.18).

There was also archaeological evidence of the overseers' horse tack and vehicles (Table 4.6). A circular copper and pewter bridle ornament with an applied bear's or fox's head was found in the antebellum refuse (Figure 4.6). In addition, the refuse midden yielded five brass rivets with washers that are believed to have come from a buggy or wagon (Watkins 1968:169–170). At least one of the Cannon's Point overseers, Seth R. Walker, owned a buggy and harness valued at $120 (Couper 1839–1854:442).

The overseer's well also yielded an unusual inventory of personal possessions. A metal rib from an umbrella was found in the well fill: Umbrellas with steel frames were manufactured in the United States after 1800 (Martin 1942:213). A brass badge or brooch with two six-pointed stars also appeared in the overseers' well (Otto 1975:276) as well as the most remarkable artifact at any of the Cannon's Point sites—a glass disc or lens (Figure 4.7). One side of the disc was convex, but the flat side bore the following inscription: "PATENT/ GL/Hugh F. Grant/1829." The word PATENT was machine-engraved; the remainder of the legend had been engraved in script with a diamond. Since the convex side had been ground by hand, the glass may have been a lens from the lighthouse built at St. Simons village on the southern tip of the island (Charles Fairbanks, 1974, personal communication).

Hugh Fraser Grant, whose name appeared on the glass artifact, was the son of Robert Grant, a well-known Glynn County planter. Hugh Grant would have been 18 years old in 1829. Hugh may have served as the overseer at Cannon's Point before his marriage to Mary Elizabeth Fraser on April 27, 1831. After his marriage, Hugh Grant moved to Georgetown, South Carolina, to manage rice plantations owned by the Rev. Hugh Fraser, his father-in-law. In 1833 Robert Grant transferred the title of the Elizafield rice plantation (Figure 2.1) to his son Hugh who relocated to Glynn County, Georgia (Anonymous: n.d.c; Glynn County Courthouse n.d.:Deed Book H:353–356; House 1954:4–8; Rogers 1970:195, 268–269; U.S. Bureau of the Census 1850a, 1850b). Although there was no documentary evidence in the "Hugh F. Grant Papers" to corroborate Hugh Grant's presence at Cannon's Point in 1829 (Lilla Hawes, 1974, written communication), there was some tentative evidence in the 1830 Glynn County census. A young white man in the age category of 15–20 years is listed as residing at Cannon's Point Plantation. This youth was not one of John Couper's sons because William Audley Couper would have been 12 years old and James Hamilton Couper would have been 36 years old. Hugh Grant, however, would have been 19 years old at that time (U.S. Bureau of the Census 1830).

Although several planters' sons served as overseers on Cannon's Point, their elite status was poorly reflected in the archaeological evidence of their material living conditions. At times, tidewater supervisors were treated as social equals by their planter employers—this was especially true for plantation managers. Common overseers, however, did not fare as well. One anonymous tidewater overseer wrote that overseeing was a solitary and dangerous profession;

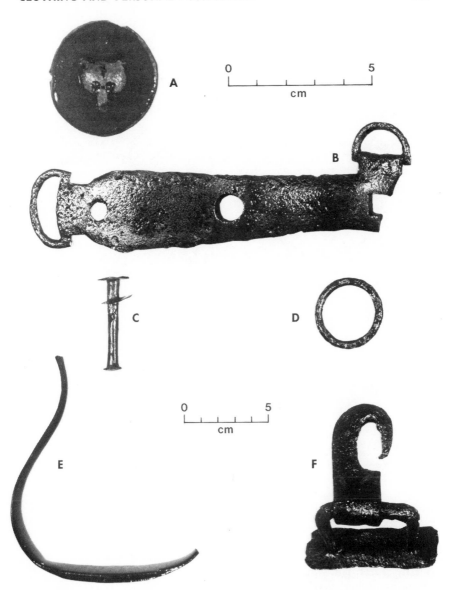

Figure 4.6. Horse equipment and vehicle items. (A) copper and pewter bridle ornament with applied bear head from the overseer's house refuse; (B) cast iron fitting, possibly from a horse collar; (C) brass vehicle rivet; (D) harness ring from the northern third slave cabin refuse; (E) brass stirrup from the surface of the northern third slave cabin refuse; (F) wrought iron trace hook from the southern chimney arch of the overseer's house.

Figure 4.7. Engraved glass disc or lens from the overseer's house well.

there was little social contact with fellow whites and there was frequent exposure to disease. But according to the author, the greatest problem was that the planters regarded their overseers as mere dependents "who are to be kept at a distance—as hirelings, who are hardly worth the wages of their daily labor." He claimed that many planters looked down upon their overseers as members of an "inferior and degraded caste" (Anonymous 1836:189–190).

Overseers on Cannon's Point seem to have shared this ambivalent treatment. On the one hand, the Cannon's Point overseers were provided with a house that was comparable to that of many small planters and middle-class townspeople. On the other hand, the overseers' modest wages and their limited perquisites and privileges yielded foodstuffs, possessions, and lifeways that bore a strong resemblance to those of their slave charges.

The similarities among the foodways and household artifacts of the Cannon's Point overseers and slaves should not come as a shock: Over 50 years ago in an article in the *Journal of Negro History* (1930:14–25) Avery Craven claimed that black slaves, poor whites, and middling whites such as overseers often lived in modest dwellings, ate essentially the same foods, and furnished their households in like fashion. Thus, despite racial, legal, and symbolic differences existing among black slaves, poor whites, and middling whites in the Old South, these people often experienced a basically similar material existence. On Cannon's Point, only the higher quality of the overseer's house seriously contested Craven's basic generalization, but Cannon's Point was one of the largest plantations of the Old South—a "showplace" plantation which "had everything fixed up nice" (Chapter 5). On the smaller plantations and slaveholding farms of the Old South, archaeologists may expect to find even greater similarities in the housing, foodways, possessions, and lifestyles of black slaves and their white overseers.

CHAPTER 5

The Planters' Living Conditions

Valuable Sea Island Plantation
and
A Gang of 126 Negroes For Sale

This plantation is one of the most healthy, productive and desirable residences on the seaboard of Georgia, and having been for twenty years under a regular system of manuring, is now in a high state of fertility.

On the premises are a dwelling house, and an excellent gin and cotton house, with basements of tabby; a hospital, workshop, corn, and negro houses . . . , and a stable and other outhouses of wood . . . .

The health of this plantation has been remarkable, and it enjoys the advantages of regular sea breezes and an abundant supply of fish and oysters.

The gang which contains 126 negroes is orderly, and in every respect a very valuable one. With very few

123

> exceptions, the negroes composing it have been ac-
> customed to a firm and mild discipline.
>
> Couper 1855

From 1845 to 1861 the only year-round white residents on Cannon's Point were the hired overseers who supervised the slave force
and policed the plantation. James Hamilton Couper and his family
used Cannon's Point only as a summer home to escape the malarial
fevers on Altama Plantation. But in earlier years, John Couper and
his family resided year-round on the Cannon's Point estate, managing both the hired overseers and the slave force (Chapter 2). From
1796 to 1845 John Couper struggled with a temperamental cash
crop—long-staple cotton (*Gossypium barbadense*)—a West Indian
species that was highly susceptible to unseasonable frosts, blights,
insect pests, and storms (Couper 1831; Spalding 1831; Stephens
1976). Not only was long-staple difficult to grow, but its market
prices fluctuated wildly through the years, depending on the world
wide cotton supply and economic conditions. To successfully grow
long-staple cotton, one needed fertile soils, a large and experienced
slave force and, of course, luck. Even with these, the yearly profits
were not great. As an example, one exceptionally well-managed tidewater cotton plantation yielded only a 4.37% return on the investment over a 40-year period. Occasionally, however, the weather and
the market prices combined to produce fabulous cotton yields and
profits (Johnson 1930:102; Rose 1964:6–9, 124–128). When John
Couper and his business partner James Hamilton purchased the
Cannon's Point estate in December 1793, the price of long-staple
cotton was booming. Couper, however, was searching for more than
an investment because in 1796 he moved his family to Cannon's
Point to take up permanent residence. On the mainland, planters
often left their plantations during the malarial summer months,
leaving the slaves under the direction of white overseers or black
supervisors. But on the sea islands where malaria was rare, planters
could reside year-round, devoting their full attention to plantation
duties. By 1820, there were 14 plantations on St. Simons Island,
including Cannon's Point, and most of these estates were managed
by their planter-owners (Cate 1930:75; Gray 1941:Vol. 2, 677; Kemble 1863:195; Wightman and Cate 1955:55; Wylly 1897:12).

As planters viewed it, a resident planter's duties were to "look to
the proper cultivation of the various crops and to supervise the establishment" (Wylly 1910:26). W. W. Hazzard, a St. Simons cotton
planter, left a written account of his plantation management for the

tidewater agricultural journal, *The Southern Agriculturist*. During the yearly agricultural work cycle, Hazzard's slaves followed a strict schedule of tasks: land-clearing, fencing, listing, ditching, planting, cultivating, and harvesting. And within the limitations set by Georgia state slave laws, Hazzard established a system of rules and regulations that would not only ensure completion of the agricultural work cycle but would maintain discipline and harmony (Hazzard 1831). Slaves who violated plantation rules were punished in the following fashion:

> If one negro [sic] steals from another, or from me, the driver is required to take of the marauder's goods and chattles an equal quantity, and restore the loss or the thief is certainly punished if he cannot make restoration, or if fair promises are made, time is allowed for restoration. Drunkenness, if riotous, would be punished by lying in the stocks all night and drinking a pint of warm water. If a negro is sick a pint of corn is deducted from his allowance every day: because if he is really sick the nurse supplies him with good gruel, he therefore, does not require corn, and if he is merely shamming, a reduction of rations, like stopping a sailor's grog, will induce him to be more active in the performance of his duties. (Hazzard 1831:352)

Hazzard's plantation regime, however, was tempered by paternalism because it was in "the interest of a master to preserve the health, vigour, and life of his servant, which produces a moral connexion [sic] and attachment betwixt master and servant, that freak, violence or misrule seldom severs" (Hazzard 1831:352). Therefore, slaves were allowed a series of privileges:

> To encourage industry and increase the comfort and contentment of these people, I allow every one, a task of ground, and a half task for each child capable of working . . . . They manage it their own way and the entire produce is appropriated to their own purposes not subject to my control, and raise with it as many poultry as they please. (Hazzard 1831:352–353)

John Couper was also known for the paternalistic treatment of his slaves who were allowed to garden, raise stock, hunt, fish, and trade after their daily tasks were completed (see Chapter 3). Fanny Kemble Butler, who later wrote a bitter indictment of slavery, admitted that John Couper had "bestowed much humane and benevolent pains" to better his slaves' condition (Kemble 1863:224). But despite his paternalistic concerns, John Couper was a believer in firm discipline for slaves. He detested abolitionists who represented a threat to his plantation regime. In a letter written in the late 1840s shortly before his death, John Couper strongly criticized the new Episcopalian priest from the "hot bed of abolitionism:"

> I believe Mr. Brown for aught I know to be a good man-but being from the hot bed of abolitionism, I distrust him . . . . I find Mr. Brown commences his meeting *with our slaves* without asking any leave. . . . It would be less dangerous to suffer Negroes preaching sermons at night than [?]. Look to Jamaica—the preachers aided by abolitionists in England have ruined that Island, and done no good to the Negroes—
>   The same game is playing here—and will succeed—if not soon checked. (Couper to King n.d.a).

By relying on his overseers and slave drivers to enforce the plantation rules, John Couper and James H. Couper maintained the plantation regime. In addition to maintaining slave discipline and supervising the crop cycle, the Coupers managed the plantation finances. Most planters, including John Couper, borrowed money to establish their ventures, and they continued to operate by borrowing against future crops (Chapter 2). Each year, the Coupers purchased slave provisions, tools, and other plantation supplies on credit from their factors or commission merchants. After the cotton harvest, the factors marketed the crop, deducting service charges, interest, and the cost of goods purchased on credit (Haskins 1955:1–2). From the 1830s to the 1850s, the Coupers relied on three factorage houses in Charleston, South Carolina: Richard M. Carnochan; Mitchell and Mure; and Robert Mure (Couper 1839–1854). After Carnochan's death in 1841 (Schirmer 1969:122), John Couper switched to Mitchell and Mure. After John Couper's death in 1850, Robert Mure assumed the responsibility for marketing the Cannon's Point crop and supplying the plantation (Couper 1839–1854).

When cotton prices were low, income from cotton sales often failed to cover plantation expenses and carrying charges. In 1846, as an example, Mitchell and Mure marketed the Cannon's Point cotton crop, which consisted of 34 bags of quality long-staple cotton, selling at only $.23 to $.25 per pound, and five bags of stained cotton, selling at $.07$\frac{1}{2}$ per pound. After service charges were deducted, the cotton crop realized only $2405.76. In turn, plantation expenditures totalled $3027.80. The major outlay was $1429.36 for plantation provisions including food, clothing, and medicine for the slaves. Additionally, expenses for hiring slave craftsmen totalled $1197.62; the overseer's salary for 13 months was $271.66; and the Coupers purchased $129.16 of plantation tools and supplies. Although costs such as the hiring of slaves could be reduced, the costs of slave provisions were unrelenting. But when cotton prices recovered during the early 1850s, the plantation operated at a profit. In 1852 sales of cotton netted $2767.39 after service charges, while plantation expenditures totalled $2008.09. Cotton sales in 1853 brought in $2566.12 after charges, and expenditures for that year were only $2006.24 (Couper 1839–1854).

In earlier decades, however, long-staple cotton planting was a more profitable pursuit on Cannon's Point. John Couper estimated his 1824 cotton crop would have been worth $90,000 at current market prices (Couper 1828). In addition to cotton, the plantation also produced food crops and livestock that supported the plantation inhabitants. In return for his financial investment and his managerial duties, the planter monopolized the plantation surplus—the cash crops, food crops, and livestock produced on the plantation. Although planters diverted some of the plantation surplus to cover the subsistence needs of their slaves and overseers (Chapters 3 and 4), they disposed of the rest as they saw fit: Planters could reinvest profits in more land, slaves, and equipment, or they could devote the profits to maintain the lifestyle that their social position demanded (Wolf 1959:136–138). Some historians have contended that the planters' love for high living dissipated the profits needed for reinvestment and economic growth. Others have argued that only the wealthiest planters were "conspicuous consumers." For these elite planters, a lavish lifestyle was actually a form of business expense, designed to impress outsiders, peers, and even the southern white and black masses (see Pease 1969:381–383).

THE SOCIAL SCENE

The Coupers were considered conspicuous consumers among planters. Although John Couper made "many heavy and costly improvements" during the five decades he lived on Cannon's Point, he also enjoyed a lavish lifestyle—a huge house, a staff of house servants, a bounteous table, a well-stocked wine cellar, and a library filled with rare books and works of art. During his lifetime, Cannon's Point became a "showplace plantation" where elite travelers could be assured of a hospitable welcome (Wylly 1914; Wylly 1897: 14, 57). His son James continued the tradition of hospitality but

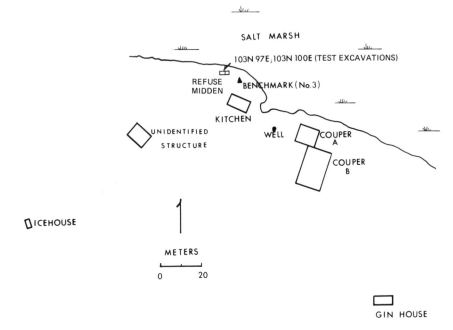

Figure 5.1.   The Cannon's Point planter's house site.

with a difference: "The father sought the company that filled his house whereas it was the company that sought the son" (Holmes 1976:137).

In addition to feting travelers, the Coupers entertained their fellow tidewater planters. As Charles Lyell wrote in his account of tidewater plantation life: "The landed proprietors here visit each other in the style of English country gentlemen, sometimes dining out with their families and returning at night, or, if the distance to be great, remaining to sleep and coming home the next morning" (Lyell 1849:Vol. 1, 329–330). A plantation mistress such as Rebecca, John's wife, or Caroline, James's wife, spent much of her time planning these dinner parties. The mistress would oversee the butchering of the beef, mutton, and pork for dinner, reserving the best cuts for the planter's table and giving the rest to the slaves. She would also review the fishermen's catch of seafood, selecting the best for the night's dinner. And finally, she would supervise the cooks' efforts. Several of Rebecca's recipes have survived including one for "Catfish Soup" and another for "Orange Cordial." When dinner was served at 4:30 P.M., the mistress hosted the visitors, kinspeople, and friends who were staying at Cannon's Point (R. Couper n.d.a, n.d.b; Wylly 1910:24–25).

The Coupers entertained their guests in the parlor and dining room of their "new dwelling house" (Couper B, Figure 5.1) which was completed by the time of Aaron Burr's visit in 1804. Yet, when the Coupers first moved to Cannon's Point in 1796, they occupied the "old dwelling house" (Couper A)—a 1½-story structure that had been built by Daniel Cannon, a carpenter who first owned the tract in the 1730s (Cate n.d.a; Lovell 1932:74–75; Wightman and Cate 1955:43, 55).

THE PLANTERS' HOUSE SITE

The old dwelling house had tabby basement walls which had been poured in courses around vertical hewn timbers. Tabby (a kind of concrete made from crushed shells, sand, shell-lime, and salt-free water) was poured into wooden forms with morticed ends that were kept apart by spreader pins (Spalding 1830, 1844). The windows and doorways of this tabby basement had been framed with vertical square posts. The exterior dimensions of the basement were 25.3 by 25.9 feet (7.7 by 7.9 m), and there were two interior partitions that formed four rooms (Figure 5.2). Along the north and south walls were 2½-story chimneys with heavy bases of tabby brick which had arches to lighten the mass. The north chimney stack was made of tabby bricks though it had clay brick fireboxes (Figure 5.3). The southern chimney was fashioned from clay brick and it was probably a replacement for an earlier chimney lost in the 1804 hurricane (see Van Doren 1929:182). On the west wall of the basement was a porch stoop constructed of poured tabby and tabby brick; along the east wall were the foundation pillars for a verandah. The pillars were of tabby brick and hewn-post construction (Otto 1975:123).

When extant, the tabby basement walls, which were capped with rows of tabby brick, supported a 1½-story frame superstructure (Figure 5.2). According to a member of the Shadman family who lived in the house after the Civil War (Chapter 2), this old dwelling house had a central hall, two rooms, a loft, and even a dairy room in a corner of the porch (Cate n.d.b). This "central-hall-and-two-rooms" house was a common folklike house style in the tidewater South (Historic Preservation Section 1974:71); it was derived from the English "hall-and-parlor" house (see Kniffen 1965:565). But the old Cannon house was too small for the growing Couper family,

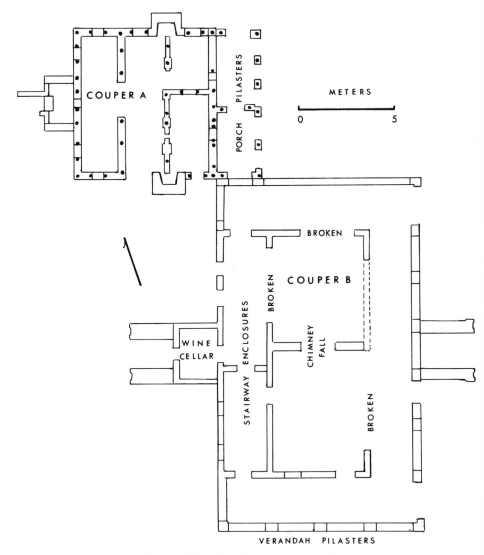

Figure 5.2. The Coupers' house site.

which included two sons (John, Jr., and James) as well as a daughter Isabella (Cate n.d.c). Excluding the hall, basement, and loft, the old dwelling house provided only an estimated 362 square feet of living space (Otto 1975:135). During the late 1790s, Couper began work on a new house adjoining the Cannon structure.

The new building also had a poured tabby basement, measuring

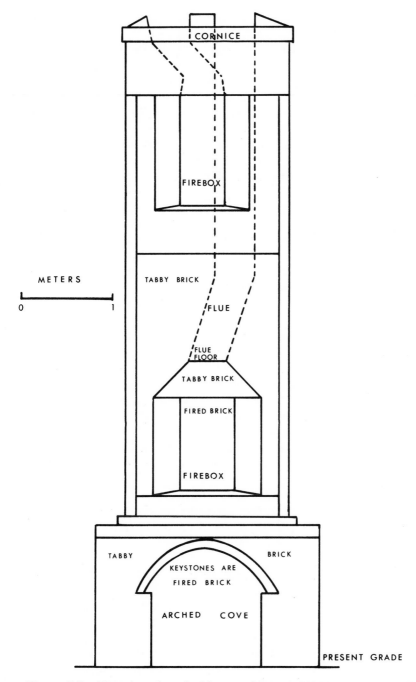

Figure 5.3. Elevation of north chimney of Coupers' "old dwelling house." Floor of hearth is 0.06 m below datum.

131

35.4 by 60.0 feet (10.8 by 18.3). The windows and doorways in the tabby walls were framed by wooden bucks nailed to tenons set in mortices near the tops and bottoms of the sides. On the western side there were double tabby walls which enclosed a stairway and stairs leading to a butler's pantry (Cate n.d.b) (Figure 5.4). Along the northern, eastern, and southern tabby walls were the verandah pilasters—constructed of poured tabby around hewn logs. The major unit of the basement enclosed a large square room with a fallen chimney and a dividing wall. In the ruined fireplace were the remains of a steatite box with a double-sloped roof, possibly a warming oven for foods brought from the detached kitchen (see Figure 5.1). This tabby basement supported a massive $2\frac{1}{2}$-story frame structure. On the first floor were the dining rooms, the parlor, and library. Porch stoops on the eastern and western sides gave access to the first floor. Surrounding the first floor was a wide verandah where the guests promenaded. Bedrooms and dressing rooms were located on the second floor, and on top there was a loft with dormer windows (Cooney 1933:40; Lovell 1932:74−75). When extant, there may have been as many as 10 rooms and three stairways in the new dwelling house as well as a wine cellar under the western stoop. There was perhaps 1786 square feet of living space, excluding stairways, basement, and loft (Otto 1975:135−136).

As was the case with most tidewater plantation houses, the Couper house complex had a detached kitchen to spare the inhabitants the smells, noises, and danger of fire. The Couper kitchen was a spacious one-story frame building set on a poured tabby floor, measuring 19.4 by 39 feet (5.9 by 11.9 m). The kitchen possessed an elaborate brick chimney with baking ovens, warming ovens, and a huge hearth (Figures 5.5 and 5.6). Here Sans Foix, the Coupers' black cook, and his staff prepared the meals that slave waiters carried to the butler's pantry of the mansion (Figure 5.4) (see Lovell 1932:115; Wightman and Cate 1955:57).

The Coupers also had an icehouse to store the New England ice that was used to chill wines (Figure 5.1). The Couper icehouse had a tabby-lined pit with two compartments. The deeper, larger compartment had a tabby floor, packed sawdust insulation, and a drainage pipe. The shallower compartment may have held sawdust to repack the ice blocks (Otto 1975:131). The pit fill yielded household rubbish as well as a dime dating to 183(8?), indicating that the ice pit was filled in during late antebellum times. A frame structure may have enclosed the ice pit, or the ice could have been covered

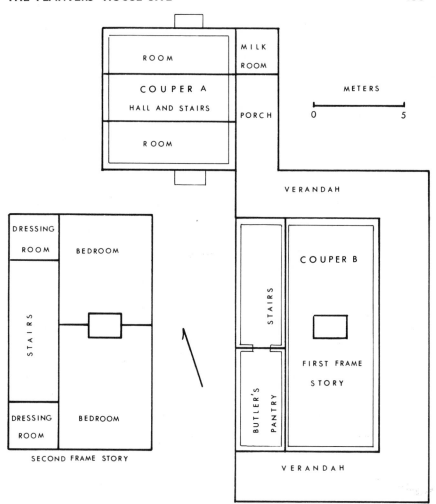

Figure 5.4. The frame stories of the Couper house. (Adapted from Cate "Cannon's Point-Plans for House" nd.)

with layers of straw, shingles, and sod (Bonner 1964:184; Booth 1971: 115).

Water for the planter's kitchen and house came from a well located just west of the mansion (Figure 5.1). It was a ring well lined with wedge-shaped bricks, unlike the pit-dug wells at the overseer and slave sites (Noël Hume 1969b:145–146). The planter's well had been cleaned out periodically until the Couper house burned in

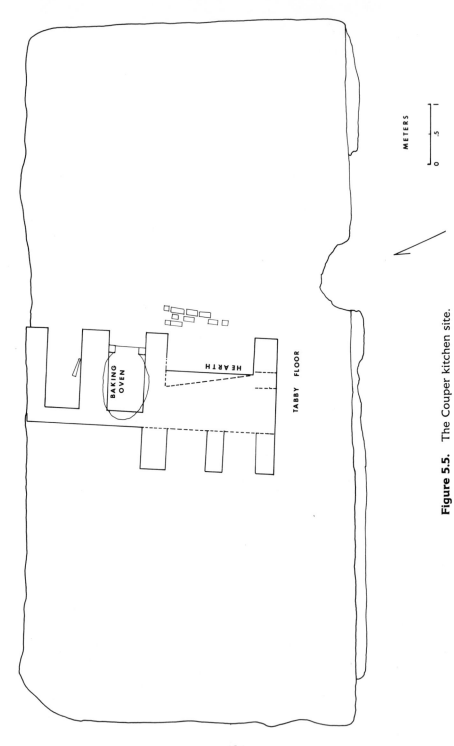

Figure 5.5. The Couper kitchen site.

BAKING OVEN

HEARTH

TABBY FLOOR

METERS

0   .5   1

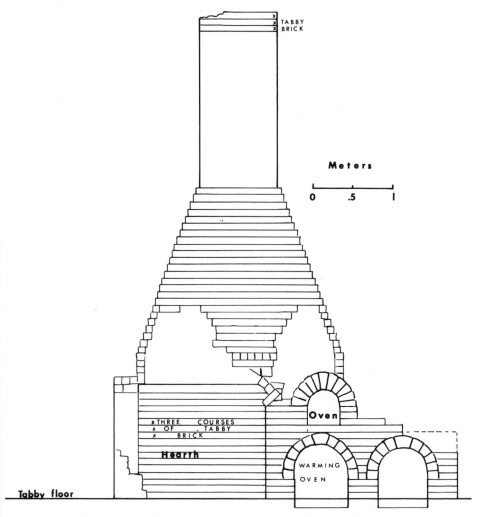

Figure 5.6.   The east face of the Couper kitchen chimney.

1890. It yielded few artifacts other than coins from James Hamilton
Couper's numismatic collection (Fairbanks 1976:171).

East of the Couper's house lay the ruins of the cotton gin houses
where cotton was ginned, moted, and stored (Figure 5.1). By 1804
John Couper had two cotton gin houses, each of which contained
three ox-driven Eve's roller gins, and he was building a third cotton
house (Editor 1804). Excavation of one of the gin house sites yielded
a cast iron hub for a wooden-band wheel—possibly one of the large

wheels that powered the wooden rollers of the Eve's gin (Figure 5.7) (Editor 1833:245; Simon 1973). But by the 1840s, Eve's gins were giving way to McCarthy roller gins. (In 1840 Fones McCarthy of Alabama devised an improved roller gin which had a leather-covered roller that pulled the staple through; a thin steel bar, operating vertically in front of the roller, separated the seed from the long-staple lint. This moving bar was powered by connecting rods linked to a crank [Gray 1941:Vol. 2, 736; USDA 1964:2]). A portion of a McCarthy gin crank was found at the gin house site along with a small cast iron band wheel which may have driven the crank (Figure 5.8; USDA 1964:Figure 1). In 1845 the Coupers are known to have purchased six new cotton gins from Mitchell and Mure, their Charleston factors (Couper 1839–1854:208). These were probably McCarthy gins.

During antebellum times, the mundane cotton houses as well as the Couper mansion and kitchen were surrounded by groves and gardens. Arriving at Cannon's Point by boat, Charles Lyell left this description of the Couper home:

> We found Mr. Couper's villa, near the water's edge, shaded by a verandah and a sago tree. There were also many lemon trees some-what injured by the late frost; but the olives of which there is a fine grove here, are unharmed, and it is thought they may one day be cultivated with profit in the sea-islands. We also admired five date palms, which bear fruit. They were brought from Bussora in Persia, and have not suffered by the cold. The oranges have been much hurt. (Lyell 1849:Vol. 1, 339)

In addition to the olive, orange, lemon, and date palm groves, the Coupers possessed an orchard containing plum, peach, nectarine, fig, guava, and pomegranate trees. Fanny Kemble Butler fondly re-membered John Couper's extensive vegetable garden which sup-plied turnips, cabbages, califlowers, green peas, salad greens, and several kinds of grapes. Kemble claimed that Couper had one of the few kitchen gardens on the island (Couper 1810a, 1810b; Editor 1833:249, 252; Kemble 1961:237–238, 267; Lovell 1932:75). Few visitors to Cannon's Point failed to comment on the Coupers' elabo-rate gardens and groves, but none saw fit to mention the refuse midden that lay to the north of the kitchen (Figure 5.1). Yet, this neglected feature of the Couper "villa" contained the most signifi-cant evidence about the household life of the Couper family and their guests. In the extensive kitchen refuse midden, field crews excavated two squares (Figures 5.1, 5.9) with trowels, and all exca-vated materials were water-screened with $\frac{1}{8}$-inch mesh to maximize

Figure 5.7. Long-staple cotton processing technology. (A) cast iron crank fragment, possibly from a McCarthy's gin; (B) cast iron hub from a large wooden-band wheel, possibly from an Eve's gin; (C) cast iron pestle, probably used in packing bags of long-staple cotton.

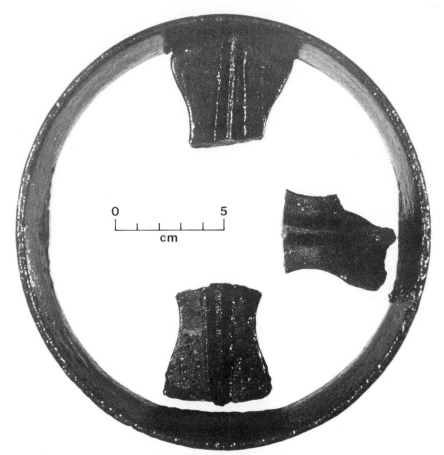

Figure 5.8. Long-staple cotton processing technology. A band wheel, possibly from a McCarthy's gin.

the recovery of artifacts and food bones. Though the surface zone (A) contained postbellum artifacts including wire nails (Nelson 1963), the underlying three zones II–IV (B-D), contained no artifacts whose known beginning date of manufacture was later than 1860 (Table 5.1). The zones below IV (E-G) contained only small samples of historic artifacts or late prehistoric materials. Thus, only Zones II–IV (B-D) could be reliably dated to the antebellum years, and only materials from these zones were compared with the antebellum refuse from the third slave cabin and the overseer's house site.

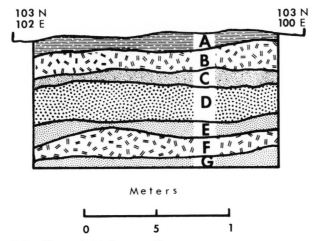

Figure 5.9. Planter's kitchen profiles.

South wall profile of square 103N 100E—Couper kitchen refuse. (A) humus with crushed shell; (B) loosely compact shell with light-grey sandy soil and crushed shell (Zone II); (C) black sandy soil with charcoal and some crushed shell (Zone III); (D) dark-grey sandy soil with crushed shell and few whole shells (Zone IV); (E) light-grey highly compact sandy soil with crushed shell (Zone V); (F) loosely compact whole shell and light-grey sandy soil (Zone VI); (G) light-brown sterile sandy soil. The surface at stake 103N 102E is 1.40m below datum.

THE PLANTER FAMILY'S DIET

Among the most numerous remains recovered from the planter's kitchen refuse were the food bones, including those from the plantation livestock—cattle, sheep, hogs, and poultry (Table 5.2). Since the Coupers monopolized the plantation herds, they achieved a steady supply of meat and dairy products such as the cheese that was made on the plantation. Most of the Cannon's Point cattle, sheep, and hogs ranged on Long Island (now Sea Island), an uninhabited barrier island owned by the Coupers (Figure 1.1). Each spring the slave stock-keepers rounded up the livestock on Long Island and transported choice animals to the plantation where they were fattened on turnips and cowpeas (J. Couper n.d.b, 1832:286–290).

By translating bone weights to their equivalent edible meat weights, we found the Coupers far preferred beef to other domestic

TABLE 5.1
Dating the Couper Kitchen Refuse (Zones II–IV)

Ceramic hallmarks	1800	1810	1820	1830	1840	1850	1860	1
Zone II								
"Clews/Warranted/ Staffordshire"[a] (1815–1834)			⊢———————⊣					
Zone III								
"Clews/Warranted/ Staffordshire" (1815–1834)			⊢———————⊣					
"Davenport" with anchor[b] (1805–1820)	⊢———————⊣							
"Jackson's Valencia"[c] (1831–1835)				⊢——⊣				
Zone IV[d]								
"Clews/Warranted/ Staffordshire" (1815–1834)			⊢———————⊣					
"Davenport" with anchor (1805–1820)	⊢———————⊣							
Zone III								
"McDougall/Glasgow" (Post-1846)						⊢———————		

[a]Stefano (1974:324).
[b]Coysh (1970:26).
[c]Godden (1963:132).
[d]Zone IV contains percussion caps; it postdates 1822 (Noël Hume 1969a:215).

meats (Table 5.3). An examination of the beef bones revealed the Coupers ate cattle that ranged in age from young steers to old, fattened work oxen. An unerupted third molar came from a steer less than 24–30 months old, whereas a heavily sculptured phalanx came from an old adult, possibly one of the work oxen that John Couper fattened on rutabagas (Couper 1832:286–290; Otto 1975:334; Silver 1963:254, 262). The high ratios of cattle bones to individual animals suggested the Coupers often enjoyed fresh beef (Table 3.11; Chaplin 1971:67). Some beef, nevertheless, was salted on the plantation. In one document, "To Salt Meat in Hot Weather," John Couper described the lengthy process of preserving beef for the planter's table. Joints were trimmed to shape; and the spine, ribs,

TABLE 5.2
Planter's Kitchen Faunal Remains

Taxa (genus and species)	Specimens		Weight		Minimum individuals	
	Number	%	gm	%	Number	%
Didelphis marsupialis (opossum)	5	0.2	3.0	0.1	2	1.1
Sylvilagus sp. (rabbit)	19	0.7	2.4	0.1	3	1.7
cf Neotoma floridana (Florida wood rat)	2	<0.1	0.2	<0.1	2	1.1
Mus musculus (domestic mouse)	3	<0.1	0.2	<0.1	2	1.1
Rattus norvegicus (norway rat)	9	0.3	1.2	0.1	3	1.7
Procyon lotor (raccoon)	20	0.7	16.0	0.8	5	2.8
Mustela vison (mink)	8	0.3	1.5	0.1	3	1.1
Sus scrofa (domestic pig)	61	2.3	170.7	8.1	5	2.8
Odocoileus virginianus (white-tailed deer)	4	0.2	23.4	1.1	1	0.6
Bos taurus (domestic cattle)	48	1.8	893.5	42.2	4	2.2
cf Ovis aries[a] (domestic sheep)	63	2.3	200.7	9.5	5	2.8
Gallus gallus (domestic fowl)	6	0.2	5.5	0.3	3	1.7
Chelydra serpentina (snapping turtle)	3	<0.1	0.6	<0.1	1	0.6
Kinosternon cf subrurum (E. mud turtle)	5	0.2	0.8	<0.1	2	1.1
Malaclemys terrapin (diamondback turtle)	918	33.9	410.8	19.4	14	7.7
Chrysemys sp. (pond turtle)	39	1.4	40.1	1.9	4	2.2
Trionyx cf ferox (soft-shell turtle)	96	3.5	82.3	3.9	7	3.9
cf Coluber constrictor (black racer)	1	<0.1	0.1	<0.1	1	0.6
Elaphe sp. (rat snake)	4	0.2	0.3	<0.1	2	1.1
Alligator mississipiensis	5	0.2	23.8	1.1	3	1.7
Bufo cf terrestris (southern toad)	11	0.4	0.5	<0.1	3	1.7

(continued)

TABLE 5.2 (*Continued*)

Taxa (genus and species)	Specimens		Weight		Minimum individuals	
	Num-ber	%	gm	%	Num-ber	%
Rana sp. (frog)	2	<0.1	0.2	<0.1	2	1.1
Carcharinus sp. (requi-em shark)	2	<0.1	0.3	<0.1	1	0.6
Dasyatis sp. (stingrays)	45	1.7	3.7	0.2	5	2.8
cf *Rhinoptera bonasus* (cow-nosed ray)	114	4.2	14.0	0.7	5	2.8
Acipenser oxyrhynchus (sturgeon)	81	3.0	19.8	0.9	4	2.2
Lepisosteus osseus (long-nosed gar)	167	6.2	16.8	0.8	4	2.2
cf *Brevoortia* sp. (men-haden)	76	2.8	0.8	<0.1	3	1.7
Arius felis (marine cat-fish)	265	9.8	31.6	1.5	19	10.4
Bagre marinus (gaff-topsail catfish)	305	11.3	67.3	3.2	18	9.9
Caranx cf *hippos* (cre-valle jack)	1	<0.1	0.3	<0.1	1	0.6
cf *Chloroscombrus chrysurus* (bumper)	1	<0.1	0.1	<0.1	1	0.6
Archosargus pro-batocepalus (sheeps-head)	97	3.6	41.1	1.9	8	4.4
Bairdiella chrysura (sil-ver perch)	20	0.7	0.7	<0.1	3	1.7
Cynoscion nothus (sil-ver sea trout)	1	<0.1	0.1	<0.1	1	0.6
Cynoscion regalis (weak fish)	3	0.1	0.5	<0.1	3	1.7
Cynoscion sp. (sea trout)	1	<0.1	0.1	<0.1	1	0.6
Leiostomus xantharus (spot)	4	0.2	0.2	<0.1	2	1.1
Menticirrhus sp. (king-fish)	7	0.3	0.3	<0.1	3	1.7
Micropogon undulatus (Atlantic croaker)	17	0.6	1.0	<0.1	5	2.8
Pogonias cromis (black drum)	81	3.0	29.3	1.4	4	2.2
Sciaenops ocellatus (red drum)	5	0.2	6.4	0.3	3	1.1

(*continued*)

TABLE 5.2 (*Continued*)

Taxa (genus and species)	Specimens		Weight		Minimum individuals	
	Number	%	gm	%	Number	%
Mugil sp. (mullet)	75	2.8	1.9	0.1	6	3.3
Paralichthys sp. (flounder)	12	0.4	1.0	<0.1	5	2.8
	2712		2115.1		182	
Other Taxa						
Unidentified Rodentia	8		0.5		—	
Unidentified small mammal	137		6.9		—	
Unidentified medium mammal	281		44.5		—	
Unidentified large mammal	1085		888.5		—	
Unidentified *Artiodactyla* (even-toed hoofed mammal)	2		7.4		—	
Unidentified mammal	1108		152.7		—	
Unidentified *Aves* (bird)	266		37.6		—	
Unidentified Chelonia	1442		248.0		—	
Cheloniidae (marine turtles)	82		78.5		4	
Lacertilia	2		0.2		1	
Unidentified *Serpentes*	5		0.2		—	
Unidentified *Reptilia*	1		0.2		—	
cf *Salientia*	19		0.7		—	
Unidentified small *Sciaenidae*	31		0.7		—	
Unidentified large *Sciaenidae*	20		20.5		—	
Carangidae (jacks)	1		0.1		—	
Ariidae	662		63.1		13	
Unidentified *Osteichthyes*	1705		196.2		—	
Unidentified bone	465		53.8		—	
	7322		1800.3		18	
	10034		3915.4		200	

[a]See Hole, Flannery, and Nealy (1969).

TABLE 5.3
Domestic Food Animals from the Plantation Sites

	Slave cabin		Overseer's house		Planter's kitchen	
	Number	%	Number	%	Number	%
Minimum number of individuals (MNI)						
Domestic rabbit	1	8	—	—	—	—
Domestic cat?[a]	—	—	1	20	—	—
Domestic hog	3	25	2	40	5	29
Domestic cattle	3	25	1	20	4	24
Domestic sheep	2	17	—	—	5	29
Domestic chicken	3	25	1	20	3	18
	12		5		17	
Identifiable bone fragments						
Domestic rabbit	4	4	—	—	—	—
Domestic cat?	—	—	11	21	—	—
Domestic hog	60	63	33	62	61	34
Domestic cattle	16	17	8	15	48	27
Domestic sheep	10	11	—	—	63	35
Domestic chicken	5	5	1	2	6	3
	95		53		178	
Bone weights (in gms)						
Domestic rabbit	0.7	<1	—	—	—	—
Domestic cat?	—	—	1.9	2	—	—
Domestic hog	86.5	29	49.2	45	170.7	13
Domestic cattle	157.4	53	58.4	53	893.5	70
Domestic sheep	43.0	15	—	—	200.7	16
Domestic chicken	8.8	3	0.7	<1	5.5	1
	296.4		110.2		1270.4	

[a]Since the cat bones displayed butchering marks, the cat may have been consumed as food, butchered for fishbait, or used in a folk medicinal remedy.

and tenderloin were separated from the abdominal walls. Meat was rubbed with pepper, saltpeter, and salt, packed in salt boxes, and later transferred to barrels of salt brine. Since planters preferred such cuts as hind limbs, shoulders, and tenderloins, they usually gave the "offal"—the viscera, heads, necks, backbones, tails, and lower legs—to the slaves (Ball 1859:137–138; J. Couper n.d.c; Hilliard 1969:4–5). The archaeological evidence at Cannon's Point tentatively confirmed this distribution of plantation beef. The planter's kitchen refuse yielded a variety of cattle elements including femurs; in turn, the third slave cabin refuse produced cattle, teeth, vertebrae, ribs, and fragments from a scapula and pelvis, indicating slaves ate flesh from cattle heads, backbone, forelegs, and side meats. Cattle femurs were absent in the slave cabin refuse, suggesting the planter family may have kept the preferred hind limbs which produced rump and round roasts (Otto 1975:333–334).

Though the planter family preferred beef, they also consumed mutton, pork, and chicken. Most of the sheep bones in the planter's refuse were from mature adults, possibly the wethers which were mentioned in one of John Couper's agricultural articles (Couper 1832; Otto 1975:334). Pork was less common fare than mutton, but the pork came from a wider age range of animals. A newly erupted pig's first molar came from a shoat slightly older than 6 months, whereas a badly worn adult hog premolar represented the other age extreme (Otto 1975:334; Silver 1963:256, 265). Given the low ratio of pork bones to individuals, much of the Coupers' pork may have been commercial meat (Table 3.11). This may explain the purchases of hams and small barrels of bacon in the Couper household accounts (Couper 1839–1854). Surprisingly, the planter's refuse yielded few chicken bones (Table 5.2) even though Fanny Kemble referred to the Coupers' "charming, nicely-kept poultry yard," and the Coupers often purchased slave-grown poultry (Hall 1829:Vol. 3, 224; Kemble 1863:225).

Despite the apparent abundance of fresh and salt meats, there were occasional shortages. In a letter to his brother, John Couper wrote of such a time:

> My wife has just disturbed me in a fury, unexpected company have dropped in near dinner, some Lamb killed two days ago is sower [sic]—we have rec'd [sic] no beef . . . our fisherman has returned with bad luck—it blows too hard-it is too late to kill poultry—so Bacon and eggs . . . . Tomorrow . . . Terrapin and sheepshead [fish]—not sheep's head—we are Christians, taking no care for tomorrow. (Couper 1828)

In this revealing letter, Couper mentioned the slave fisherman who would supply seafood the next day. In the tidewater, planters commonly appointed slave fishermen and hunters to furnish the planter's table with fish and game. After taking their pick, planters gave some of the excess to the slaves and overseers (Johnson 1930:142; Woofter 1930:35).

Unexpectedly, we found that wild game, fish, and reptiles composed almost one-half of the planter family's meat diet (Table 3.10).

Though small forest mammals such as raccoons, opossums, and rabbits were rarely eaten by the planter's family (Table 3.8), venison was more common fare. The Coupers, their guests, or their slave hunters probably shot the deer on the neighboring barrier islands (such as Little St. Simons and Long Island) since St. Simons Island had few standing forests during the antebellum years (see Hazzard 1825). Fish and turtles, nevertheless, were more important sources of wild flesh than mammals (Table 3.8). By fishing regularly in the outlying sounds, the Coupers' slave fishermen caught such fish as spots, jacks, and bumpers as well as black and red drums. And by regularly visiting the landward marshes and the freshwater streams of the coastal mainland, the fishermen collected snapping, mud, soft-shell, and pond turtles. The slave fishermen also visited the beaches of Little St. Simons and Long Island to capture marine turtles when the females came ashore to lay eggs in the early summer. Diamondback turtles were more commonly eaten than any other turtle species (Table 3.8) since these tasty reptiles were once abundant in the salt marshes and tidal streams (see Dahlberg 1972:323–353; Hazzard 1825; Larson 1969:31; Ursin 1972:95). Even alligator bones appeared in the planter's kitchen refuse. In antebellum times alligators must have been choice game items. For example, Aaron Burr, a visitor at Cannon's Point penned the following in a letter to his daughter: "You perceive that I am constantly discovering new luxuries for my table. Not having been able to kill a crocodile [alligator], I have offered a reward for one, which I mean to eat, dressed in soup, fricassee, and steak. Oh! how I long to partake of this repast" (Van Doren 1929:182).

Thus, by sending out their slave fishermen and hunters, the Coupers enjoyed a wider variety of wild game, fish, and reptiles than the slaves and overseers. Significantly, no deer, spot, jack, bumper, mud and pond turtle, marine turtle, or alligator bones were identified in either the slave or overseer refuse middens (Tables 3.6, 4.2). Such animals were commonly found on the barrier islands, in the deeper sounds, or in the landward marshes and streams (Tables 3.9, 4.3, 5.4)—habitats that the field slaves and overseers rarely visited (Figures 3.3, 5.10). Given their limited leisure time, slaves and overseers did most of their food collecting on Cannon's Point or in the neighboring tidal streams and marshes, therefore collecting a narrower range of game, fish, and turtles.

In addition to enjoying a wider array of wild foods and monopolizing the plantation meat supplies, the Coupers purchased quantities of commercial foods by using credit on future cotton sales.

TABLE 5.4

Habitats Used by the Planter Family's Slave Hunters and Fishermen for Food Collecting[a]

Aquatic habitats	Terrestrial habitats

Ocean waters off the beach
  Jacks
  Bumpers
Sounds
  Jacks?
  Spots
  Croakers
  Black drums
  Red drums
Sounds, tidal rivers, and creeks
  Snapping turtles?
  Diamondback turtles
  Alligators?
  Requiem sharks
  Stingrays
  Cow-nosed rays
  Sturgeons
  Gars
  Menhaden
  Marine catfish
  Gafftop-sail catfish
  Jacks?
  Bumpers?
  Sheepshead
  Silver perch
  Silver sea trout
  Weakfish
  Sea trout
  Spots?
  Kingfish
  Croakers?
  Black drums?
  Red drums?
  Mullet
  Flounders
Streamside salt marsh
  Diamondback terrapins
	Cannon's Point forests and secondary growth
	  Opossums
	  Rabbits
	  wood rats
	  raccoons
	  minks
	Barrier island forests
	  white-tailed deer (and small forest mammals?)
	Barrier island beaches
	  sea turtles
	Salt marsh
	  Raccoons?
	  Minks?

(continued)

TABLE 5.4 (*Continued*)

Aquatic habitats	Terrestrial habitats
Landward marsh and streams	
Snapping turtles	
Mud turtles	
Diamondback terrapins?	
Pond turtles	
Soft-shell turtles	
Alligators	
Freshwater ponds	
Frogs (snapping, mud, pond, and	
Soft-shell turtles?)	
Freshwater river	
Sturgeons	

[a]Sources: Dahlberg (1972); Dahlberg and Heard (1969); Goldman (1910); Hazzard (1825); Larson (1969); Shelford (1963); Teal (1962); Ursin (1972).

As Charles Lyell noted in his travelogue, the tidewater planters derived a "considerable part of their food . . . from the produce of their lands," but they also kept large stores of groceries as was "the custom in country houses in some parts of Scotland" (Lyell 1849:1, 330). According to the Cannon's Point accounts kept by James H. Couper, the Coupers purchased wheat flour, buckwheat, crackers, soda biscuits, sugar, butter, lard, tea, and Java coffee (Couper 1839–1854). Barrels of flour were a rather common entry in the plantation household accounts, and it is known that elite southern whites preferred breads of wheaten flour to corn bread—a slave staple food (Hilliard 1972:50, 56).

Drawing on this abundance of commercial and plantation foods, Sans Foix, the Coupers' cook, supervised the kitchen staff as they prepared foods for the planter family's table. Most seafoods, including terrapins, were probably cooked in soups and chowders. Even catfish, rays, and sharks contributed to the elegant seafood soups served at the Couper house (R. Couper n.d.b). In turn, choice cuts of beef, mutton, pork, and venison could have been roasted in the spacious kitchen hearth (Figure 5.6). Saw marks were present on many of the beef, mutton, and pork bones, indicating the carcasses had been carefully divided into joints for roasting. Vegetables from the Coupers' kitchen garden could have been steamed in kettles, while breads and pastries baked in the oven (Figure 5.6).

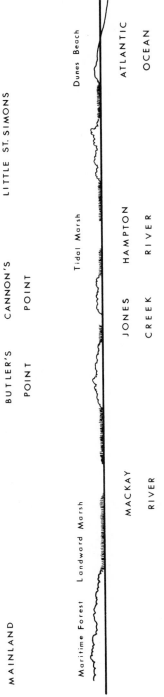

Figure 5.10. Idealized habitat cross-section of Cannon's Point and outlying areas. (Adapted from Dahlberg 1972; Larson 1969).

Sans Foix—who had studied with Cupidon, the black chef of the Marquis de Montalet, a Sapelo Island planter—was a renowned cook. As an example of his culinary skills, in December 1821 Sans Foix cooked the dinner for a meeting of the St. Clair Club, whose members included the leading planters of St. Simons Island. The first course included clam broth and chicken mulligatawny; the second course consisted of fish, shrimp pies, crab in the shell, roasts, and steamed vegetables—all of which were served with wines. This was followed by a simple dessert of marmalade tartlets, dried fruits, and nuts. After clearing the dishes, John Couper's slave waiters— Sandy, Johnny, and Dick—served the planters a punch of rum, brandy, sugar, lemon juice, and peel (Wightman and Cate 1955:57; Wylly 1916:55–56).

THE PLANTER'S TABLEWARE AND CERAMICS

Despite their wealth, the Coupers possessed few European or Oriental porcelains, which are usually regarded as indicators of elite status (see Stone 1970a). Rather the bulk of the Coupers' table-wares, teawares, and chamberwares were transfer-printed pearl-wares and whitewares (Table 3.24). Transfer-printed wares reached their height of popularity in the United States from 1790 to 1850. Although transfer-printing was first applied to creamware in the late eighteenth century, none of these rarer black on creamware examples were recovered from the plantation sites (Noël Hume 1973:240– 242; Table 3.24). By the 1790s the techniques of transfer-printing cobalt blue on pearlware had been perfected, and transfer-printing later appeared on the whitewares that were being produced from the 1820s on (Coysh 1970:7; Whiter 1970). (Transfer-printing required engraved copper plates coated with ink. Workers applied papers or bats of glue to the engraved plates and then transferred the inked designs to the earthenware biscuit. Central designs and the rim borders were usually applied separately. After washing off the pa-pers, the print was fixed by heating. Then glaze could be applied before the final firing in a glost oven [Coysh 1970; Whiter 1970]).

Transfer-printing generally appeared on earthenwares that were intended for daily use. With transfer-printing, even semiskilled workers could decorate enormous quantities of earthenware. And during the early 1800s, Great Britain captured the world market for lead-glazed, refined utilitarian earthenwares (Miller 1980:1–2). By the 1820s transfer-printing became the most common method of

decorating earthenwares, so over 50% of all the earthenwares produced from 1800 to 1825 in Great Britain were transfer-printed blue
on white. The United States was the principal foreign market for
transfer-printed earthenwares and by 1841 almost 40% of the yearly
British production was entering American ports (Godden 1963:11;
Noël Hume 1973:247).

Transfer-printed decorations were very sensitive to changing
fashion. During the first few decades of production, pseudo-Oriental
designs such as "Blue Willow" predominated, but from the 1820s to
the 1840s scenic designs proved most popular. One partial plate
from a "Park Scenery" set by G. Phillips pottery (1834–1848) was
recovered from the planter's icehouse fill (Figure 3.5). Scenic designs remained popular into the 1840s, when floral designs began to
supersede them (Godden 1963:113, 1971:88). From the 1790s to
the 1850s, the planter family acquired, used, and discarded dozens
of transfer-printed plates, platters, tureens, tea cups, saucers,
pitchers, basins, and chamberpots. Almost 80% of the ceramic
sherds recovered from the planter's kitchen refuse were transfer-
printed wares. In contrast, transfer-printed wares composed only
one-sixth of the overseers' ceramics and only one-fifth of the slaves'
ceramics (see Table 3.14).

Since transfer-printed wares were so sensitive to chronological
change, this may explain why the mean ceramic date of the planter's
ceramic assemblage—which was largely transfer-printed—more
closely approximated the median date of occupation of the planter's
sites than the mean ceramic dates from the slave and overseer sites.
The ceramics from the antebellum refuse Zones (II–IV) of the planter's refuse yielded a mean ceramic date of 1818.1 (Table 3.12).
From documents, we knew that the Coupers lived year-round at
Cannon's Point from 1796 to 1845, and that they occupied the plantation only during the summer months from 1845 to 1861 (Chapter
2). The median date of the Coupers' year-round occupation (1820)
was almost identical to the mean ceramic date (1818.1) of the antebellum refuse zones. At the planter's kitchen, there was a much
closer correspondence between the ceramics' date of manufacture
and their acquisition, use, and discard than at the slave and overseer sites where the mixed, outmoded ceramics yielded mean ceramic dates that were earlier than the probable spans of occupation
(see Chapters 3 and 4).

The banded, edge, hand-painted, and undecorated wares that
were so plentiful at the slave and overseer sites were comparatively
rare at the planter's kitchen. During the early 1800s banded, edge,

hand-painted, and undecorated wares all coexisted with transfer-printed wares. But by the 1820s transfer-printing became the most common method of decorating utilitarian earthenwares, even though "the technique had taken the best part of thirty years to win out" (Noël Hume 1973:247). During most of the antebellum period, the undecorated wares were usually the cheapest of the refined earthenwares; in turn, the edge and banded wares were somewhat more costly; the hand-painted wares were generally more expensive. than edge and banded wares; and finally, transfer-printed wares tended to be the most costly earthenwares, though their prices declined somewhat with mass production (Miller 1980:3–4). Thus, the differences in cost may explain the abundance of the cheaper undecorated, edge, banded, and hand-painted wares at the slave and overseer sites and the abundance of the more costly transfer-printed wares at the planter's site (Table 3.13), yet as suggested earlier, the explanation may be more complex than differences in cost. The various earthenwares of the antebellum period may have appealed to differing groups of ceramic consumers who had differing ceramic needs. At the slave and overseer sites, most of the ceramics were tablewares, and many of these tablewares were serving bowls. At the slave cabin, the banded, hand-painted, and undecorated serving bowls composed over 40% of the tableware items; at the overseer's house, banded, painted, and undecorated serving bowls were almost 25% of the tablewares; but, at the planter's kitchen, such banded, painted, and undecorated serving bowls composed less than 10% of the tablewares—instead, 70% of the planter's tablewares were transfer-printed plates, platters, soup plates, and tureens (Table 3.13).

These differences in ceramic forms may well reflect differences in food preparation and consumption practices in the slave, overseer, and planter households. Slaves and overseers often combined their foods in one-pot meals which they consumed from serving bowls; yet, the overseers' servants had the utensils to cook more foods separately and thus served more meals on transfer-printed, edge, and undecorated flatware. The planters' servants, however, cooked a wide variety of roasted meats, soups, vegetables, and breads in the kitchen hearth and served them on blue transfer-printed earthenware platters and tureens (Otto 1977:104).

In addition to their large, matched sets of transfer-printed tablewares, the Coupers had an impressive array of tea, dairy, storage, and chamberwares—pitchers, wash basins, and chamber pots for the dressing rooms and bedrooms of the mansion (Table 3.14, Figure 5.4). In fact, almost half of the planters' ceramics were used for purposes other than food consumption (Table 3.14). Numbers of salt-glazed and alkaline-glazed stoneware storage vessels once held preserved meats and vegetables.

PLANTER LUXURIES

The luxuries that the planters afforded themselves were luxuries in the truest sense of the meaning. The kitchen midden revealed dozens of fragments from liquor bottles, most of which once held wines. In addition to the light-green "champagne bottles," most of the olive-green cylindrical bottles were medium- to light-hued, the sorts of bottles that usually held wines (Tables 3.21, 3.22) (Noël Hume 1974:197–198). The written record attested to the variety of wines that John Couper stocked in his cellar (Figure 5.2) and chilled with ice from his icehouse (Figure 5.1). When Aaron Burr visited St. Simons Island, John Couper sent him an assortment of "French Wines, consisting of Claret, Sauterne, and Champagne, all excellent" (Van Doren 1929:174). John Couper's son James, however, never stocked Claret or other French still wines. The wines he served at dinner parties were always sherry, Madeira, and on special occasions, champagne (Wylly 1916:62). The Coupers also purchased "case" bottles of Holland gin and other "spirits" (Table 3.22) as well as demijohns of brandy which were used to make "Orange Cordial" (Couper 1839–1854:100; R. Couper n.d.b).

After their dinner parties, the Coupers offered cigars to their male guests (Wylly 1916:62). Clay pipe fragments rarely appeared in the planters' refuse (Table 3.20); it is known that elite whites preferred to smoke "Segars" rather than "Negro pipes." The best antebellum cigars were "Spanish" which were fashioned from Cuban leaves and packed in cedar boxes (Heiman 1962:87–88, 94).

Few planters could match the Coupers' elaborate dinner parties with their abundance of meats, wines, cordials, and "Segars" (Pease 1969:390–391). Even fewer could match James Hamilton Couper's collection of books, artworks, and memorabilia. Charles Lyell, the famous British geologist, described James's library: "On my return to Cannon's Point, I found in the well-stored library of Mr. Couper, Audubon's *Birds*, Michaud's *Forest Trees*, and other costly works on natural history; also Catherwood's *Antiquities of Central America*, folio edition" (Lyell 1849:Vol. 1, 342). James Couper's nephew, Charles Spalding Wylly, a frequent visitor to Cannon's Point, claimed the collection was worth $40,000, including a "very valuable portfolio of copies of Rafael's cartoons" and a "Virgil of extremely old date, which I in particular remember his telling me was the most valuable single volume on his shelves." In addition, the walls of the Couper library were adorned with engravings—copies of Lorraine, Rembrandt, and others (Lovell 1932:216; Wylly 1916:62–63). Finally, there were James Couper's collections of fossils, marine shells, minerals, and coins. The bulk of these collections, however, were lost during the Civil War, for a Union naval surgeon visiting the abandoned Couper mansion during the war noted that "large quantities of [fossil] bones and minerals are scattered around the floor" (Barnes and Barnes eds., 1963:57). Over a century later, archaeologists recovered several foreign mineral samples near the Couper mansion ruins, and three Roman coins were found in the planter's well (Fairbanks 1976:171).

The Yale-educated James Couper impressed guests with his erudition. He was a "host who never said a word that was not well-considered and prepared, whose hours for work, for exercise, for reading, for writing, were parcelled out in a systematic memoranda and whose store of information was immense." On the other hand, his father John was renowned for his personality—"his integrity, kindness, and genial humor." Their wives possessed both wit and beauty. In 1804 Aaron Burr described John's wife Rebecca as "still young, tall, comely, and well bred" (Burr in Jones 1957:89, 182). In 1849 Frederika Bremer referred to Caroline, James's wife, as the "youthful, pretty and happy mother" of eight intellectually precocious children (Wylly 1916:14, 57).

PLANTER CLOTHING

The Coupers, their wives, and their children dressed the part of elite hosts. From their Charleston factors, they purchased such ready-to-wear clothing as coats, pantaloons, shirts, vests, cravats, beaver hats, socks, boots, ladies' hose, lace boots, walking slips, kerchiefs, and shawls as well as yards of such fabrics as satinette, merino, and English prints. The clothing purchases also included packages of "Metal Buttons" and "Pantaloon Buttons" (Couper 1839–1854).

The planter's kitchen refuse yielded numbers of brass buttons that had once fastened coats, waistcoats, and vests. In addition, the planter's refuse contained numerous one-hole bone discs (Table 3.18) which may have fastened pantaloons, shirts, and undergarments. If covered with cloth, these bone discs may also have been used on gentlemen's coats and waistcoats (South 1974:190). Although one 14-mm brass button from the planter's kitchen refuse had an exact counterpart in the slave refuse, indicating the slaves used some of the planters' discarded dress garments, the planters' clothing and fasteners stood in stark contrast to those of the slaves. Most of the slaves' fasteners were four- and five-hole bone buttons and four-hole iron buttons (Table 3.18) which had once fastened work clothes that were hand-made from white Welsh plains and Osnaburgs (Chapter 3). In contrast, most of the planter family's fasteners were brass buttons and one-hole bone discs that had once secured ready-to-wear coats, vests, and undergarments.

TRAVEL AND HOSPITALITY

In addition to luxury garments, a final aspect of the planters' conspicuous consumption was travel. The Coupers regularly visited Savannah and Charleston for business and pleasure. One former Hopeton slave described James H. Couper's mode of travel: "In doze days deah wuz no way tuh git tuh Savannah cep by boat an wen Mr. Couper wannh go, he use a boat bout fifty foot long an bout six foot wide. He take six strong oahsmen and dey would make it in ten aw twelve hours" (Georgia Writers' Project 1972:173). As for traveling about St. Simons Island, the Coupers possessed horses and vehicles. The 1850 Cannon's Point inventory listed five "carriage [and] riding horses" and two "carriages and buggys" (Couper 1839–1854).

The Coupers' carriages, plantation boats, clothing, library, dinner parties, and their mansion itself established a pattern of conspicuous consumption that impressed dozens of foreign, northern, and local guests (Holmes 1976:137, 142) and contributed to Cannon's Point being known as one of the true "showplace" plantations of the Old South. As the renowned traveler Frederick Law Olmsted discovered in the tidewater region, owners of showplace plantations "had everything fixed up nice" and "kept a kind of open house and were always ready to receive company." At such a plantation, a visitor could spend a month or so and not spend a cent. Consequently, showplace plantations "always had a great many Northerners going to see them" (Olmsted 1861:Vol. 1, 230). On showplaces such as Cannon's Point, guests always saw the best side of plantation life—

charming hosts, lavish accommodations, banquets, and a retinue of "willing" house servants.

The Coupers' lavish hospitality could be maintained only through the efforts of their household slaves. On Cannon's Point in 1823, there were six full-time house servants as well as five skilled workers and 63 adult field slaves. The household slaves included the cook Sans Foix, his staff, and the maids; the skilled slaves may have included the planter's fisherman. Thus, at least one-tenth of John Couper's adult slave force spent their days caring for the Couper family and their many guests (see Hazzard 1825). Charles Lyell believed that the famed hospitality of tidewater planters was possible only because of the house slaves: "The sacrifices . . . made by the planter are comparatively small, since he has a well-trained establishment of servants, and his habitual style of living is so free and liberal, that the expense of a few additional inmates in the family is scarcely felt" (Lyell 1849:Vol. 1, 329).

One is tempted to blame John Couper's financial problems and eventual bankruptcy on his extravagant entertaining. His generous hospitality drained off profits that possibly should have been reinvested in more land, field slaves, and equipment. Since detailed account books are not available for the first five decades of the plantation's history, it is impossible to test this assumption. John Couper, however, recognized that his financial problems lay with the vulnerability of his cash crop—long-staple cotton. It was the loss of several valuable cotton crops in the 1800s and not extravagant living that reduced him to bankruptcy in 1828 (see Chapter 2).

Moreover, the Coupers' hospitality may be considered as a kind of business expense, showing foreign and northern visitors the better side of plantation slavery. Whether their guests defended or detracted slavery, all were impressed with the Coupers and their well-ordered plantation. Upon returning to Europe and the North, several of these guests penned highly favorable accounts of the Coupers' plantation regime at a time when plantation slavery was coming under increasingly vocal attack both abroad and at home (e.g., Bremer 1853; Hall 1829; Lyell 1849; Murray 1857).

CHAPTER 6

Cannon's Point Plantation and Status Patterning in the Archaeological Record

A plantation such as Cannon's Point could best be defined as an agricultural and social unit where there was a sharp separation between the owner, the supervisors, and the workers; where the aim was year-round commercial agriculture; where there was specialization in one or two cash crops; and where the owner was a businessman first and a farmer second. A plantation was also an instrument of force, creating and maintaining a hierarchy of planters, overseers, and slaves. This force was backed by the state slave codes, which allowed the planters to coerce slaves into producing a surplus of not only cash crops but also food crops, livestock, and labor (see Wolf 1959:136).

In turn, the planters, overseers, and slaves had differing access to the plantation surplus. Law and custom allowed the planter family to monopolize the surplus and use it as they saw fit. Some of the plantation surplus went to feeding the planter family and providing them with the goods and services they needed to live in a socially acceptable style. The Coupers had their pick of the plantation gardens, groves, and livestock herds; in addition, they selected about six slaves to work as house servants. Some of the surplus was sold to cover debts and to purchase luxuries, equipment, land, and slaves (Chapter 5), and finally, the Coupers directed some of the plantation surplus to cover the subsistence needs of their hired white overseers and the dozens of black slaves living on Cannon's Point (see Wolf 1959:137–138). In return for their services, the Cannon's Point overseers received the use of a house, probably the loan of a servant or two, and a yearly income ranging from $200 to $400. Using credit on their incomes, overseers had to purchase their food and clothing as well as luxuries (Chapter 4). In return for their work, the Cannon's Point slaves received the use of a cabin as well as foods, textiles, and occasional gifts (Chapter 3).

At Cannon's Point, the plantation surplus (cash crops, food crops, livestock, and labor) was inequitably distributed among the plantation inhabitants on the basis of racial, social, and economic status, creating marked differences in material living conditions, that is, the quality and quantity of housing, foods, and possessions. Most whites and blacks in the Old South, however, dwelt on farms and small plantations where the racial, social, and economic differences among the inhabitants were not always expressed in their material lives. A typical white farmer might own 200 acres of land, a few dozen livestock, and several black slaves; yet, both he and his slaves might work together in the fields, live in hewn-log cabins, eat corn bread and bacon, wear homespun garments, and devote their leisure hours to hunting and fishing (Craven 1930; Otto 1981b). On such small farms the surplus was more equitably distributed among free whites and black slaves, producing overall similarities in their material living conditions.

This perplexing situation in Old South society should stand as a reminder to archaeologists who are excavating habitation sites in complex societies and are faced with the difficult task of correlating the archaeological remains with the status of the former site inhabitants. As archaeologists excavate the tangible remains of material living conditions—the quality and quantity of housing, food remains, and artifacts—they must determine the former site inhabitants' access to material wealth and labor. Then, in turn, they must determine the racial, ethnic, and social status of former site inhabitants (see Chapter 1).

There are at least three approaches to the problem of status-related patterning in the archaeological record. The first, and traditional, approach has been to infer the status of the site inhabitants from the quality and quantity of the excavated remains. Many archaeologists have assumed that there is a perfect correlation between living conditions, access to material wealth, and status. But this is not always the case in complex societies (Laumann *et al*, 1970:63–65). Furthermore, this approach offers no controls or safeguards: Archaeologists have no means of checking the accuracy of their inferences about status patterning as long as they continue to excavate sites and analyze archaeological remains depending only on inference (Fontana 1968:180). Lewis Binford has long urged archaeologists to test the accuracy of their inferences and assumptions about the archaeological record by testing them against independent sets of data (Binford 1968:13, 1978:330–331).

Fortunately, historical archaeologists have access to such an independent set of data—historical documents—that offer a second approach to the problem of status patterning. Among the most useful historical documents are the probate inventories of households which executors of estates conducted on the death of estate holders; these inventories record the personal and chattel property of householders, especially their movable household artifacts (see Stone 1970a:73, 1977:53). By researching probate inventories, archaeologists can discover which types of artifacts and even which livestock (see Bowen 1975) were used by people of differing status.

This approach was pioneered by Garry Wheeler Stone in his analysis of the ceramics listed in Suffolk County, Massachusetts, probate inventories. Stone used the inventories to trace the introduction and diffusion of porcelains, stonewares, and refined earthenwares in eighteenth-century Boston. He found that porcelains, in particular, were sensitive indicators of status in Boston households. Porcelains were first acquired by Boston's merchant elite, quickly diffused to the lesser merchants and shop-keepers, but only slowly diffused among the craftsmen and other townspeople (Stone 1970a:73). Stone, however, also recognized the problems in using probate inventories: sketchy descriptions of artifacts; neglect of more common artifacts and undue concern with rare, expensive ones; and the neglect of slaves' and servants' possessions in county inventories (Carr 1977:64; Stone 1970a:73–74, 77, 1977:57). More importantly, probate inventories are not available for all areas and periods in the United States (Adams 1977:15).

Documents such as deeds, maps, census manuscripts, tax lists, travelogues, autobiographies, and even oral testimonies—sources more widely available than probate inventories—can provide archaeologists with a third approach to the problem of status patterning because these documents can be used as controls to identify the people who once lived at the archaeological sites. With the help of such documents, archaeologists can often identify the true status of site inhabitants—their race, ethnicity, occupation, affluence, or poverty. Then, by holding status as a known constant, archaeologists can demonstrate how known status differences and access to material wealth produce patterning in archaeological remains. And if archaeologists can compare sites, contexts, or artifactual assemblages that date to the same period in time, they can also hold time as a known constant. Thus, by using documentary and chronological controls, archaeologists can demonstrate how known status differences produce patterning in archaeological remains dating to the same period in time (see South [1972:100]; South [1977:231–232]; and for a discussion of pattern recognition at historic sites see South [1978]).

ARCHAEOLOGICAL REMAINS AS REFLECTIONS OF KNOWN STATUS DIFFERENCES

The Stone documents approach is the approach used at Cannon's Point Plantation. Documents attested to the presence of white planters, white overseers, and black slaves on the same plantation during the same period in time (Chapter 2). Then we identified the dwelling sites that they once occupied by using documents and by using controlled analogies with the settlement patterns of well-documented tidewater plantations (Otto 1975:passim). Using documents and artifacts to date ruins and refuse midden contexts, we compared house sites, food remains, and artifacts that dated to the antebellum period of occupation (see Chapters 3–5). By holding status and time as known constants, we hoped to demonstrate how known status differences and access to the plantation surplus were reflected in the archaeological remains of housing, foods, and possessions.

Documents also suggested that the archaeological record of material living conditions could have revealed several kinds of status patterning. If, for example, similarities appeared in the housing, foods, and artifacts at the white planter and overseer sites, this would have revealed "white dominance patterning," reflecting the higher racial and legal status of the free white planters and over-seers. And if differences appeared in the housing, foods, and ar-tifacts at the planter, overseer, and slave sites, this would have re-vealed a "hierarchical pattern," reflecting the known social or occupational divisions among the planter-managers, hired over-seers, and slave laborers. Lastly, if similarities appeared in the ar-chaeological remains at the overseer and slave sites, and if these remains were inferior to those of the planter's, this would reveal a "wealth-poverty pattern," reflecting the affluence of the planters and the relative poverty of overseers and slaves (Chapter 1).

Housing

To demonstrate status patterning in the housing of Cannon's Point inhabitants, we collected architectural, archaeological, and written evidence concerning construction materials, and tech-niques; expected durability; available living space; and the amenities available to occupants.

At both the planter and overseer sites, the materials used to construct the overseer's and planter's houses were homogeneous, and the workmanship was of professional quality. The overseer's frame house rested on brick pilasters fashioned from the same type of brick used to build the symmetrical chimney stacks. The planter's "new" frame dwelling, completed in 1804 (Chapter 5), rested on carefully poured tabby walls; in addition, one type of brick had been used to build the single massive chimney stack. In contrast, the frame slave cabin rested on low tabby and clay brickbat piers, and the dirt-floored hearth and low chimney had been built from clay and tabby bricks. Thus, the similarities in construction materials and techniques at the overseer's and planter's house sites suggested a white dominance patterning.

The poorer construction materials and workmanship devoted to the third slave cabin demonstrated its temporary nature. The frame structure was raised only slightly from the ground and was therefore more susceptible to decay and termites than frame dwellings that were raised several feet from the ground surface. The overseer's frame house rested on sturdy brick pilasters, whereas both the plan-ter's old and new frame houses rested on massive tabby basements. Moreover, the Coupers' dwellings survived the destructive hur-ricanes of 1804 and 1824. During the 1804 hurricane Aaron Burr watched as the gale destroyed several plantation outbuildings, one of the chimneys on the Couper house, and part of the verandah.

Burr did not report on the survival of the slave cabins, though he may have included these with destroyed outbuildings (Van Doren 1929:182). And in the aftermath of the 1824 hurricane, John Couper reported losing several outbuildings and 12 slave cabins. His old and new houses also sustained "considerable damage" (Ludlum 1963:116–117). Yet, Couper's mansion survived the storm while most of the plantation slave cabins were destroyed. In fact, the third slave cabin in the northern quarters, built during or after the 1820s, may have been a replacement for one of the destroyed cabins (Chapter 3).

In contrast to the slave cabins, the overseer's and planter's houses were built to last. The tabby walls of the planter's house and the brick pilasters of the overseer's house are still largely intact. Again, the similarities in the expected durability of the planter and overseer dwellings suggested white dominance patterning.

The available living space of the plantation dwellings, nevertheless, revealed hierarchical patterning, reflecting the social differences existing among the plantation inhabitants. The planter's house may have possessed as many as 16 rooms excluding stairways, halls, lofts, and storage areas; the overseer's home contained four rooms; and the slave cabin enclosed a single room. Therefore, the planter's dwelling had four times as many rooms as the overseers' home and 16 times as many rooms as the slave cabin. The rooms of the planter's house offered an estimated 2130 square feet of living space, excluding halls, stairways, and lofts; the overseer's four rooms may have provided 790 square feet of living space; and the slave cabin had perhaps 340 square feet of space (see Chapter 3–5). Thus, the planters mansion may have had 2.7 times as much living space as the overseers' home which in turn offered 2.3 times as much space as the slave cabin.

The amenities available to the occupants, however, revealed white dominance patterning: The planter's home complex possessed a spacious detached kitchen; the dwelling itself had three chimney stacks with multiple fireplaces; the specialized storage areas included a dairy room, a wine cellar, a butler's pantry, and an icehouse; and finally, there was a brick-lined ring well. The overseer's homestead possessed a similar array of amenities: a possible detached kitchen; the house itself had two chimney stacks with double fireplaces; the storage areas included chimney recesses as well as a provision house; and there was a wood-lined pit well. The slave cabin, of course, lacked the detached kitchens, multiple fireplaces, and specialized storage areas of the white dwellings. The slaves cooked their meals in the hearth, probably stored their foods on shelves, and they shared a shallow barrel-lined pit well with the occupants of three other cabins.

In summary, the evidence about the plantation inhabitants' housing revealed both white dominance and hierarchical patterning, reflecting the preeminence of free whites in the plantation hierarchy as well as the occupational differences among the plantation inhabitants.

Foods

In order to demonstrate status patterning in the food resources of the plantation inhabitants, we collected archaeological and written evidence concerning their food collecting equipment, wild foods which supplemented their diets, and domestic foods that composed the bulk of their diets.

The antebellum refuse middens at the plantation sites yielded small samples of fishing and hunting equipment. The slave, overseer, and planter refuse contained lead slip-sinker weights which were used for hook-and-line fishing (Table 3.5). Ammunition also appeared at all three sites. Even the slaves' antebellum refuse yielded lead shot, a percussion cap, and a dark-grey gunflint. The overseers' refuse produced a similar inventory—lead shot, a percussion cap, and a dark-grey gunflint (Table 3.5). Apparently the slaves and overseers used flintlocks as well as the percussion-lock firearms which began to replace flintlocks after the 1820s (Noël Hume 1969a:215; Witthoft 1966:33). The slaves and overseers, however, used the dark-grey English gunflints which are easily distinguished from the amber French gunflints (Table 3.5) which appeared in the planters' refuse (see Noël Hume 1969a:220). As John Witthoft has noted: "As late as 1840, French flint held sway over other kinds. It was preferred then, as it is today, because it is superior material" (Witthoft 1966:32). Since the planters' slave hunters used a type of gunflint that was qualitatively superior to the gunflints used by slaves and overseers, the small sample of gunflints from the plantation sites suggested possible wealth-poverty patterning.

Although they had access to firearms, the slaves and overseers may have lacked boats, and they had only limited leisure time for food collecting. As a result, they utilized the habitats on or near Cannon's Point—plantation forests, salt marshes, and tidal streams such as Jones Creek—collecting a similar range of common wild animals. The planter family, on the other hand, could appoint slave fishermen and hunters who had the time and transportation needed to visit the outlying habitats of the Altamaha estuary—barrier islands, deep sounds, landward marshes, and coastal freshwater streams—to collect a greater variety of the available fish, turtle, and mammal species. It is known that the Coupers assigned slaves for food collecting (Couper 1828), and it is known that the Coupers possessed plantation boats that could be used for traveling to outlying habitats. During the hurricane of September 1824 John Couper lost a four-oared canoe with a locker in the stern (Darien *Gazette*, 23 November 1824). With such a canoe, the planters' slave fishermen and hunters could have collected a greater variety of wild animals for the planter's table.

The planters' kitchen refuse yielded the bones of deer, alligators, marine turtles, mud and pond turtles, sharks, cownosed rays, jacks, bumpers, silver trout, weak fish, and spots—animals whose bones did not appear in the slave and overseer refuse (Tables 3.6, 4.2, 5.2). Significantly, these animals are found in the outlying habitats of the Altamaha estuary that the slaves and overseers apparently visited only rarely. At the slave and overseer sites, bones from the same 15 local species composed 63% and 68% of the identifiable wild animal taxa in the antebellum refuse. With the exception of the black and red drums, these wild animals were common denizens of the forests and marshes of St. Simons Island and the smaller tidal streams such as Jones Creek. Given the greater diversity of wild food animals at the planter's kitchen, and the similar range of locally found species at the slave and overseer sites, the wild food resources of the plantation inhabitants suggested wealth-poverty patterning.

In addition to collecting similar wild animals, the slaves and overseers consumed remarkably similar domestic foodstuffs. Slaves received rations of corn, rice, rice flour, molasses, and vegetables as well as some salt and fresh meat. Overseers, in turn, purchased corn, rice, rice flour, and molasses as well as barrels of salt meat. Both slaves and overseers found it necessary to supplement their meat supplies by fishing, hunting, and raising small stock such as chickens and hogs, and both slaves and overseers ate more pork and less beef than the planter family (Table 3.11) who monopolized the plantation herds. In addition to fresh beef and mutton from the Cannon's Point herds, the Coupers had access to an abundance of vegetables, fruits, and commercial foods. Given the superior food resources of the planter family and the strong similarities in the slave and overseer foodstuffs, the written and archaeological evidence of domestic foods also revealed wealth-poverty patterning.

In summary, the evidence about the plantation inhabitants' foods generally revealed a wealth-poverty patterning reflecting the lower economic status of slaves and overseers and their limited access to the plantation surpluses.

Possessions

To demonstrate status patterning in the household and personal possessions of the plantation inhabitants, we collected archaeological and written evidence about food-related artifacts such as ceramics (see Cloutier 1976), medicines, and possessions used in recreation and status consumption such as liquors, tobacco, and horse tack and vehicles.

Since the antebellum refuse contexts at the plantation sites yielded relatively large samples of ceramic sherds (>175) (Table 3.24), this presented an opportunity to test whether status patterning would appear in early nineteenth-century ceramic assemblages. Although many archaeologists have assumed that they could infer "the relative socioeconomic level of a population and define any major status differences which existed at a site by means of the distributional analysis of ceramics" (Miller and Stone 1970:100), this assumption has rarely been tested (Fontana 1968:180; South 1972:100). In his significant article on the mean ceramic date formula, Stanley South wrote that status differences may be more readily apparent in seventeenth-century ceramic assemblages rather than in eighteenth-century ceramics because during the eighteenth century, British ceramics, in particular, were mass produced and were rapidly distributed throughout the Western world, including north America. Consequently, archaeological investigations at a variety of eighteenth-century sites in America—all dating to the same period but occupied by people of differing status—reveal in each site a very similar distribution of ceramic types (see South 1972:100). South, however, did not consider nineteenth-century American sites, although the distribution of ceramic types at such sites might reveal status patterning.

By comparing the ceramics from known slave, overseer, and planter refuse middens that dated to the antebellum period (Chapters 3–5), we found significant differences in the distribution of nineteenth-century ceramics. At the slave and overseer sites, the banded, edge, and undecorated earthenwares composed about 70% of the total ceramic sherds in the antebellum refuse. In contrast, banded, edge, and undecorated sherds were rare in the planters' refuse, constituting only 12% of the total sherds; instead, almost 80% of the planters' ceramic sherds came from transfer-printed wares (Table 3.13). Since the chi-square statistic demonstrated that the differences in the ceramic type frequencies at the Cannon's Point sites were statistically significant (Appendix B, Test 1), the distribution of ceramic types clearly revealed wealth-poverty patterning, reflecting the known economic status differences existing among the Cannon's Point inhabitants. Apparently, the planter family purchased transfer-printed earthenwares for their own use, and provided their slaves and overseers with assemblages of banded, edge, and undecorated wares (see Otto in South 1977:93–99).

Recently, George Miller researched the wholesale price-fixing lists of the British Staffordshire potters (1770s–1850s) who dominated the American ceramics market. Miller found that Staffordshire potters classified their earthenwares in terms of their decorative techniques and ranked them accordingly by price. Miller discovered that the most expensive ceramics were the transfer-printed wares, followed in value by the hand-painted wares, the minimally decorated edge and banded wares, and lastly the undecorated or "common" earthenwares (Miller 1980:3–5). Yet, as Stanley South suggested in his article on the mean ceramic date formula, classification of ceramics by shape rather than type may be a "more sensitive indicator of *function* and possible socioeconomic level" (South 1972:99). To test this statement, we reclassified the Cannon's Point ceramics, deriving minimum numbers of ceramic vessels, partially reconstructing vessels, and identifying shapes and probable function by comparison with type examples in the University of Florida Archaeological Laboratory and with illustrations in Godden (1963, 1966), Whiter (1970), Coysh (1970, 1972), Webster (1971), and various site reports. Classification by shape revealed a higher percentage of storage vessels (jugs and jars) and a lower percentage of tableware (platters, plates, tureens, and bowls) at the planter's kitchen than at the overseer site or at the slave site (Table 3.16). Surprisingly, teawares and coffeewares appeared at all three sites (Table 3.14). At eighteenth-century military and domestic sites in North America, the appearance of teawares is often regarded as an indicator of higher status since only officers and the more affluent families acquired the utensils for the status-enhancing afternoon tea-drinking ritual (see Roth 1961:64, 66; South 1977:40–41, 230–231). But at Cannon's Point, an early nineteenth-century site, slaves and overseers as well as planters consumed luxury beverages such as tea and coffee, acquiring the necessary cups, saucers, pots, and other accoutrements. One possible significant difference was that the slave and overseer teawares and coffeewares represented mixed assemblages of transfer-printed and undecorated items of varying shapes and sizes. In contrast, planter teawares and coffeewares shared many of the same transfer-printed designs and shapes, indicating they had come from large, matched sets. Thus, the heterogeneity of the slave and overseer teawares and the homogeneity of the planter teawares hinted at wealth-poverty patterning.

More striking differences, however, appeared in the tableware collections from the plantation sites. At the planter's site, the vast majority of tableware items (over 80% of the total) were serving flat-ware vessels such as plates, platters, and soup plates. Bowl shapes were rather rare, composing only 8% of the tableware items. But at the overseer's site, sherds of bowl shapes—hemispherical shapes and "common" bowls with flaring, carinated sides (Godden 1966: 173; Van Rensselaer 1966:341)—composed almost one quarter of the tableware. At the slave site such bowl shapes constituted over 40% of the total tablewares (Table 3.16). Since the chi-square statistic showed that the differences in the tableware shape frequencies at the Cannon's Point sites were statistically significant (Test 2), the differences in bowl and flatware shapes at the plantation clearly revealed hierarchical patterning, reflecting the known social status differences among the Cannon's Point inhabitants.

In classifying the ceramic shapes, we noted that most of the planter serving flatware was transfer-printed, whereas most of the bowls at the overseer and slaves sites were banded or slip-decorated. We found that transfer-printed flatware composed over 60% of the planters' tableware forms, 28% of the overseers' tableware, and only 11% of the slaves' tableware. In contrast, banded-ware bowls composed 29% of the slaves' tableware forms, 17% of the overseers' tableware, and only 6% of the planters' serving vessels (Table 4.4). Again, the chi-square statistic demonstrated that the differences in the distribution of ceramic forms at the plantation sites were statically significant (Test 3): The distribution of ceramic forms clearly revealed hierarchical patterning.

The hierarchical patterning in the ceramic shapes and forms from the plantation sites may be explained in terms of differing functions of ceramic vessels in the foodways systems of planters, overseer, and slaves. At the planter's house meat and breads were served on transfer-printed platters accompanied by tureens of vegetables and soups: These foods were consumed from transfer-printed plates and soup plates (Chapter 5). At the overseer's site meats and breads were served on platters but were often accompanied by slow-simmer foods served in bowls (Chapter 4). And at the slave cabin foods were also served on flatware but bowls of stews, hominy, and pileau were daily fare (Chapter 3). Thus, the ceramics from the plantation sites appear to have reflected hierarchical differences in the preparation and consumption of foods in the planter, overseer, and slave households.

In addition to ceramic sherds, the antebellum refuse at the plantation sites contained relatively large samples of medicine bottle fragments (>58). Medicine bottle sherds composed 31% of the total glassware in the slave refuse, 43% of the total glass sherds in the overseer refuse, and only 17% of the total glass container sherds in the planter refuse (Table 3.21). The high percentages of medicine bottle fragments in the overseers' refuse corroborated the known distribution of medicines on antebellum plantations. Since overseers kept the medicines, one would expect higher frequencies of medicine bottles at overseer sites. Therefore, the distribution of medicine bottles on Cannon's Point suggested hierarchical patterning, reflecting the known occupations of the plantation inhabitants.

The liquor bottles from the plantation sites more clearly revealed status patterning. The antebellum refuse at the plantation sites yielded relatively large samples (>58) of liquor bottle fragments. Bottle sherds were identified by color, shape, and probable function (Table 3.22). Classifying the liquor bottle sherds from the plantation sites showed that olive-green bottle sherds were most common in the slave refuse, composing almost 85% of the total. Although the slaves in the third cabin obtained some wines and gins, they generally consumed the brewed beverages and ciders that filled the dark olive-green bottles (Chapter 3). In contrast, the planters' and overseers' refuse yielded more sherds of case bottles, which usually held gin and distilled spirits (Chapters 4–5). The chi-square statistic indicated that the frequencies of olive-green and case bottle sherds at the plantation sites were statistically significant (Test 4); as a result, the distribution of liquor bottles revealed white dominance patterning, reflecting the higher racial and legal status of plantation whites.

The distribution of clay tobacco pipes also suggested white dominance patterning. Clay pipe fragments were far more plentiful in the slave refuse midden than in the white planter and overseer refuse (Table 3.20). The written evidence from the tidewater area corroborated this distribution of pipes at Cannon's Point, for local newspaper advertisements invariably referred to clay pipes as "Negro pipes" (Chapter 3).

The small samples of glass beads at the plantation sites also hinted at white dominance patterning. The refuse at the white planter and overseer sites yielded only an occasional bead. The slave refuse, however, produced eight beads—all of which were cornerless, hexagonal types, and most of which were blue (Table 3.19).

Finally, the antebellum refuse contexts at the plantation sites contained small samples of horse tack and vehicles. Surprisingly, the slave refuse contained a single iron harness ring (Table 4.6) that could have come from a draft animal or a riding horse. Tidewater slaves rarely had access to riding animals, though some favored slaves on Thomas Spalding's Sapelo Island plantation were allowed to own horses (Wylly 1910:51). More horse tack appeared in the overseers' refuse as well as several vehicle rivets (Table 4.6, Figure 4.6). The planters' kitchen refuse yielded a harness buckle, and documents attested to the planter's ownership of carriages, buggys, and horses (Chapter 5). Thus, both archaeological and written evidence suggested white dominance patterning. The slaves may have had access to riding horses, but the plantation whites had carriages and buggys as well as horses.

In summary, the household and personal possessions of the plantation inhabitants revealed several kinds of status-related patterning. The distribution of ceramic types clearly revealed wealth-poverty patterning, but the frequencies of ceramic shapes and forms revealed hierarchical patterning. The distribution of medicine bottles at the plantation sites suggested hierarchical patterning, but the liquor bottles clearly revealed white dominance patterning. The distribution of clay tobacco pipes, glass beads, and horse tack and vehicles also suggested white dominance patterning.

Other data categories, nevertheless, revealed little status patterning since the evidence was inadequate for meaningful comparisons. Furniture is known to be a reliable indicator of status differences in contemporary households (see Lasswell 1965), but there was little archaeological and written evidence about the furniture of Cannon's Point slaves (Table 3.3). Material items once used in daily work were also poorly represented in the archaeological record (Table 3.5). And though numerous fragments of cooking utensils appeared in the slave and overseer refuse, there was little archaeological evidence of the planters' cooking equipment in the kitchen refuse (Table 3.5). Some glass tableware sherds were recovered from the slave and planter refuse, but only a tiny sample came from the overseers' refuse (Table 3.21). Cutlery was also poorly documented in the archaeological record (Table 4.5). Finally, relatively large samples of buttons and other fasteners were found in the slave and planter refuse which revealed interesting differences in the distribution of button types. In the slaves' refuse, four- and five-hole bone and iron buttons were relatively plentiful, whereas the planters' refuse contained more one-hole bone discs (Table 3.18). The overseers' refuse, however, contained only a tiny sample of clothing fasteners (Table 3.18), and there was no direct written evidence concerning the overseers' garments (Chapter 4).

The complexity of status-related patterning in the material possessions of the Cannon's Point inhabitants demonstrates the limitations of the traditional approach of inferring status from the quality and quantity of archaeological remains. At Cannon's Point certain kinds of artifacts revealed certain kinds of status patterning, and several kinds of artifacts revealed no evidence of status patterning. Rather than trying to infer the status of former site inhabitants from the quality and quantity of their artifactual remains, historical archaeologists may find it more profitable to analyze documents (such as probate inventories) to determine which artifacts were used in households whose inhabitants differed in known status; or, they can use documents as controls to identify the true status of the former inhabitants at archaeological sites. Then by comparing the archaeological remains from a series of well-documented sites with inhabitants of known status, archaeologists may ultimately derive patterns that will allow them to accurately predict status at other sites where the status of the inhabitants is undocumented. To date, historical archaeologists using this approach have convincingly demonstrated status patterning at archaeological habitation sites at St. Augustine, Florida—a Spanish colonial outpost during the sixteenth to the eighteenth centuries where the inhabitants are known to have differed in racial, ethnic, social, and economic status (see Cumbaa 1975a, 1976, n.d.; Deagan 1974, 1976, 1983; Fairbanks 1976).

Thus the findings from Cannon's Point Plantation may be presented in the form of a hypothesis for future testing at other Old South plantation sites. If corroborated and refined by excavations at other documented plantation sites, this pattern may one day be used to accurately predict the identity and status of site inhabitants at undocumented plantation sites.

Hypothesis: At Old South tidewater plantations known to have been occupied by white planters, white overseers, and black slaves, one may expect to find status-related patterning in the archaeological and written records of material living conditions—the quality and quantity of housing, foods, and possessions—because of differing access to the plantation surplus.

Subhypothesis: In terms of housing, such data categories as construction materials, expected durability, and amenities available to occupants should reveal patterning that reflects racial status differences; and the available living space of domestic structures should reveal patterning that reflects social status differences.

Subhypothesis: In terms of food resources, such data categories as the food collecting equipment, wild food supplements, and domestic foodstuffs should reveal patterning that reflects economic status differences.

Subhypothesis: In terms of household and personal possessions, such data categories as ceramic types should reveal patterning that reflects economic status differences; ceramic shapes and forms should reveal patterning that reflects social status differences; and liquor bottles, clay pipes, glass beads, and horse tack and vehicles should reveal patterning that reflects racial status differences.

ARCHAEOLOGICAL REMAINS AS INDEPENDENT EVIDENCE FOR INTERPRETING STATUS

At Cannon's Point Plantation a controlled comparison of known slave, overseer, and planter sites showed that housing reflected known racial and social status differences, while foods reflected known economic status differences, and household and personal possessions reflected known racial, social, and economic differences. Since plantation archaeology is still in its infancy, it remains to be seen whether future plantation excavations will corroborate or challenge the findings from Cannon's Point. Yet, preliminary evidence from several slave cabin sites and free black sites suggests that the findings from the Cannon's Point slave cabin are not unique but may be part of a wider pattern—a pattern of Afro-American archaeological visibility that may ultimately allow archaeologists to predict the presence of black Americans at sites where their presence may not be documented in the written record.

Housing

At Cannon's Point, Rayfield, and Kingsley plantations, the slave cabins were rather large rectangular or square units, measuring 17 by 20 feet; 18 by 18 feet; or as much as 19 by 25 feet. And at Andrew Jackson's Hermitage Plantation near Nashville, Tennessee, Sam Smith found comparable slave cabins with rectangular dimensions (Smith 1976:97). Yet, many, if not most, tidewater slave cabins were much smaller units often measuring only 12 by 12 feet (Rose 1964:121). Such smaller and more typical tidewater cabins closely resembled the basic West African building units of 10 × 10 feet (Vlach 1978:132–136). At two antebellum free black ruins in New England—the Black Lucy site, Andover, Massachusetts, and the Parting Ways site, Plymouth, Massachusetts—archaeological excavations revealed housing units of 12 by 12 feet that also recalled the West African norm (Baker in Schuyler 1980:35; Deetz 1977: 144–149).

Food Remains

At the Cannon's Point third slave cabin, most large mammal bones had been cleaved or broken open with axes or cleavers. No saw marks were apparent on the bones, indicating that the carcasses were not regularly divided into cuts and joints for roasting but were probably stewed in one-pot meals (Chapter 3). Examining the food bones from the Black Lucy site, V. G. Baker found that the vast majority of cattle, sheep, and hog bones had been chopped and cleaved open, "suggesting that stews, not roasts, are the main bill of fare" (Baker in Schuyler 1980:34). And at the Parting Ways site, virtually all of the food bones had been chopped open rather than sawed (Deetz 1977:152).

The food bones at archaeological sites may contain other indicators of Afro-American status. At Cannon's Point, for example, the relative importance of opossums and raccoons in the diets of the plantation inhabitants revealed hierarchical patterning. By translating the weights of opossum and raccoon bones into their equivalent edible meat weights, one finds that the Cannon's Point slaves ate more opossum than raccoon meat, the overseers ate about the same amount of opossum and raccoon meat, and the planter family ate far more raccoon than opossum meat (Table 3.8). At the Hermitage Plantation cabins, the food bones also suggested that black slaves ate more opossums than raccoons (Smith 1976:Table 23). It has long been known that slaves preferred tender opossums to tough, stringy raccoons, and this preference for opossums set blacks apart from southern whites (Glassie 1968:115). If this black preference for opossum meat is corroborated at other documented Old South sites, the frequencies of opossums and raccoons may prove one day to be reliable indicators of racial and social status at undocumented Old South sites.

Ceramics

The refuse midden at the Cannon's Point third slave cabin yielded numerous banded, edge, and undecorated wares. In fact, banded ware sherds alone accounted for 25% of the total ceramic sherds (Chapter 3). At Andrew Jackson's Hermitage Plantation and at the Castalian Spring farm-resort in middle Tennessee, Sam Smith also found higher percentages of banded-ware sherds at the slave cabins than at the sites occupied by higher status whites (Smith 1975:86, 1976:155). But whereas banded-ware sherds comprised 25% of the total sherds in the third slave cabin refuse, the middle Tennessee slave cabin sites yielded "at most about 7 or 8 percent" banded-ware sherds, so the pattern appeared "in an attenuated form" (Smith 1977:159). Smith, however, noted that the banded-ware sherds usually came from bowl forms, and when he added the hand-painted and other bowl sherds to the banded-ware totals, he found "a 34 percent frequency for this type of container" (Smith 1975:86).

The third slave cabin site, of course, yielded numerous sherds from banded, painted, and undecorated bowls. Such bowl shapes accounted for 44% of the total identifiable tableware items at the slave site, whereas serving flatware comprised 49% of the tablewares (Table 3.16). And when Baker classified the ceramic shapes from the Black Lucy site, he found that serving bowl shapes represented 41% of the total of 49 tableware items, whereas serving flatware composed 51% of the tablewares. Baker also classified the ceramics from the Parting Ways site. Again, he found the same pattern: Serving bowls accounted for 53% of the total of 81 tableware items, while serving flatware composed 46% of the tablewares (Baker in Schuyler 1980:34). Given these remarkable similarities in the frequencies of serving bowl shapes at the Cannon's Point slave cabin and the two free black sites, Baker hypothesized that "the presence of serving bowls exceeding 40 percent of all tableware, plus chopped faunal remains . . . appear distinctive of Afro-American sites, both slave and free" (Baker in Schuyler 1980:34).

The comparative evidence from the antebellum New England free black sites suggests that one-pot, slow-simmer meals were not confined to the black slaves of the Old South who lacked both cooking utensils and the time for food preparation. Several kinds of disparate foods could be combined in one kettle and left to simmer for hours while slave women engaged in other tasks. The indirect evidence of one-pot meals at the Black Lucy and Parting Ways sites, nevertheless, indicates that such meals may represent a continuity from the West African past. Among traditional West African peoples, it was common practice to stew grains, vegetables, and meats with pepper in ceramic vessels (see Chapter 3).

Medicine Bottles

The Cannon's Point and Kingsley slave cabins yielded fragments of small cylindrical glass vials that presumably once held medicines (Chapter 3). Sam Smith, however, was fortunate enough to find complete pharmaceutical vials in the floor areas of several Hermitage slave cabins. Noting the traces of mercury inside, Smith astutely concluded that the vials once held calomel or mercurous chloride—"a standard plantation treatment" for sick slaves (Smith 1977:156–157). The presence of such pharmaceutical vials may prove to be reliable status indicators at sites once occupied by slaves, especially if vials are found in conjunction with blue, cornerless, hexagonal glass beads.

Glass Beads

Glass beads appeared at the Cannon's Point, Rayfield, and Kingsley slave cabins: virtually all of them were blue, faceted beads (Chapter 3). Sam Smith found similar faceted beads at the Castalian Spring slave cabins as well as the First Hermitage area, which was used as a slave quarters after the 1820s (Smith 1975:88–89, 1976:244). Yet, when Smith excavated two Hermitage dwelling sites that were believed to be "brick Negro houses," the sites yielded none of the familiar blue, faceted beads. Possibly, the absence of such beads may be explained by the presence of only male slaves in these brick cabins (Smith 1977:159–161). If Smith's interpretation is corroborated by future slave cabin excavations, the blue, faceted beads may prove to be useful indicators of the presence of black slave women at Old South archaeological sites.

Afro-American Archaeological Visibility

Excavations at a number of slave and free black house sites have yielded a tentative pattern based on several architectural, faunal, and artifactual characteristics. If this pattern can be corroborated by excavations at other known Afro-American antebellum sites, it may ultimately be possible to accurately predict the presence of black Americans at undocumented sites. Yet, as V. G. Baker has pointed out, the archaeological remains from lower-class Afro-American sites should be compared with those from lower-class Euro-American sites to determine whether such characteristics as serving bowls, chopped food bones, and one-pot meals are the result of race or class. To date, however, only a handful of lower-status free white sites have been excavated and reported in the southern states (see Morse and Morse 1964; Otto and Gilbert 1984; Price and Price 1978; Smith 1980). Therefore, our tentative Afro-American archaeological pattern is offered as an hypothesis for future testing at both lower-status white and black sites.

Hypothesis The presence of Afro-Americans at antebellum archaeological sites may be predicted by the presence of building units such as 12 by 12 feet or by relatively high frequencies of chopped food bones, opossum remains, banded ware sherds, serving bowl shapes, calomel bottles, and faceted beads.

THE PROMISE OF PLANTATION ARCHAEOLOGY

Although the excavation of plantations and slaveholding farms will add to our historical knowledge of the living conditions of southern blacks and whites, the true promise of plantation archaeology may lie in the realm of behavioral archaeology (Otto 1982:442–444; see South 1979:223). Not only were plantations agricultural production units but they were also habitation sites where the occupational rankings among the inhabitants were often expressed in their material living conditions (Wolf 1959). In this respect, plantations resemble military sites where archaeologists have often found that differences in military rank were expressed in living conditions (see

South 1974:213, 1977:230–231). Plantations, however, offer additional advantages to archaeologists since plantation inhabitants included people who differed in sex, race, and wealth as well as occupational rank. Of all archaeological habitation sites, plantations may offer the most profitable situation for confronting that elusive but perennial archaeological problem: "How are status differences reflected in the archaeological record?"

In addition to the problem of status patterning in the archaeological record, plantation archaeology may aid anthropologists in their studies of African cultural survivals in the Americas. Anthropologists of Afro-America have long been concerned with the persistence of African cultures in the New World. Among Caribbean Afro-Americans, it is believed that the African cultural heritage is particularly strong. Surprising little, however, is known about the African slave antecedents of modern Caribbean cultures. Far more is known about the institutional aspects of slavery than about the slaves themselves. Since the vast majority of Caribbean slaves were nonliterate, it was invariably white observers—government officials, travelers, and planters—who left descriptions of slave life (see Handler 1971). Though relatively abundant, these white-authored sources have the same inherent limitation: They are ethnohistorical sources that record the observations of outsiders who were only partly aware of the reality of Caribbean slave life. Public officials and travelers were not only superficial observers, but preconceived biases colored their perceptions of slave life. Even plantation whites were not fully aware of the totality of black slave life (Chapter 1). For within the work and household contexts of plantation daily life, black slaves drew upon the African past and the American present to create a unique social and cultural world that is only partially documented in the written record (Mintz 1976:18, 43).

Recognizing the limitations in the written accounts of Caribbean slavery, anthropologist Jerome Handler and archaeologist Frederick Lange planned to excavate a plantation slave quarters on Barbados, the British West Indian sugar colony. Through archaeological excavations, they hoped to investigate "settlement patterns, house construction, size and spatial relationships, household furniture and utensils, and culinary practices" (Handler and Lange 1978:6). Such aspects of Barbadian slave household life were only sketchily documented in the written sources.

On Barbados, however, thin soils and deep-plowing had taken their toll of the plantation slave quarters. Handler and Lange failed to locate any slave habitation sites. But by relying on oral testimonies collected from the descendants of slaves, they located an undisturbed slave cemetery at Newton Plantation, perhaps the most fully documented plantation on the island. Excavating about one-sixth of the cemetery, they recovered over 90 burials, the largest number of New World slave interments ever found. The earlier burials, which generally antedated 1750, lacked coffins and were east-headed in orientation. In turn, later burials often had coffins and were west-headed. To interpret this change in slave mortuary practices, the investigators suggested that the east-headed burials may have been oriented toward Africa, where the slaves hoped their souls would return after death. Conversely, the west-headed burials may have reflected Christian influences, since Christian dead were often placed so they would rise facing toward the east on Judgement Day. Thus, in the Newton slave cemetery, the researchers may have found an archaeological microcosm of wider changes occurring in Barbadian slave culture as African-born traditional slave populations gave way to American-born, Christian slaves (Handler and Lange 1978).

Handler and Lange not only found tangible evidence of African cultural survivals, but they also found evidence of the process of African and European cultural interchange in the New World—a process of mutual learning, adaptation, and cultural change that began 500 years ago and continues to the present. Despite the persistence of some African cultural survivals in the Americas, the dominant theme in the evolution of Afro-American cultures has been the process of black-white cultural interchange or mutual acculturation. African slaves brought much of their culture with them in their minds, reproducing some of their speech and behavior in the New World. But for both African slaves and their European masters, the new American setting demanded that they "innovate, fabricate, synthesize and adapt" (Mintz 1970:6–7), learning from each other as well as from the Native American inhabitants. In order to fully understand this process it becomes necessary to study the free whites who once lived among the black slaves as well as the slave themselves.

Although Handler and Lange persuasively presented the ethnographic case for African cultural persistence in the Barbadian slave burials, they presented little information about the burial customs of contemporary white Christian Barbadians (Handler and Lange 1978:212). Such comparative data would have greatly strengthened their interpretation of changing slave burial practices. This neglect of white Barbadians is the only major flaw in an otherwise superb effort in Afro-American archaeology. For even on Barbados, where black slaves composed the vast majority of the inhabitants, blacks did not live in cultural isolation. There was always some social interaction and cultural interchange occurring between the black majority and the white Barbadian minority (see Watson 1975).

Archaeological evidence of this process of black-white cultural interchange should appear at plantation sites in the New World. Plantation inhabitants not only included dozens or even hundreds of black slaves but also handfuls of whites—overseers, clerks, craftsmen, and of course, planters. Despite class and ethnic barriers, some interaction always occurred among plantation whites and blacks (Mintz 1976:18–20). By excavating and comparing plantation sites once occupied by blacks and whites, we could delineate the differences as well as the similarities in their housing, foods, possessions, and mortuary customs. And by synthesizing the archaeological and written records, we can examine more fully the process of black-white cultural interchange as well as the survival of African cultural traits in slave households and social life.

At sixteenth-, seventeenth-, and eighteenth-century plantation sites, archaeologists may expect to find strong continuities from the African cultural past. But at many nineteenth-century plantation sites, archaeologists may be disappointed in their search for tangible evidence of African cultural survivals. At Cannon's Point, Rayfield, and Kingsley slave cabins, investigators found few Africanisms in the archaeological record of slave household life (Chapter 3). But at Cannon's Point, archaeological and historical investigations revealed many similarities in the foodways and household possessions of black slaves and white overseers (Chapters 3 and 4). And as archaeologist Robert Schuyler has pointed out, such similarities in the archaeological records of black and white households may be of greater significance than the persistence of African cultural traits. Cultures are adaptive systems that do not exist or survive in historical vacuums. Perhaps, the "primary contribution of Afro-American archaeology may not be evidence for perserverance but rather evidence of human ability to constantly alter or even totally invent new cultural patterns" (Schuyler 1980:1–2).

Statistical Tests

TEST 1: CERAMIC TYPE AND STATUS

Null hypothesis: The two classifications—status and ceramic types—are independent.

Alternative hypothesis: The two classifications are dependent.

Rejection region: Reject the null hypothesis if χ^2 exceeds the tabulated value of χ^2 for $a = 0.05$ and $df = (r - 1)(c - 1)$ or $df(4)(2) = 8$. The tabulated value of χ^2 is 15.5.

Ceramic type	Status			
	Slave	Overseer	Planter	Total
Banded	138 (56.7)	54 (18.7)	13 (129.6)	205
Blue-and-green edge	67 (28.2)	9 (9.3)	26 (64.5)	102
Transfer-printed	116 (302.5)	25 (99.7)	953 (691.8)	1094
Undecorated	157 (91.0)	64 (30.0)	108 (208.1)	329
Others	65 (65.0)	27 (21.3)	142 (148.0)	234
	543	179	1242	1964

$\chi^2 = 770$

Since 770 > 15.5, the null hypothesis is rejected and the two classifications (status and ceramic type) are assumed to be dependent.

The strength of this association can be tested with the contingency coefficient:

$$C = \sqrt{\frac{\chi^2}{n + \chi^2}} = \sqrt{\frac{770}{1964 + 770}} = \sqrt{0.2816} = 0.5307;$$

$$C_{max} = \sqrt{\frac{r - 1}{r}} = \sqrt{\frac{4}{5}} \qquad = \qquad 0.8944;$$

$$C_{adj} = \frac{C}{C_{max}} = \frac{0.5307}{0.8944} \qquad = \qquad -0.5934.$$

The value for C_{adj} suggests a strong association.

TEST 2: CERAMIC SHAPE AND STATUS

Null hypothesis: The two classifications—status and ceramic shape—are independent.

Alternative hypothesis: The two classifications are dependent.

Rejection region: Reject the null hypothesis if χ^2 exceeds the tabulated value of χ^2 for $a = 0.05$ and $df = (r - 1)(c - 1) = (2)(2) = 4$. The tabulated value of χ^2 is 9.49.

	Status			
Ceramic shape	Slave	Overseer	Planter	Total
Serving bowls	35 (16.6)	19 (16.1)	12 (33.3)	66
Serving flatware	39 (57.7)	56 (56.2)	135 (116.1)	230
Other tableware shapes	6 (5.8)	3 (5.6)	14 (11.6)	23
	80	78	161	319

$\chi^2 = 45.4$

Since 45.4 > 9.49, the null hypothesis is rejected and the two classifications (status and ceramic shape) are assumed to be dependent.

The strength of this association can be tested with the contingency coefficient:

$$C = \sqrt{\frac{\chi^2}{n + \chi^2}} = \sqrt{\frac{45.4}{319 + 45.4}} = \sqrt{0.1246} = 0.3530;$$

$$C_{max} = \sqrt{\frac{r - 1}{r}} = \sqrt{\frac{2}{3}} = 0.8165;$$

$$C_{adj} = \frac{C}{C_{max}} = \frac{0.3530}{0.8165} = 0.4323.$$

The value for C_{adj} suggests a rather strong association.

TEST 3: CERAMIC FORM AND STATUS

Null hypothesis: The two classifications—status and ceramic forms—are independent.

Alternative hypothesis: The two classifications are dependent.

Rejection region: Reject the null hypothesis if χ^2 exceeds the tabulated value of χ^2 for $a = 0.05$ and $df = (r - 1)(c - 1) = (2)(2) = 4$. The tabulated value of $\chi^2 = 9.49$.

	Status			
Ceramic form	Slave	Overseer	Planter	Total
Banded-ware bowls	23 (11.3)	13 (11.0)	9 (22.7)	45
Transfer-printed serving flat-ware	15 (34.4)	22 (33.5)	100 (69.1)	137
Other tableware forms	42 (34.4)	43 (33.5)	52 (69.1)	137
	80	78	161	319

$\chi^2 = 58.1$

Since $58.1 > 9.49$, the null hypothesis is rejected and the two classifications are assumed to be dependent.

The strength of this association can be tested with the contingency coefficient:

$$C = \sqrt{\frac{\chi^2}{n + \chi^2}} = \sqrt{\frac{58.1}{319 + 58.1}} = \sqrt{0.1541} = 0.3926;$$

$$C_{max} = \sqrt{\frac{r - 1}{r}} = \sqrt{\frac{2}{3}} = 0.8165;$$

$$C_{adj} = \frac{C}{C_{max}} = \frac{0.3926}{0.8165} = 0.4809.$$

The value for C_{adj} suggests a rather strong association.

TEST 4: LIQUOR-BOTTLE TYPES AND STATUS

Null hypothesis: The two classifications—status and liquor bottle types—are independent.

Alternative hypothesis: The two classifications are dependent.

Rejection region: Reject the null hypothesis if χ^2 exceeds the tabulated value of χ^2 for $a = 0.05$ and $df = (r - 1)(c - 1)$ or $df = (2)(2) = 4$. The tabulated value of χ^2 is 9.5.

Liquor bottle type	Slave	Overseer	Planter	Total
		Status		
Olive-green	313 (290.4)	43 (45.9)	247 (266.7)	603
"Champagne"	41 (39.5)	9 (6.2)	32 (36.3)	82
Case	13 (37.1)	6 (5.9)	58 (34.1)	77
	367	58	337	762

$\chi^2 = 37.8$

Since $37.8 > 9.5$, the null hypothesis is rejected, and the two classifications (status and liquor bottle types) are assumed to be dependent.

The strength of the association can be tested with the contingency coefficient:

$$C = \sqrt{\frac{\chi^2}{n + \chi^2}} = \sqrt{\frac{37.8}{762 + 37.8}} = \sqrt{0.0473} = 0.2175;$$

$$C_{max} = \sqrt{\frac{r - 1}{r}} = \sqrt{\frac{2}{3}} \qquad = 0.8165;$$

$$C_{adj} = \frac{C}{C_{max}} = \frac{0.2175}{0.8165} \qquad = 0.2664.$$

The value of C_{adj} suggests a rather strong association.

Bibliography

Adams, William H.
1977   Silcott, Washington: Ethnoarchaeology of a rural American community. *Laboratory of Anthropology, Reports of Investigations, No. 54.* Pullman: Washington State University.

Agricola
1845   Overseers. *Southern Agriculturist (NS) 6:428–430.*

Ames, Mary
1969   *From a New England woman's diary in Dixie in 1865.* New
[1906] York: Negro Universities Press.

Anderson, Jay A.
1971   *"A solid sufficiency": An ethnography of yeoman foodways in Stuart England.* Ph.D. dissertation, Department of Folklore, University of Pennsylvania.

Anderson, James
1976   Aunt Jemima in dialectics: Genovese on slave culture. *Journal of Negro History* 61:90–157.

Anonymous
1833   On the management of slaves. *Southern Agriculturist* 6:284.

Anonymous
    1836   The education and treatment of overseers, drivers, and slaves.
             The Southern Agriculturist 9:189–191.
Anonymous
    n.d.a   Couper, James H. Name card files, Georgia State Archives,
             Atlanta.
    n.d.b   Couper, John. Name card files, Georgia State Archives,
             Atlanta.
    n.d.c   Grant, Hugh F. Name card files, Georgia State Archives,
             Atlanta.
Anthony, Ronald W.
    1979   Descriptive analysis and replication of historic earthenware:
             Colono wares from the Spiers Landing Site Berkeley County,
             South Carolina. *The Conference on Historic Site Archaeology
             Papers 1978* 13:253–268.
Ascher, Robert, and Charles H. Fairbanks
    1971   Excavation of a slave cabin, Georgia, USA. *Historical Archae-
             ology* 5:3–17.
A.S.D.
    1838   On raising negroes. *Southern Agriculturist* 11:77–80.
Baker, H. G.
    1962   Comments on the thesis that there was a major centre of plant
             domestication near the headwaters of the River Niger. *Journal
             of African History* 3:229–233.
Baker, V. G.
    1980   Archaeological visibility of Afro-American culture: An example
             from Black Lucy's garden, Andover, Massachusetts. In
             Archaeological perspectives on ethnicity in America, edited
             by Robert L. Schuyler. New York: Baywood.
Ball, Charles
    1859   Fifty years in chains; or the life of an American slave. New
             York: Dayton.
Barnes, Elinor, and James A. Barnes (eds.)
    1963   *Naval surgeon-blockading the South (1862–1866): The di-
             ary of Dr. Samuel Pellman Boyer.* Bloomington: Indiana Uni-
             versity Press.
Baron, Stanley
    1962   *Brewed in America: A history of beer and ale in the United
             States.* Boston: Little, Brown.
Bascom, William
    1941   Acculturation among the Gullah negroes. *American An-
             thropologist* 43: 43–50.
Basden, G. T.
    1966   *Among the Ibos of Nigeria.* London: Cass.
    [1921]

Berge, Dale T.
  1968   The Gila Bend stage station. *The Kiva* 33:169–243.
Binford, Lewis R.
  1968   Archaeological perspectives. In *New perspectives in archae-
            ology,* edited by S. R. and L. R. Binford. Chicago: Aldine.
  1978   Dimensional analysis of behavior and site structure: Learning
            from an Eskimo hunting stand. *American Antiquity* 43:330–
            361.
Blassingame, John W.
  1972   *The slave community: Plantation life in the antebellum
            South.* New York: Oxford University Press.
  1975   Using the testimony of ex-slaves: Approaches and problems.
            Journal of Southern History 41:473–492.
  1976   Status and social structure in the slave community. In
            Perspectives and irony in American slavery, edited by Harry
            Owens. Jackson: University Press of Mississippi.
Blassingame, John W. (ed.)
  1977   *Slave testimony.* Baton Rouge: Louisiana State University
            Press.
Bonner, James C.
  1944   Profile of a late ante-bellum community. *American Historical
            Review* 49:663–680.
  1964   *A history of Georgia agriculture 1732–1860.* Athens: Univer-
            sity of Georgia Press.
  1965   Plantation and farm: The agricultural South. In *Writing
            southern history-essays in honor of Fletcher M. Green,* edited
            by Arthur S. Link and Rembert W. Patrick. Baton Rouge: Loui-
            siana State University.
Booth, Sally S.
  1971   *Hung, strung, and potted: A history of eating in Colonial
            America.* New York: Potter.
Botume, Elizabeth
  1968   *First day amongst the contrabands.* New York: Arno Press.
  [1893]
Bowen, Joanne
  1975   Probate inventories: An evaluation from the perspective of zoo-
            archaeology and agricultural history at the Mott Farm.
            Historical Archaeology 9:11–25.
Bremer, Frederika
  1853   *The homes of the New World: Impressions of America* (2 vols.,
            translated by Mary Howitt). New York: Harper.
Brown, John
  1972   *Slave life in Georgia: A narrative of the life, sufferings, and*

escape of John Brown, a fugitive slave, edited by F. N. Boney. Savannah: Beehive Press.

Brunswick *Advocate*

1837– Newspapers on microfilm at the University of Georgia Library
1839   at Athens.

Burr, Aaron

1957   A refugee on a Georgian plantation. In *The plantation South,* edited by Katharine Jones. Indianapolis: Bobbs-Merrill.

Cahalane, Victor H.

1947   *Mammals of North America.* New York: MacMillan.

Campbell, Robert S., and Wesley Keller

1973   Range resources of the Southeastern United States. *American Society of Agronomy, Special Publication* 21.

Carawan, Guy, Candie Carawan, and Robert Yellin

1967   *Ain't you got a right to the tree of life.* New York: Simon and Schuster.

Carr, Lois Green

1977   The uses of inventories: A warning. *The conference on historic site archaeology papers 1976,* (Vol. 11), pp. 64–68.

Cate, Margaret Davis

1930   *Our todays and yesterdays.* Brunswick, Georgia: Glover.

n.d.a   "Cannon, Daniel." Folder on file at the Margaret Davis Cate Collection, Brunswick Junior College Library, Brunswick, Georgia.

n.d.b   "Cannon's point-plans for house: Couper-Fraser material." Folder on file at the Margaret Davis Cate Collection.

n.d.c   "[Couper] Genealogy." Folder on file at the Margaret Davis Cate Collection.

Chaplin, Raymond E.

1971   *The study of animal bones from archaeological sites.* New York: Seminar Press.

Cloutier, Jean-Pierre

1976   *Fort William: Food-related artifacts.* Toronto: Ontario Government Bookstore.

Coleman, Kenneth

1958   *The American Revolution in Georgia, 1763–1789.* Athens: University of Georgia Press.

Collins, Donald R.

1966   How bullets were made. *Civil War Times Illustrated* 4:22–25.

Cooney, Lorraine M. (comp.)

1933   *Garden history of Georgia,* edited by Hattie C. Rainwater. Atlanta: Peachtree Garden Club.

Coulter, E. Merton

1940   *Thomas Spalding of Sapelo.* Baton Rouge: Louisiana State University Press.

Couper, Alex W.
   1861   Letter to J. M. Couper, 12 August. On microfilm, John Couper
            Collection (1775–1963), University of Georgia Library at
            Athens.
Couper, James H.
   1826–   Hopeton Plantation Account Book, No. 185, James Hamilton
   1852   Couper Plantation Records (1826–1854), Southern Historical
            Collection, University of North Carolina Library at Chapel Hill.
   1839–   *Hopeton Plantation Journal*, 185. James Hamilton Couper
   1854   Plantation Records.
   1851   Letter to James Couper, 5 May. On microfilm, John Couper
            Collection (1775–1963), University of Georgia Library at
            Athens.
   1855   Valuable Sea Island Plantation and Gang of 126 Negroes for
            Sale. Advertisement in November 1, Albany *Patriot*.
            Newspaper on file at Albany Public Library, Albany, Georgia.
   1860   Letter to James Couper, 31 October. On microfilm, John Cou-
            per Collection (1775–1963), University of Georgia Library at
            Athens.
   1864   Tax Returns-Confederate States. On microfilm, Couper Fami-
            ly Papers (1775–1960), Georgia State Archives, Atlanta.
Couper, John
   1828   Letter to James Couper, 24 May; M-186. On file at the South-
            ern Historical Collection, University of North Carolina Library
            at Chapel Hill.
   1831   On the origin of Sea-Island Cotton. *Southern Agriculturist*
            4:243–244.
   1832   On the employment of oxen as substitutes for horses in agri-
            cultural operations. *Southern Agriculturist* 5:286–290.
   1835   General observations on the Olive, Orange, and Date Trees
            growing in Georgia; and the method of cultivating the Ruta
            Baga Turnip as a second crop after Corn. *Southern Agri-
            culturist* 8:350–352.
   1839   Letter to Hamilton Couper, [?] March. On microfilm, John
            Couper Collection (1775–1963), University of Georgia Library
            at Athens.
   1842   Letter to James H. Couper, 24 June. Typescript on file at the
            Margaret Davis Cate Collection, Brunswick Junior College Li-
            brary, Brunswick, Georgia.
   n.d.a   Letter to member of the King family, undated, Folder 138,
            Thomas Butler King Papers (1763–1925), Southern Historical
            Collection, University of North Carolina Library at Chapel Hill.
   n.d.b   "Cheese", Manuscript in Folder 60-Recipes, Cures, and Farm-
            ing Directions, William Audley Couper Papers (1795–1930).

Southern Historical Collection, University of North Carolina Library at Chapel Hill.

n.d.c   "To Salt Meat in Hot Weather," Manuscript in Folder 60, William Audley Couper Papers (1795–1930), Southern Historical Collection, University of North Carolina Library at Chapel Hill.

Couper, John, Jr.

1810a   Letter to Ann Couper, 21 June. On file, Fraser-Couper Family Papers (1810–1817), Georgia Historical Society Library, Savannah.

1810b   Letter to Ann Couper, 31 August. On file, Fraser-Couper Family Papers (1810–1817), Georgia Historical Society Library, Savannah.

Couper, Rebecca

n.d.a   Orange Cordial. On file, Fraser-Couper Family Papers (1850–1884), Georgia Historical Society Library, Savannah.

n.d.b   Catfish Soup. On file, Fraser-Couper Family Papers (1850–1884), Georgia Historical Society Library, Savannah.

Coysh, A. W.

1970   *Blue and white transfer ware 1780–1840.* David and Charles, Newton Abbot, U.K.

1972   *Blue-Printed Earthenware 1800–1850.* Rutland, Vermont: Tuttle.

Craven, Avery O.

1930   Poor Whites and Negroes in the Antebellum South. *Journal of Negro History* 15:14–25.

Crosby, Alfred W.

1972   *The Columbian exchange: Biological and cultural consequences of 1492.* Westport, Connecticut: Greenwood Press.

Crum, Mason

1940   *Gullah: Negro life in the Carolina Sea Islands.* Durham: Duke University Press.

Cumbaa, Stephen L.

1975a   Patterns of resource use and cross-cultural dietary change in the Spanish Colonial Period. Ph.D. dissertation, Department of Anthropology, University of Florida.

1975b   A reconsideration of Freshwater Shellfish exploitation in the Florida Archaic. *The Florida Anthropologist* 29:49–59.

1976   *The Historic (Re)Past: 18th Century Dietary Reconstruction.* Paper presented at the Annual Meeting of the Society for American Archaeology, St. Louis Missouri.

n.d.   A contribution to usable weight calculations in Paleonutritional Studies. Paper on file at the Zooarchaeological Laboratory, Florida State Museum, Gainesville.

Curtin, Phillip
1969   *The Atlantic Slave Trade-A Census.* Madison: University of
        Wisconsin Press.
Curtin, Phillip (ed.)
1967   *Africa remembered: Narratives by West Africans from the Era
        of Slave Trade.* Madison: University of Wisconsin Press.
Dahlberg, Michael D.
1972   An ecological study of Georgia Coastal Fishes. *Fishery Bul-
        letin, U.S. Fish and Wildlife Service* 70:323–353.
1975   *Guide to coastal fishes of Georgia and nearby states.* Athens:
        University of Georgia Press.
Dahlberg, Michael D., and Richard W. Heard III
1969   Observations on Elasmobranchs from Georgia. *Quarterly
        Journal of the Florida Academy of Sciences* 32:21–25.
Dahlberg, Michael D., and Eugene Odum
1970   Annual cycles of species occurrence, abundance, and diversity
        in Georgia Estuarine Fish populations. *The American Mid-
        land Naturalist* 83:382–392.
Daly, Patricia
1969   Approaches to Faunal analysis in archaeology. *American An-
        tiquity* 34:146–153.
Darien *Gazette*
1812–   Newspapers on microfilm at the University of Georgia Library
1828   at Athens.
David, Paul A. *et al.*
1976   *Reckoning with slavery: A critical study in the quantitative
        history of American Negro slavery.* New York: Oxford Univer-
        sity Press.
Davidson, Basil
1968   *Africa in history: Themes and outlines.* New York: Macmillan.
Davis, David Brian
1974   Slavery and the Post-World War II historians. *Daedalus*
        103:1–16.
Deagan, Kathleen A.
1974   Sex, status, and role in the Mestizaje of Spanish Colonial Flor-
        ida. Ph.D. dissertation, Department of Anthropology. Univer-
        sity of Florida.
1976   *Archaeology at the Greek Orthodox Shrine.* Gainesville: Uni-
        versity Presses of Florida.
1983   *Historical archaeology in St. Augustine.* New York: Academic
        Press.
Deetz, James
1973   Ceramics from Plymouth 1635–1835: The archaeological evi-

dence. In *Ceramics in America* edited by Ian M. G. Quimby. Charlottesville: University Press of Virginia.

1977   *In small things forgotten, the archaeology of early American life.* New York: Anchor Press.

Duffy, John
1959   Medical practice in the Ante-Bellum South. *Journal of Southern History* 25:53–72.

Duncan, John
1967   *Travels in Western Africa in 1845 and 1846.* London: John-
[1847]   son Reprint.

Dunton, John
1972   Building hardware excavated at the fortress of Louisbourg, Manuscript Report 97. Ottawa: National and Historic Parks Branch, Department of Indian Affairs and Northern Development.

Durrenberger, E. Paul
1965   Anderson's Mill (41 TV 130). *Bulletin of the Texas Archaeological Society* 36:1–70.

Editor
1804   Extract of a letter from John Couper. Article in May, Savannah *Columbian Museum and Savannah Advertiser* (1796–1821). Newspaper on microfilm, University of Georgia Library at Athens.

Editor
1833   Account of an Agricultural Excursion Made into the South of Georgia in the Winter of 1832. *Southern Agriculturist* 6:157–169, 243–252.

Elkins, Stanley
1959   *Slavery: A problem in American institutional and intellectual life.* Chicago: University of Chicago Press.

Elliot, William
1828   On the cultivation and high prices of Sea-Island Cotton. *Southern Agriculturist* 1:151–163.

Engel, Beth, and Geneva Stebbins
1974   *Pages from the Past-St. Simons Island 1880–1886.* Jessup, Georgia: Sentinel Press.

Fagan, Brian
1965   *Southern Africa during the Iron Age.* New York: Praeger.

Fairbanks, Charles H.
1972   *The strategy of digging in St. Augustine.* Paper presented at the Annual Meeting of the Society for Historical Archaeology, Tallahassee, Florida.

1974   The Kingsley Slave Cabins in Duval County, Florida, 1968. *The Conference on Historic Site Archaeology Papers 1972* 7:62–93.

1976   Spaniards, planters, ships, and slaves: Historical archaeology
         in Florida and Georgia. *Archaeology* 29:165–172.
1977   Backyard archaeology as a research strategy. *The Conference
         on Historic Site Archaeology Papers 1976* 11:133–139.

Ferguson, Leland B.
1975   Analysis of ceramic materials from Fort Watson: December
         1780–April 1781. *The Conference on Historic Site Archae-
         ology Papers 1973* 8:2–28.
1979   Review of Handler and Lange: Plantation slavery in Barbados.
         American Antiquity 44:384.
1980   Looking for the "Afro" in Colono-Indian Pottery. In
         Archaeological perspectives on ethnicity in America, edited
         by Robert L. Schuyler. New York: Baywood.

Flanders, Ralph B.
1933   *Plantation slavery in Georgia.* University of North Carolina
         Press.

Fleming, J. Arnold
1923   *Scottish pottery.* Glasgow: Maclehouse, Jackson.

Fogel, Robert, and Stanley L. Engerman
1974a   *Time on the cross: The economics of American Negro Slavery.*
         Boston: Little, Brown.
1974b   *Time on the cross: Evidence and Methods-A Supplement.*
         Boston: Little, Brown.

Fontana, Bernard L.
1965   The Tale of a nail: On the ethnological interpretation of histor-
         ic artifacts. *The Florida Anthropologist* 8:85–96.
1968   Bottles, buckets, and horseshoes: The unrespectable in Amer-
         ican archaeology. *Keystone Folklore Quarterly* 13:171–184.

Fontana, Bernard L., and J. C. Greenleaf
1962   Johnny Ward's ranch: A study in historic archaeology. *The
         Kiva* 28:1–115.

Forten, Charlotte
1864   Life on the Sea Islands. *Atlantic Monthly* 13:587–596,
         666–676.

Foster, George M.
1953   What is folk culture? *American Anthropologist* 55:159–173.
1960   Culture and Conquest: America's Spanish Heritage. *Viking
         Fund Publications in Anthropology* 27.

Fredrickson, George
1975   Review of Roll, Jordan, Roll by Eugene Genovese. *Journal of
         American History* 62:131.

French, Austa Malinda
1862   *Slavery in South Carolina and the ex-slaves.* New York:
         French.

Genovese, Eugene D.
  1969   The treatment of slaves in different countries: Problems in the
          applications of the comparative method. In *Slavery in the
          New World* edited by Laura Foner and Eugene D. Genovese.
          Englewood Cliffs, New Jersey: Prentice-Hall.
  1970   Commentary: An historian's view. *Agricultural History*
          44:143–148.
  1974   *Roll, Jordan, Roll: The world the slaves made.* New York:
          Pantheon Books.
Georgia Writers' Project
  1940   *Drums and shadows: Survival studies among the Georgia
          Coastal Negroes.* Athens: University of Georgia Press.
  1972   *Drums and shadows.* New York: Anchor Books.
Glassie, Henry
  1968   *Pattern in the material folk culture of the Eastern United
          States.* Philadelphia: University of Pennsylvania Press.
Glynn County Courthouse
  n.d.   Deed Books ABEF, CD, G, G, N, and BB; Wills and Appraise-
          ments D-G; and Marriage Records A. Ms. on file at Glynn
          County Courthouse, Brunswick, Georgia.
Godden, Geoffrey A.
  1963   *British pottery and porcelains 1780–1850.* New York: Barnes.
  1966   *An illustrated encyclopedia of British pottery and porcelain.*
          New York: Crown.
  1971   *The illustrated guide to Mason's Patent ironstone china.* New
          York: Praeger.
Goldman, Edward A.
  1910   Revision of the Wood Rats of the Genus *Neotoma. North Amer-
          ican Fauna* 31.
  1918   The Rice Rats of North America. *North American Fauna* 43.
Goodenough, Ward H.
  1963   *Cooperation in change.* New York: Sage.
Gray, Lewis C.
  1941   *History of agriculture in the Southern United States to 1860*
          (2 vols). (Washington, D.C.: Carnegie Institution).
Gutman, Herbert G.
  1975a   *Slavery and the numbers game: A critique of time on the
          cross.* Urbana: University of Illinois Press.
  1975b   *Time on the cross: The economics of American Negro slavery:
          The world two cliometricians made. Journal of Negro History*
          60:53–227.
  1976   *The Black family in slavery and freedom, 1750–1925.* New
          York: Pantheon Books.
Hall, Basil
  1829   *Travels in North America in the Years 1827 and 1828* (3 vols).
          Edingurgh: Cadell. [Margaret Davis Cate, noted tidewater his-

torian, identified the St. Simons Island plantation that Hall
visited as Cannon's Point. See copy of Hall (1829) on file at the
Margaret Davis Cate Collection].

Hall, Edward T.
1977   *Beyond culture*. New York: Anchor Press.

Hall, Margaret
1931   *The aristocratic journey*, edited by Una Pope-Hennessy. London: Putnam's.

Handler, Jerome
1971   *A guide to source materials for the study of Barbados history
1627–1834*, Carbondale, Illinois: Southern Illinois University
Press.

Handler, Jerome, and Frederick Lange
1978   *Plantation slavery in Barbados: An archaeological and historical investigation*. Cambridge, Massachusetts: Harvard
University Press.

Hanson, Lee H.
1971   Pipes from Rome, New York. *Historical Archaeology* 5:92–99.

Hart, John Fraser
1978   Cropland concentrations in the South. *Annals of the Association of American Geographers* 68:5.

Haskins, Ralph W.
1955   Planter and cotton factor in the Old South: Some areas of
friction. *Agricultural History* 29:1–14.

Hawes, Lilla
1974   Written communication, 12 December. Savannah: Director,
Georgia Historical Society.

Hazzard, William Wigg
1825   History of Glynn County-1825. Typescript of ms. on file at the
Margaret Davis Cate Collection.
1831   On the general management of a plantation. *Southern Agriculturist* 4:350–354.

H. C.
1834   On the management of Negroes. *Southern Agriculturist* 7:369.

Heard, George A.
1938   St. Simons Island during the War Between the States. *Georgia
Historical Quarterly* 22:249–272.

Hedin, Raymond
1981   Muffled voice: The American slave narrative. *Clio* 10:129–
142.

Heiman, Robert K.
1962   *Tobacco and Americans*. New York: McGraw-Hill.

Heslin, James J.
1975   Written communications. 3 March and 20 May. Director, New
York Historical Society.

Higgins, W. Robert
    1971   The geographical origins of Negro slaves in Colonial South
            Carolina. *South Atlantic Quarterly* 70:34–47.
Higginson, Thomas W.
    1962   *Army life in a Black regiment.* Boston: Beacon Press.
    [1870]
Hilliard, Sam B.
    1969   Hog meat and cornpone: Food habits in the Antebellum
            South. *Proceedings of the American Philosophical Society*
            113:1–13.
    1972   *Hog meat and hoecake: Food supply in the Old South
            1840–1860.* Carbondale: Southern Illinois University Press.
Historic Preservation Section
    1974   *Historic preservation handbook.* Atlanta: Department of Nat-
            ural Resources.
Hole, Frank, K. V. Flannery, and J. A. Neely
    1969   Prehistory and human ecology of the DehLuran Plain.
            Memoirs of the Museum of Anthropology 1. Ann Arbor: Uni-
            versity of Michigan Press.
Holland, Rupert S. (ed.)
    1969   *Letters and diary of Laura M. Towne: Written from the Sea
    [1912] Islands of South Carolina 1862–1884.* New York: Negro Uni-
            versities Press.
Holmes, James
    1976   *"Dr. Bullie's" notes: Reminiscences of Early Georgia and of
            Philadelphia and New Haven in the 1800s,* edited by Delma
            Eugene Presley. Atlanta: Cherokee.
Holt, Thomas
    1976   On the cross: The role of quantitative methods in the recon-
            struction of the Afro-American experience. *Journal of Negro
            History* 61:158–172.
House, Albert V. (ed.)
    1954   *Planter management and capitalism in Ante-Bellum Geor-
            gia: The journal of Hugh Fraser Grant, Ricegrower.* Columbia
            University Press, New York.
Hudson, Charles
    1966   Folk history and ethnohistory. *Ethnohistory* 13:52–70.
Humphrey, Richard V.
    1969   Clay pipes from Old Sacramento. *Historical Archaeology*
            3:12–33.
Johnson, Guion Griffis
    1930   *A social history of the Sea Islands.* University of North Car-
            olina Press.
Jones, Bobby Frank
    1965   A cultural middle passage: Slave marriage and family in the
            Ante-Bellum South. Ph.D. dissertation, Department of Histo-
            ry. University of North Carolina.

Jones, Olive
  1971   Glass bottles: Push-ups and Pontil Marks. *Historical Archae-
            ology* 5:62–73.
Kemble, Frances Anne
  1863   *Journal of a residence on a Georgian plantation in 1838–
            1839.* New York: Harper.
  1961   *Journal of a residence on a Georgian plantation in 1838–
            1839,* edited by John A. Scott. New York: Knopf.
Kidd, Kenneth E. and Martha A. Kidd
  1970   A classification system for glass beads for the use of field ar-
            chaeologists. In *Occasional Papers in Archaeology and Histo-
            ry* 1.
King, Anna
  1854–   Plantation Record, Thomas Butler King Papers, File 1252, Se-
  1864   ries D, Southern Historical Collection, University of North
            Carolina Library at Chapel Hill.
King, Roswell, Jr.
  1828   On the management of the Butler Estate, and the cultivation
            of sugar cane. *Southern Agriculturist* 1:523–530.
Kingsbury, Pamela
  1974   Staffordshire transfer-printed ware from the Thayer collec-
            tion. *Antiques* 105:169–173.
Kniffen, Fred
  1965   Folk housing: Key to diffusion. *Annals of the Association of
            American Geographers* 55:549–577.
Larson, Lewis H.
  1969   Aboriginal subsistence technology on the southeastern coast-
            al plain during the Late Prehistoric Period. Ph.D. Disserta-
            tion, Department of Anthropology, University of Michigan.
Lasswell, Thomas E.
  1965   *Class and stratum.* Boston: Houghton.
Laumann, Edward O., *et. al.*
  1970   *The logic of social hierarchies.* Chicago: Markham.
Leeds, Anthony, and Andrew P. Vayda (eds.)
  1965   *Man, culture, and animals: The role of animals in human
            ecological adjustments.* Washington, D.C.: American Asso-
            ciation for the Advancement of Sciences.
Leigh, Frances Butler
  1883   *Ten years on a Georgia plantation since the war.* London:
            Bentley.
Lovell, Caroline Couper
  1932   *The Golden Isles of Georgia.* Boston: Little, Brown.
Ludlum, David M.
  1963   *Early American hurricanes 1492–1870.* Boston: American
            Meteorological Society.
Luscomb, Sally C.
  1972   *The collectors encyclopedia of buttons.* New York: Crown.

198 BIBLIOGRAPHY

Lyell, Charles
    1849   *A second visit to the United States of North America* (2 vols). New York: Harper.
MacFarlane, Suzanne
    1975   The ethnoarcheology of a slave community: The Couper Plantation site. M.A. thesis, Department of Anthropology. University of Florida.
Mallard, Robert Q.
    1892   *Plantation life before emancipation.* Richmond: Whittet and Shepperson.
Martin, Edgar W.
    1942   *The standard of living in 1860.* Chicago: University of Chicago Press.
Mathewson, R. Duncan
    1973   *Archaeological analysis of material culture as a reflection of sub-cultural differentiation in 18th Century Jamaica.* Paper presented at the Bicentennial Symposium, Eighteenth Century Florida and the Caribbean, Florida International University, Miami.
Miller, George L.
    1972   The application of the south mean ceramic date formula to a Nineteenth Century site. *The Conference on Historic Site Archaeology Papers 1971* 6:193–194.
    1980   Classification and economic scaling of 19th Century ceramics. *Historical Archaeology* 14:1–40.
Miller, Grant L., and Sherrell C. Jorgenson
    1969   Seasonal abundance and length frequency distribution of some marine fishes in coastal Georgia. *U. S. Fish and Wildlife Service, Data Report* 35.
Miller, J. Jefferson, and Lyle M. Stone
    1970   Eighteenth Century Ceramics from Fort Michilimackinac. *Smithsonian Studies in History and Technology No.* 4. Washington, D.C.: Smithsonian Institution Press.
Mintz, Sidney
    1970   Creating culture in the Americas. *Columbia University Forum* 13:4–11.
    1976   An anthropological approach to the Afro-American past. *Occasional Papers in Social Change, No.* 2. Philadelphia: Institute for the Study of Human Issues.
Miracle, Marvin P.
    1965   The introduction and spread of Maize in Africa. *Journal of African History* 6:39–55.
Monteiro, Joachim J.
    1968   *Angola and the River Congo* (2 vols). London: Cass.
Morse, Dan F., and Phyllis A. Morse
    1964   The Brake site: A possible Early 19th Century log cabin in

Stewart County, Tennessee. *The Florida Anthropologist* 17:165–176.

Mullin, Gerald W.
1972   *Flight and rebellion: Slave resistance in Eighteenth Century Virginia.* New York: Oxford University Press.

Murray, Amelia M.
1857   *Letters from the United States, Cuba and Canada.* New York: Putnam.

Myers, Robert Manson
1972   *The children of pride: A true story of Georgia and the Civil War.* New Haven: Yale University Press.

Nelson, Lee H.
1963   Nail Chronology as an aid to dating old buildings. *History News* 19:25–27.

Nichols, Frederick D.
1957   *The early architecture of Georgia.* Chapel Hill: University of North Carolina Press.

Noël Hume, Ivor
1969a   *A guide to artifacts of Colonial America.* New York: Knopf.
1969b   *Historical archaeology.* New York: Knopf.
1969c   Pearlware: Forgotten milestone of English ceramic history. *Antiques* 95:390–397.
1973   Creamware to Pearlware: A Williamsburg perspective. In *Ceramics in America,* edited by Ian M. G. Quimby. Charlottesville: University of Virginia Press.
1974   *All the best rubbish.* New York: Harper.

Official Records
1901   *Union and Confederate Navies in the War of rebellion* (Series I, Vol. 12). Government Printing Office, Washington, D.C.

Ojo, G. J. A.
1966   *Yoruba culture.* London: University of London Press.

Olmsted, Frederick Law
1861   *The cotton kingdom: A travellers observations on cotton and slavery in the American slave states.* New York: Mason.
1968   *A journey in the seaboard slave states, with remarks on their*
[1856] *economy.* Detroit: Negro Universities Press.

Olsen, Stanley J.
1963   Dating early plain buttons by their form. *American Antiquity* 28:551–554.
1965   Liquor bottles from Florida military sites. *American Antiquity* 31:105–107.

Omwake, H. G.
1961   Peter Dorni White Kaolin Pipes. *Bulletin of the Archaeological Society of New Jersey* 18–19:12–15.

Osofsky, Gilbert
1969   *Puttin' On Ole Massa.* New York: Harper.

Otto, John S.
  1975a   *The theoretical possibilities of plantation archaeology.* Paper
           presented at the Annual Meeting of the Society for Historical
           Archaeology, Charleston, South Carolina.
  1975b   Status differences and the archaeological record: A com-
           parison of planter, overseer, and slave sites from Cannon's
           Point Plantation (1794–1861), St. Simons Island, Georgia.
           Ph.D. dissertation, Department of Anthropology, University of
           Florida.
  1977   Artifacts and status differences—A comparison of ceramics
           from planter, overseer, and slave sites on an Antebellum plan-
           tation. In *Research strategies in historical archaeology,*
           edited by Stanley South. New York: Academic Press.
  1979   Slavery in a coastal community—Glynn County (1790–1861).
           Georgia Historical Quarterly 64:461–468.
  1981a   Oral traditional history in the southern highlands.
           Appalachian Journal 9:20–31.
  1981b   The case for folk history: Farm slavery in the southern high-
           lands. *Southern Studies* 21:167–173.
  1982   Afro-American archaeology. *Plantation Society in the Amer-
           icas* 1:440–444.
Otto, John S., and G. D. Gilbert
  1984   Archaeological excavations at a "Plain Folk" log cabin site,
           Meade County, Kentucky. *Filson Club History Quarterly*
           58:40–53.
An Overseer
  1836   On the conduct and management of overseers, drivers and
           slaves. *Southern Agriculturist* 9:225–231.
An Overseer
  1855   The duties of an overseer. *DeBow's Review* 18:339–345.
Owens, Leslie Howard
  1976   *This species of property: Slave life and culture in the Old
           South.* New York: Oxford University Press.
P.
  1837   Overseers. *Southern Agriculturist* 10:505–506.
P. C.
  1838   Rules for the government of overseers. *Southern Agriculturist*
           11:344–346.
Park, Mungo
  1888   *The life and travels of Mungo Park.* Edinburgh: Nimmo, Hay
           and Mitchell.
Parsons, Charles G.
  1970   *Inside view of slavery or a tour among the planters.* Detroit:
  [1855]   Negro History Press.

Parsons, Elsie C.
    1923   Folklore of the Sea Islands, South Carolina. *Memoirs of the
            American Folk-Lore Society* 16.
Pearson, Elizabeth Ware (ed.)
    1969   *Letters from Port Royal 1862–1868.* New York: Arno Press.
Pease, Jane
    1969   A note on patterns of conspicuous consumption among sea-
            board planters, 1820–1860. *Journal of Southern History*
            35:380–389.
Phillips, Ulrich B.
    1918   *American Negro slavery.* New York: Appleton.
    1929   *Life and labor in the Old South.* Boston: Little, Brown.
Phillips, Ulrich B. (ed.)
    1969   *Plantation and frontier documents 1649–1863.* New York:
    [1910] Franklin.
Phillips, Ulrich B., and James D. Glunt (eds.)
    1927   *Florida plantation records.* St. Louis: Missouri Historical
            Society.
A Planter
    1836   Notions on the management of Negroes. *Southern Agri-
            culturist* 9:580–584, 625–627.
A Practical Planter
    1831   A more general use of the Plough recommended to the planters
            of the lower county. *Southern Agriculturist* 4:393–402.
Price, Cynthia R., and James E. Price
    1978   Pioneer settlement and subsistence on the Ozark Border: Pre-
            liminary report on the Widow Harris cabin site. *The Con-
            ference on Historic Site Archaeology Papers 1977,* 12:145–
            169.
Puckett, Newbell Niles
    1968   *Folk beliefs of the Southern Negro.* New York: Negro Univer-
    [1926] sities Press.
Ransom, Roger L.
    1974   Was it really all that great to be a slave? *Agricultural History*
            48:578–585.
Rawick, George
    1972   *From sundown to sunup: The making of the Black communi-
            ty.* Westport, Connecticut: Greenwood.
Rawick, George (ed.)
    1972   *The American slave: A composite autobiography.* Westport,
            Connecticut: Greenwood.
Reimold, Robert J.
    1974   *Toxaphene interactions in Estuarine Ecosystems: Fourth An-

nual Report to Hercules, Inc., Sapelo Island. The University of Georgia Marine Institute.

Rogers, George C.
1970 *The history of Georgetown County, South Carolina.* Columbia: University of South Carolina Press.

Rose, Willie Lee
1964 *Rehearsal for reconstruction: The Port Royal experiment.* New York: Vintage Books.

Roth, Rodris
1961 Tea drinking in 18th Century America: Its etiquette and equipage. *Contributions from the Museum of History and Technology* 14:61–91.

Russell, William Howard
1954 *My diary north and south.* New York: Harper.
[1863]

Savannah *Georgian*
1832 Newspapers on File at the Wimberley George de Renne Library, University of Georgia at Athens.

Scarborough, William K.
1964 The plantation overseer: A re-evaluation. *Agricultural History* 38:13–20.
1966 *The overseer: Plantation management in the Old South.* Baton Rouge: Louisiana State University Press.

Schiffer, Michael B.
1972 Archaeological context and systemic context. *American Antiquity* 37:156–165.

Schirmer, Jacob F.
1969 The Schirmer diary. *South Carolina Historical Magazine* 70:122–125.

Schuyler, Robert L.
1970 Historical and historic sites archaeology as anthropology. *Historical Archaeology* 4:83–89.
1980 Afro-American culture history. In *Archaeological perspectives on ethnicity in America,* edited by Robert Schuyler. New York: Baywood.

Seabrook, Whitemarsh B.
1831 On the variety of cotton, proper to be cultivated on the Sea Islands. *Southern Agriculturist* 4:337–346.

Shelford, Victor E.
1963 *The ecology of North America.* Urbana: University of Illinois Press.

Shofner, Jerrell, and William Rogers
1962 Sea Island Cotton in Ante-Bellum Florida. *Florida Historical Quarterly* 40:373–380.

Shyrock, Richard H.
1930 Medical practices in the Old South. *The South Atlantic Quarterly* 29:160–178.

Silver, I. A.
 1963 The ageing of domestic animals. In *Science in archaeology*, edited by Don Brothwell and Eric Higgs. New York: Basic Books.
Simon, Donald W.
 1973 Excavations at "North Cabin"—Couper Plantation, Cannon's Point, St. Simons Island, Georgia. Unpublished paper on file, Department of Anthropology, University of Florida at Gainesville.
Simons, J. Hume
 1849 *The planter's guide and family book of medicine: For the instruction and use of planters, families, and country people*. Charleston, South Carolina: M'Carter and Allen.
Sitterson, J. Carlyle
 1953 *Sugar country: The cane sugar industry in the South 1753–1950*. Lexington: University of Kentucky Press.
Sleen, W. G. N. van der
 n.d. *Handbook on beads*. York, Pennsylvania: Liberty Cap Books.
Smith, Julia Floyd
 1973 *Slavery and plantation growth in Antebellum Florida 1821–1860*. Gainesville: University Presses of Florida.
Smith, M. G.
 1965 The Hausa of Northern Nigeria. In *Peoples of Africa*, edited by James L. Gibbs. New York: Holt.
Smith, Samuel D.
 1975 *Archaeological explorations at the Castalian Springs, Tennessee, historic site*. Nashville: Tennessee Historical Commission.
 1977 Plantation archaeology at the Hermitage: Some suggested patterns. *Tennessee Anthropologist* 2:152–163.
 1980 Historical background and archaeological testing of the Davy Crockett birthplace state historic area, Green County, Tennessee. *Division of Archaeology, Tennessee Department of Conservation, Research Series No. 6*.
Smith, Samuel D. (ed.)
 1976 An archaeological and historical assessment of the first Hermitage. *Division of Archaeology, Tennessee Department of Conservation, Research Series No. 2*.
South, Stanley A.
 1964 Analysis of the buttons from Brunswick Town and Fort Fisher. *The Florida Anthropologist* 17:113–133.
 1972 Evolution and horizon as revealed in ceramic analysis in historical archaeology. *The Conference on Historic Site Archaeology Papers 1971* 6:71–106.
 1974 Palmetto parapets: Exploratory archaeology at Fort Moultrie, South Carolina 38CH50. *Institute of Archaeology and An-*

thropology, Anthropological Studies 1. Columbia: University of South Carolina.

1977   *Method and theory in historical archaeology.* New York: Academic Press.

1978   Pattern recognition in historical archaeology. *American Antiquity* 43:223–230.

1979   Historic site content, structure, and function. *American Antiquity* 44:213–237.

Spalding, Thomas
1830   On the mode of constructing Tabby Buildings, and the propriety of improving our plantations in a permanent manner. *Southern Agriculturist* 3:617–623.

1831   On the introduction of Sea-Island Cotton into Georgia. *The Southern Agriculturist 4:131–133.*

Stampp, Kenneth
1956   *The peculiar institution.* New York: Knopf.

Steel, Edward M.
1964   *T. Butler King of Georgia.* Athens: University of Georgia Press.

Stefano, Frank, Jr.
1974   James and Ralph Clews, Nineteenth Century Potters, Part 1: The English Experience. *Antiques* 105:324–328.

Stephens, S. G.
1976   The Origin of Sea Island Cotton. *Agricultural History* 50:391–399.

Stone, Garry Wheeler
1970a   Ceramics in Suffolk County, Massachusetts, inventories 1680–1775—A preliminary study with diverse comments thereon, and sundry suggestions. *The Conference on Historic Site Archaeology Papers 1968* 3: Part 2. 73–90.

1970b   Reply to Cleland. *The Conference on Historic Site Archaeology Papers 1968* 3:124–126.

1977   Artifacts are not enough. *The Conference on Historic Site Archaeology Papers 1976* 11:43–63.

Sturtevant, William C.
1968   Anthropology, history, and ethnohistory. In *Introduction to cultural anthropology,* edited by James Clifton. Boston: Houghton.

Switzer, Ronald R.
1974   The Bertrand bottles. *National Park Service, Publications in Archaeology* 12.

Tams, Georg
1969   *Visit to the Portuguese possessions in South-western Africa* (2
[1845] vols). New York: Negro Universities Press.

Tannenbaum, Frank
1974   *Slave and citizen: The Negro in the Americas.* New York: Knopf.

Teal, John M.
    1958   Distribution of Fiddler Crabs in Georgia Salt Marshes. *Ecology* 39:185–193.
    1962   Energy flow in the Salt Marsh ecosystem of Georgia. *Ecology* 43:614–624.

Thompson, Robert F.
    1969   African influences on the Art of the United States. In *Black studies in the university*, edited by Armstead L. Robinson *et al.* New Haven: Yale University Press.

Thorpe, Earle
    1978   The slave community: Studies of slavery Need Freud and Marx. In *Revisiting Blassingame's The Slave Community: The scholars respond.* Westport, Connecticut: Greenwood.

Thorpe, T. B.
    1854   Cotton and its cultivation. *Harper's New Monthly Magazine* 8:447–462.

Toulouse, Julian H.
    1970   High on the Hawg: Or how the western miner lived, as told by the bottles he left behind. *Historical Archaeology* 4:59–69.
    1971   *Bottle makers and their marks.* New York: Nelson.

Towne, Laura
    1901   Pioneer work on the Sea Islands. *The Southern Workman* 30:396–400.

Trigger, Bruce G.
    1968   The determinants of settlement pattern. In *Settlement Archaeology*, edited by K. C. Chang. Palo Alto, California: National Press Books.

Tumin, Melvin D.
    1967   *Social stratification: The forms and functions of inequality.* Englewood Cliffs, New Jersey: Prentice-Hall.

Turner, Lorenzo D.
    1949   *Africanisms in the Gullah dialect.* Chicago: University of Chicago Press.

U.S. Bureau of the Census
    1820   *Population schedules of the Fourth Census of the United States, Glynn County.* Prepared by Joseph Manning (Microfilm Roll 7, The National Archives).
    1820–   Census records-Glynn County. Photostatic Copies of originals
    1860   on file at the MDCC.
    1830   *Population schedules of the Fifth Census of the United States, Glynn County.* Prepared by John Anderson (Microfilm Roll 17, The National Archives).
    1840   *Population schedules of the Sixth Census of the United States, Glynn County.* Prepared by Francis D. Scarlett (Microfilm Roll 42, The National Archives).
    1850a   *Population schedules of the Seventh Census of the United States-[White and Free Colored Population], Glynn County.*

Prepared by E. C. P. Dart (Microfilm Roll 71, The National Archives).

1850b   *Population schedules of the Seventh Census of the United States-[Slave Population], Glynn County.* (Microfilm Roll 90, The National Archives).

1853   *The Seventh Census of the United States.* Government Printing Office, Washington, D.C.

1860a   *Population schedules of the Eight Census of the United States [White and Free Colored Population], Glynn County.* Prepared by Charles C. Usher (Microfilm Roll 124, The National Archives).

1860b   *Population schedules of the Eight Census of the United States [Slave Population], Glynn County.* (Microfilm Roll 146, The National Archives).

1864   *Agriculture of the United States in 1860.* Government Printing Office, Washington, D.C.

U.S. Coast Survey

1869   Map of Altamaha Sound and Vicinity, Georgia. On file at the MDCC.

U.S. Department of Agriculture

1964   Roller-Ginning American-Egyptian Cotton in the Southwest. *USDA Handbook* 257.

U.S. Geological Survey (ed.)

1954   *Altamaha Sound, Georgia.* N3115–W8115/7.5/1954/AMS 4746 IV SE Series V 845.

Ursin, Michael J.

1972   *Life in and around the Salt Marshes.* New York: Crowell.

Van Doren, Mark (ed.)

1929   *Correspondence of Aaron Burr and his daughter Theodosia.* New York: Stratford Press.

Van Rensselaer, Susan

1966   Banded creamware. *Antiques* 90:337–341.

Vlach, John Michael

1978   *The Afro-American tradition in decorative arts.* Cleveland: Cleveland Museum of Art.

Walker, Iain C.

1971   Nineteenth Century clay tobacco pipes in Canada. *Ontario Archaeology* 16:19–35.

Walker, I. C., and LL. De S. Walker

1969   McDougall's clay pipe factory, Glasgow. *Industrial Archaeology* 6:132–146.

Walker, John W.

1971   Excavation of the Arkansas post branch of the state of Arkansas. National Park Service.

Wall, Bennett H.

1965   African slavery. In *Writing Southern history,* edited by Arthur

Link and Rembert Patrick. Baton Rouge: Louisiana State University Press.

Warner, W. Lloyd
1970   The study of social stratification. In *Readings on social stratification*, edited by Melvin M. Tumin. Englewood Cliffs, New Jersey: Prentice-Hall.

Watkins, C. Malcolm
1968   *The cultural history of Marlborough, Virginia.* Washington, D.C.: Smithsonian University Press.
1970   Artifacts from the sites of three Nineteenth Century houses and ditches at Darien Bluff, Georgia. *University of Georgia Laboratory of Archaeology Series Report 9.*

Watson, Karl
1975   *The civilized island: Barbados, a social history 1750–1816.* Ph.D. dissertation, Department of History, University of Florida.

Wax, Darold D.
1967   Georgia and the Negro before the American Revolution. *Georgia Historical Quarterly* 60:63–77.
1973   Preferences for slaves in Colonial America. *Journal of Negro History* 58:371–401.

Webster, Donald B.
1971   *Decorated stoneware pottery of North America.* Rutland, Vermont: Tuttle.

Wells, Thomas H.
1967   *The slave ship Wanderer.* Athens: University of Georgia Press.

A Well Wisher
1836   On the conduct of overseers and the general management of a plantation. *Southern Agriculturist* 9:508–511.

White, George
1849   *Statistics of the state of Georgia including an account of its natural, civil, and ecclesiastical history.* Savannah: Williams.
1854   *Historical collections of Georgia.* New York: Pudney and Russell.

Whiter, Leonard
1970   *Spode: A history of the family, factory, and wares from 1733–1833.* New York: Praeger.

Wightman, Orrin Sage, and Margaret Davis Cate
1955   *Early Days of Coastal Georgia.* St. Simons Island, Georgia: Ft. Frederica Association.

Wilson, Rex L.
1961   Clay tobacco pipes from Fort Laramie. *Annals of Wyoming* 33:120–134.

1966   Tobacco pipes from Fort Union, New Mexico. *El Palacio* 73:32–40.

Wing, Elizabeth
1965   Animal bones associated with two Indian sites on Marco Island, Florida. *The Florida Anthropologist* 18:21–28.

Winterbottom, Thomas
1969   *An account of the native Africans in the neighborhood of*
[1803]   *Sierra Leone* (2 vols). London: Cass.

Witthoft, John
1966   A history of gun flints. *Pennsylvania Archaeologist* 36:(1–2).

Wolf, Eric R.
1959   Aspects of plantation systems in the New World: Community sub-cultures and social classes. In *Seminar on plantation systems of the New World, Social Science Monographs 7.* Washington, D.C.: Research Institute for the Study of Man and the Pan American Union.

Woofter, T. J., Jr.
1930   *Black Yeomanry: Life on St. Helena Island.* New York: Holt.

Wylly, Charles Spalding
1897   *Annals and statistics of Glynn County, Georgia.* Privately printed. Margaret Davis Cate Collection, Brunswick Junior College, Brunswick.

1910   *The seed that was sown in the colony of Georgia: The harvest and aftermath, 1740–1870.* New York: Neale.

1914   *An historical account of Hopeton, Altama, and other Couper property from the acquisition of the lands early in the 19th Century by the two Scots boys-James Hamilton and John Couper.* Manuscript on microfilm, Couper Family Papers (1775–1960), Georgia State Archives, Atlanta.

1916   *Memories and annals.* Brunswick, Georgia: Glover.
[1897]

Yetman, Norman R. (ed.)
1970   *Life under the peculiar institution-selections from the slave narrative collection.* New York: Holt.

Ziegler, Alan C.
1973   Inference from prehistoric faunal remains. *Addison-Wesley Module in Anthropology* 43.

Index

Couper family, 2, 12–13, 18, 95
Couper, Caroline, 72, 128, 154
Couper, Hannah, 97
Couper, Isabella, 20, 130
Couper, James Hamilton, 17–20, 24,
    26–30, 43, 86, 94–98, 114, 118,
    124, 127, 130, 148, 153–155
  book and art collections, 153–154
  library, 153
  mineral collection, 30, 154
  numismatic collection, 135, 154
  plantation duties, 126
Couper, John, 17, 20, 23–24, 26, 95–
    96, 98, 124, 127, 135, 140, 145,
    150, 153–154, 156, 164
  attitudes toward abolitionists, 126
  paternalistic treatment of slaves, 125
  plantation duties, 126
Couper, John, Jr., 130
Couper, Rebecca, 128, 154
Couper, William Audley, 96–98, 118
Craven, Avery, 121
Cupidon, 150
Cutlery, 170

D

Dairywares, 114, 152
Darien *Gazette*, 95
Deer, 146, 164
Dembo, 86
Disease
  malaria, 26–28, 70, 115, 124
  "humoural imbalances," 69
  "morbific matter," 69–70, 115
Documentary controls, 13, 159–160,
    170
Doll, porcelain, 76
Drum fishing, 48, 107, 146
Drums and Shadows (1940), 7
Dutch ovens, 60, 113

E

Elizafield Plantation, Georgia, 97, 118
Elkins, Stanley, 5
Engerman, Stanley, 5
Ethnohistorical sources, 6, 10, 19
  definition, 6
Eve's roller gin, 23, 25, 135–136

F

Factors (cotton agents), 126
Fairbanks, Charles, 1–2, 8, 61
Fan handle, brass, 77
Fennell, E. D., 98
Fennell, J. N., 98
Feguson, Leland, 84
Fernandina, Florida, 30
First South Carolina Volunteers (U.S.),
    30
Fish, 47–56, 107, 145–146, 164
  bumpers, 146, 164
  burrfish, 107
  cownosed rays, 164
  croakers, 54, 107
  drums, 54, 56, 107, 146, 164
  flounders, 54
  gar, 54, 107
  jacks, 146, 164
  kingfish, 54
  marine catfish, 53–54, 107, 148
  menhaden, 107
  mullet, 48, 54, 107
  perch, 107
  sea bass, 107
  sea trout, 54
  shad, 107
  sharks, 148, 164
  sheepshead, 54, 107, 145
  silver perch, 54
  silver trout, 164
  spots, 146, 164
  stingrays, 54, 107, 148
  sturgeon, 54
  weakfish, 164
Fisk University, Tennessee, 7–8
Florida State Museum, Gainesville, 2
Fogel, Robert, 5
Folk subcultures, definition, 65
Folk historical sources, 6, 19
Foodways, 61, 167
Forten, Charlotte, 72
Franklin College, Georgia, 98
Fraser, Rev. Hugh, 118
Fraser, Mary Elizabeth, 118
Frederica, Georgia, 20
Furniture, 169